Praise for *What Mothers Do*

Especially When It Looks Like Nothing

"Her book is being passed from mother to mother like contraband."

—Anne Karpf, *The Guardian*

"It's a wonderful book and a great affirmation for mothers that is full-blooded and includes the whole richness of mothering. A very enrolling experience to read it."

—Janet Balaskas, founder of the Active Birth Centre, mother, grandmother

"I wish I'd had this book years ago—to show to bosses who didn't understand, to friends who couldn't grasp why I was permanently tired, and even to myself—to know that I wasn't the only one who wished for an extra eight hours in the day."

—Anne Diamond, television presenter, mother

"I love this book. A work from a pure heart and an informed head, it is at once simple and profound, as is the subject it addresses. It reads as if the author were in the room speaking to the reader. No pseudo-science, no psychobabble. Just the truth."

—Thomas Szasz, author, psychiatrist, psychoanalyst, father, grandfather

"Stadlen brings mothering experience to light and life, and will surely evoke in most mothers, 'Yes! That is what I do.' I suspect What Mothers Do *will become an enduring classic."*

—Ruth Barnett, psychotherapist, mother

"I kept thinking 'Yes! That's just what it was like!' After reading the book, I understand better my own experience of motherhood that is such an important part of me."

—Angela Buxton, mother

"On the basis of years of experience of talking with mothers, Naomi Stadlen breaks new ground in capturing those aspects of the experience of modern motherhood that are often overlooked or denigrated in the standard literature. Her book is a valuable source of insights that will be of immense value to parents and nonparents alike."

—Richard Skues, principal lecturer in social science, London Metropolitan University

what mothers do

especially when it looks like nothing

what mothers do

especially when it looks like nothing

Naomi Stadlen

Jeremy P. Tarcher/Penguin
a member of Penguin Group (USA) Inc.
New York

JEREMY P. TARCHER/PENGUIN
Published by the Penguin Group
Penguin Group (USA) Inc., 375 Hudson Street, New York, New York 10014, USA • Penguin Group (Canada), 90 Eglinton Avenue East, Suite 700, Toronto, Ontario M4P 2Y3, Canada (a division of Pearson Penguin Canada Inc.) • Penguin Books Ltd, 80 Strand, London WC2R 0RL, England • Penguin Ireland, 25 St Stephen's Green, Dublin 2, Ireland (a division of Penguin Books Ltd) • Penguin Group (Australia), 250 Camberwell Road, Camberwell, Victoria 3124, Australia (a division of Pearson Australia Group Pty Ltd) • Penguin Books India Pvt Ltd, 11 Community Centre, Panchsheel Park, New Delhi–110 017, India • Penguin Group (NZ), 67 Apollo Drive, Rosedale, North Shore 0745, Auckland, New Zealand (a division of Pearson New Zealand Ltd) • Penguin Books (South Africa) (Pty) Ltd, 24 Sturdee Avenue, Rosebank, Johannesburg 2196, South Africa • Penguin Books Ltd, Registered Offices: 80 Strand, London WC2R 0RL, England

Previously published in 2004 by Piatkus Books UK

Published simultaneously in Canada

Most Tarcher/Penguin books are available at special quantity discounts for bulk purchase for sales promotions, premiums, fund-raising, and educational needs. Special books or book excerpts also can be created to fit specific needs. For details, write Penguin Group (USA) Inc. Special Markets, 375 Hudson Street, New York, NY 10014.

ISBN 978-1-58542-591-4

Printed in the United States of America
1 3 5 7 9 10 8 6 4 2

Book design by Michelle McMillian

with thanks

My warm thanks to all the mothers who have talked about what they do, and helped me to understand a little better what being a mother is about. To my hardworking and supportive La Leche League colleagues. To Sheila Kitzinger for an inspiring breakfast conversation in 1989, and to Janet Balaskas for her support and for inviting me, in 1990, to run groups for mothers at her Active Birth Centre. To Jennifer Marsh for her encouragement. To all my friends who read early versions of these chapters, and to my daughter Rachel for her encouragement and superb logical editing. To Penny Phillips, the warmest and most understanding publisher's editor one could have. To my parents, Marianne and Hans Jacoby. To my three marvelous children, Rachel, Shoël, and Darrel. To Tony, beloved and faithful husband, soulmate, more than words can say.

contents

author's note

The identities of the mothers quoted in *What Mothers Do* are confidential, so I have developed the following system of referring to them and their families.

B indicates the name of a boy child (where gender noted).
G indicates the name of a girl child (where gender noted).
F indicates the father's name.
M indicates the mother's name.

I have given babies' ages to the lower week, the first two months. Thereafter, I have used the lower month. If a mother says her baby is "nearly four months," I still give this as three months.

In using pronouns, it is important to make a clear distinction between mother and baby. This can be confusing if both are female. So, with apologies to girl babies, I have used masculine pronouns for general statements about babies.

The term "mother" usually means the person who bears the baby, gives birth to him, and takes care of him afterward. But this is not always done by the mother alone. Fathers and grandmothers especially may be the primary daytime carers. If the parents divorce and remarry, there may be stepparents taking turns. There may be adoptive mothers as well as biological ones. When a nonprofessional person stands in for the mother in this way or takes turns with her, descriptions of what mothers do may apply to this person also. It would be clumsy to keep repeating: "Mothers or other relatives responsible for the child . . ." Observations about mothers may therefore apply to other relatives caring for the baby.

In the American edition, to avoid misunderstanding, a number of British terms and idioms have been changed to their American equivalents, including several terms and idioms spoken by mothers in conversation.

introduction

When I first went into labor, I couldn't believe that it was leading toward the birth of our baby. I couldn't think further than the drama of the present moment. But afterward, a midwife placed my first child in the crook of my arm on the hospital delivery bed. I looked down at her and my arm felt the weight of her—hot, heavy, and new. I was overcome. Every bit of her looked good. I didn't know a baby could look like that. She seemed whole, open, and trusting. Was I really worthy to take care of her? I looked down at her bright eyes, all silvery with newly born light, and the sight of her seemed to settle an inner argument with myself. She looked good, and surely this meant that life itself must be essentially good. Everything seemed clear and simple as I gazed at her wonderful face.

Back home, I found it hard to hold on to that moment in the hospital. Being a mother didn't seem clear and simple. At the same time, I felt ashamed that I wasn't finding it easier to cope. Having a baby was such an ordinary event. I thought my difficulties meant that there must be something radically wrong with me. One of the reasons I wrote *What Mothers Do* was to prove to myself that my feelings were justified. Being a mother *is* difficult. This means that we can take pride in any part of it that we do well. If mothering really were so easy, then our pride would just be vanity. I hope that when I explain some of the difficulties, other mothers will feel vindicated in finding it hard. I hope they will also discover many daily reasons for feeling pleased with themselves. I hope *What Mothers Do* can provide reasons for comfort, understanding, and encouragement to other mothers, especially during those emotional early months. Most mothers cry easily at this time. I wish I had realized that when it was me.

Just as it can seem unbelievable, during labor, that the whole process will end with the birth of a baby, so in the endless round of child care, a mother can lose sight of what all that work is for. Mothering enables a newborn to grow into a capable child.

Mothers sometimes say: “I get bored out of my mind, doing things for the baby all day.” Yet one can do at least as much boring work in an office. Still, office work can feel part of a significant whole. This provides a sense of belonging and contributing to something useful. Mothers, who are doing so much, often describe themselves as sitting around, doing nothing. They feel lonely, invisible, and unimportant. Yet their work belongs to much more than one organization. Each mother is preparing her child to belong to the society that we all share. It doesn’t seem too much to say that the whole of civilization depends on the work of mothers. Social life would be chaotic if mothers were not contributing so much. If mothers feel unimportant, then surely the value of their work is not being properly acknowledged. *What Mothers Do* is written to show not only the reasons why mothering deserves our admiration but also how much it depends on all of us. We are all connected to the world of mothers.

At the moment, the world that mothers inhabit is not a comfortable place. When a woman first starts telling people that she is expecting a baby, she can feel as though she has stepped into a war zone. For every possible question concerning herself and her baby, there are at least two opposite schools of thought. Each school of thought backs up its beliefs with an attack on the "enemy" school, with chilling predictions of what will happen if a mother falls prey to enemy influence.

Long before her baby is born, before she has set eyes on him, a mother finds herself facing decisions about how to look after him. What should she do about her job? Should she attend prenatal classes? Should she have a birth plan? What diapers should she have ready? I remember the first time I shopped for diapers. There were no disposables for sale when I was expecting my first child. I hurried into a pharmacy, assuming in my ignorance that there would be only one sort of diaper. But there was a long shelf of assorted packages. I leaned forward to try to read the various descriptions and felt as if I might faint. Everything seemed so complicated.

A whole genre of books has developed that pressure mothers to follow the authors' personal rules or guidelines because these are supposed to make motherhood easier. But how useful is a program of rules? Mothers who try to follow such rules often react by complaining that looking after a baby is dreadfully boring. This is understandable. If one is following a set of rules, looking after a baby definitely gets boring. Each individual baby is sure to seem abnormal. He is unlikely to fit any particular set of rules—which were presumably based on the needs of a completely different baby. One can easily lose the joy of getting to know someone wholly unique.

After the birth of my daughter, I looked around to find other mothers who had made the same choices that I had. But of course no one else had. Instead, we had each made some important postnatal decisions. We had chosen whether to breastfeed or to use formulas; which diapers to use; whether to use a crib or to sleep with the baby; carry the baby in a sling or wheel him in a stroller; sleep-train or not; cuddle a crying baby or leave him to cry; vaccinate the baby and, if so, which vaccines to use, in which combinations, and when; use conventional or alternative medicine; employ professional child care and, if so, which kind . . . and more. It still alarms me to think about this list. Every choice opens up into many smaller choices. We live in a tolerant society, and choice is a valuable consequence of this. However, mothers often feel categorized by their choices and cut off from other mothers who have chosen differently.

Understandably, mothers can then become defensive. I found that conversations with other mothers would often turn into competitions. One mother might say: "My baby eats more solids [or sleeps longer, or is more active] than other babies of his age." "Top that!" is the silent challenge to other mothers. In a different kind of competition, mothers vie with each other about who is the expert. "I'll tell you what *I* used for colic," one mother tells another. There is a note of authoritative command in her voice. A third sort of conversation might sound more relaxed because it includes storytelling and laughter. But the tension runs just below the surface. The bottom line is "I'm having a much more horrible time as a mother than you are." This sort of competition is for the jackpot of maximum sympathy from all the listening mothers.

Yet it doesn't have to be like this. Motherhood is not a competition. There's room for every one of us. Motherhood is huge. No one could ever fulfill all its possibilities. No one could ever make entirely good choices. All of us have times of failure. Surely no mother could ever be a total failure either. There is room for every mother to be good at something. She can then respect other mothers and feel she belongs *with* them, rather than feel in competition *against* them. Overall, being a mother is a humbling experience. There is always more to learn. Just when her child passes a particular stage, a mother is sure to hear about something much better and simpler that she could have done.

I didn't realize how competitive my conversations with other mothers were. I used to come away feeling bruised, without understanding why. Slowly, I learned that each of us was unique. It was pointless to try to find another me. Instead, I began to listen to all the mothers I met in a more openminded way. It was fascinating to see how we all differed. Most mothers had precise reasons for their choices. Their situations were unique. Paradoxically, it was when I listened to the details of mothers' individual situations that I was able to see how much we all shared.

Below the surface of our individual choices, there are underlying themes that are common to most mothers. We share them no matter where we live or when. Being a mother centers on the love a mother gives to her child. She gives it in all kinds of ways. Her style is unique. Yet our common experience of this love connects us. A mother today could read an anxious diary entry written by the mother of a feverish baby several centuries ago and immediately recognize that distant mother's concerns. Mothering also seems to be portable and infinitely adaptable. It can flourish in very unlikely situations, when it is not at all convenient or practical. It can challenge the very core of materialist thinking, which is exactly what it often does today.

Many times I have seen two mothers of small babies sit down opposite each other at a meeting. One may have given up her career to stay at home with her child. The other has chosen to continue in her job. Each may have made a difficult choice and, facing the other mother, may feel guilty for it. The at-home mother feels she is consuming without earning and wasting her education. The at-work mother is aware of how much time she is spending away from her child. Each mother probably starts by thinking that she couldn't possibly do what the other mother is doing—though perhaps she *should*. Then, as they listen to each other, they realize how much they share. The at-home mother learns how intensely the at-work mother cares about her child. The at-work mother learns that the at-home one isn't a superhuman "earth mother" but an ordinary woman who can get as frustrated at home as she herself does. Both feel warmed and strengthened by discovering that they can understand each other. It is moving to witness.

Motherhood can be a great leveler. When mothers are faced with a crying newborn, the usual social differences among them vanish. Wealth, power, and success, and often race and ideology, suddenly seem unimportant. What counts is the sharing of motherly experience. This is the moment when one mother can give such invaluable support to another. When mothers value each other, they do not resort to competitive conversations, and their generosity to each other seems boundless.

All this seems perfectly straightforward, but I didn't realize any of it when I became a mother myself. My husband and I had had unconventional childhoods, and both of us wanted to be traditional parents. This meant that his career continued along the same track, but with the added weight of him being the family breadwinner. My life, on the other hand, after I had left my job just before the birth of our first baby, seemed to roll across the points onto a completely new track that led me in an unforeseen direction.

At first, as a new mother, I felt as if I had lost all my bearings in an unfamiliar world. The very street we lived on seemed longer than before, the cars larger and louder, the shops much farther away. My daughter was a great help to me then. I discovered that she wasn't expecting me to have turned overnight into a competent mother. She simply accepted me. Slowly we worked out a rhythm of being together. It became more like being two best friends than any ideas I had had about a mother with her baby. However, I felt out of step with other women of my generation.

The media featured inspirational stories about mothers who fitted their children around their careers. The implication seemed to be that being a mother wasn't interesting. Before having children, I assumed this too. After my daughter's birth, I found time spent with her was full of interest, but I didn't know how to explain it, even to myself. We might have had a good morning together—but whatever had we been doing all that time? In the privacy of home, I would feel excited, as if I were discovering for myself how to be a mother. But what had I discovered? As soon as we went out, even if we were just standing in a line at the supermarket, I felt unsure of myself. Facing the busy operators at the checkout counters, I felt a dizzying sense of my apparent triviality. Nothing I did as a mother fulfilled a precise social need like this. What I did at home seemed invisible and intangible. Perhaps my mothering was nothing after all.

I began to get a sense of having achieved something only when our children were older. Then I could see that, one by one, each vulnerable newborn had grown into a viable person. When our youngest child reached seven, a whole phase of intense mothering seemed to be over. I would walk into our kitchen and find the three of them sitting around the table, giggling over something they had just watched on television. I didn't know what it was about, and they didn't seem keen to tell me. This was their life, which was independent of me. Even the youngest no longer needed me or included me in the old way. So this freed me. Now I could use some of my time and energy differently. There was work that I had thought I was looking forward to taking up again, but my thoughts kept returning to those amazing years of being a mother. I felt I had just come through a momentous experience. I wanted to go back and understand what it had all been about. I also admired my husband as a father and wanted to discover more about fatherhood too.

I read books, but the understanding I was looking for didn't seem to be in them. Then I discovered that I was already receiving some of the information I wanted in the way that one does when one is interested in something. I was a trained breastfeeding counselor for the National Childbirth Trust. This meant that I was answering telephone calls and making home visits to a variety of mothers. I was also invited by Janet Balaskas to become the breastfeeding counselor for the Active Birth Centre (called the Birth Centre when I joined in 1979).

Ten years later I discovered La Leche League and retrained in breastfeeding counseling. I started to take La Leche League GB meetings in central London, and for six years edited La Leche League (Great Britain) *News*. I found that a typical question about breastfeeding would open out into much wider questions about family life. In 1990 Janet Balaskas, who had founded the Active Birth Centre, invited me to hold open mornings for mothers and babies. These turned into Mothers Talking, which are weekly discussion groups for mothers.

The way I run Mothers Talking groups has developed gradually. I must have made every mistake in the book. But slowly I have discovered how to help mothers to feel at ease with each other. I have finally learned to take into account and respect each mother's right to her individual choices. I can now take a meeting at which several mothers have made very different choices from each other. Yet each mother feels safe, and we can have a civilized discussion. This allows mothers to be curious about each other's differences without feeling threatened by them. Many mothers tell me they have formed long-lasting friendships with other mothers whom they met at these groups.

One day my husband asked me why I didn't extend my experience as a breastfeeding counselor and train to become a general counselor. It was a good suggestion, as it enabled me to specialize in seeing mothers and sometimes couples who were parents. This deepened my understanding. It has been a privilege to help parents piece together their childhood experiences and to gain a clearer awareness of how these experiences influenced what they were doing with their own children. (It should go without saying that no data from my counseling practice have been included in this book.)

I now teach counseling and psychotherapy students at several London colleges. I have created a unique course called The Psychology of Motherly Love. I encourage students, many of whom are not parents, to question and discuss, and they have given me different perspectives on motherhood.

At one stage I thought I was being too easygoing. I decided to interview mothers with a consistent set of questions. I planned the questions and tape-recorded several interviews. But I soon found this approach clumsy compared with spontaneous conversation. Mothers were talking to me anyway, not to answer my questions but because they recognized my interest and wanted to tell me something. Neither they nor I thought that these conversations would provide material for a book. That idea came to me later. But I did take notes. Sometimes a mother would say something with great simplicity. Her view might not coincide with my own, but I would be impressed by how well she had expressed herself. I would make a note of what she had said, with a sense that it was too precious to lose. In this very piecemeal way, I found that I was gathering together the understanding that I was looking for.

At first, whenever a mother told me her story, the details sounded unique. Then I became more aware of larger patterns in what mothers were saying. This helped me to see beyond the details. Slowly the stories fell into a more recognizable shape. The shape was distinct, and the various parts interlocked. I could see a pattern in the way a woman changed when she became a mother. It has been difficult to separate out the various strands of this pattern to form the different chapters of this book. In essence, the experience is whole.

I had been wary of telling mothers that I had begun writing this book. This is partly because I didn't want to bring a self-conscious element into our discussions. Only one mother ever asked me if I was writing anything (I said I was, and she immediately switched the subject), so I am certain that no one could possibly have given me quotable statements "for your book." But there was also another reason. I wasn't confident of having much to say. I would start to write, yet it all seemed elusive. Eventually, I did put together some ideas about maternal tiredness and wrote a sample chapter. But when I sent it to publishers, they told me that it had all been said already.

For many years I wondered whether all this work would prove to be unpublishable. However, I kept talking to mothers. Every individual idea in this book has been shared in many discussions with many mothers. I don't impose my ideas, but I certainly don't hide them. As far as I am aware, mothers who talk to me are clear about what I think. Because I am so interested in mothering, mothers usually enjoy talking to me.

I don't make notes while mothers are talking, though I sometimes jot down key words to help me remember anything that seems important. Often, however, I haven't used those key ideas after all. As I am walking home, relaxed after a meeting, something that someone said will suddenly come back to me. At the time, I hardly noticed it. Even as I repeat the words to myself, I don't necessarily know why they are important. I can't see immediately how they fit into the whole subject of mothering. But I reach home, put down my bags, and hurry to find a pen and paper.

I am fortunate that my university degrees were in history. I have been especially impressed by rereading the work of Thucydides (who gathered much of his information for *The Peloponnesian War* from conversation). From his disciplined writing, I learned to appreciate how important it is to listen to a variety of discordant voices—and to be especially careful not to distort them, not to reduce them to one uniform harmonious choir.

My conversations with mothers are confidential, and I am concerned to keep them so. My notes have no names or dates. I myself cannot usually remember who said what. I have used a system of quoting short statements by mothers as examples of the mothering pattern, and adding the sex and age of each mother's baby (see page ix). My hope is that if a mother can identify her own words, she will feel protected by this anonymous setting. I have often been deeply moved by what mothers have said. Our conversations are sacred to me, and I hope to continue to have more such conversations long after this book has been published.

The mothers who talk to me usually live in London. Not all were born here. Most are white; some are black; others are of mixed race. They come from Britain and many other parts of Europe, North and South America, Israel, Egypt, Nigeria, South

Africa, Madagascar, India, China, Japan, Australia, and New Zealand. Most come from nuclear families, but some are from traditional extended families. Some are married, some have partners, some are single mothers, and some are in lesbian relationships. Their ages range from early twenties to mid-forties. Nearly all received good educations, and nearly all seem to have earned enough to live on before having children. This must make them a more financially independent generation than that of their grandmothers and perhaps their mothers too.

We shall see that almost all these mothers complain that they were not very well prepared for motherhood. In this respect they may be unique in the whole history of mothers. In the past, girls were prepared from a young age. They watched their mothers and learned from them and were responsible for their siblings. The mothers quoted in this book may be more articulate, more self-conscious, and more self-doubting than mothers who are better prepared.

It may not be comfortable to reinvent the mothering wheel, but mothers do manage it. It can be daunting, yet it is also exciting not to accept tradition but to think out so much afresh. So *What Mothers Do* explores some of the results of doing this. It also tries to show the overall shape of mothers' experiences. The intention is to show what mothers have already done. It is *de*scription, not *pre*scription. The longer I live, the more I dislike hearing someone telling a mother what she "ought" to do. If you happen to notice in these pages that I have trespassed from giving a description to giving any "rules," I should be grateful if you would write to tell me.

Although I have talked to a modest sample of all possible mothers, it has been enough to show me how vast is the terrain of the subject of mothering and how little we know about it. Everything around me seems to confirm its importance—and how often it is denigrated. How could I ever have doubted that there was something to say? Looking through *What Mothers Do* now that I have finished writing, it seems to me that I have hardly begun to describe it. Although these pages contain so much of what I have learned, it must be a fraction of all that still remains, waiting to be discovered. I hope *What Mothers Do* can provide two things: much-needed encouragement to mothers and a firm stepping-stone for anyone trying to understand them.

one

who understands?

When I say that I am writing a book for mothers, I receive pitying looks. “But don’t you think there are plenty of books already?” people ask. “Hasn’t it all been said before?”

No, it hasn’t. Women such as myself, whose children are grown up now, know that it hasn’t. We know how much has been left unsaid. Mothers live in a universe that has not been accurately described. The right words have not been coined. Using habitual vocabulary sends us straight down the same old, much-trodden footpaths. But there are other areas to which these footpaths do not lead. There are whole stretches of motherhood that no one has explored.

Mothers complain about their physical isolation, but surely a more fundamental isolation is about not being understood. That kind of isolation arises when a person finds it difficult to communicate an important experience to other people. “Very little has been written on the subject of motherhood,” observed Susan Griffin, the California writer. She recalled: “I was alone in a house with an infant most of the time." She wrote that, when she went out with her husband and child, "I was inarticulate. I imagined people thought me stupid. I felt stunned, dumb. But there was something I had wanted to tell. Something profound."[1] The British novelist Rachel Cusk wrote: "When I became a mother I found myself for the first time in my life without a language, without any way of translating the sounds I made into something other people would understand."[2] If two mothers whose profession was words found it so difficult to talk about motherhood, how much more difficult must it be for the rest of us? One mother commented:

> I went to a dinner party on Thursday. And I had nothing to say. I was out of it. I couldn't talk about the only things that mattered to me. And even if I had, no one would have understood me. [B, 6 months]

It is easy to fall in with the customary use of language. Another mother said:

> My boss phoned and asked if I was working. I'm so annoyed with myself because I said: "No." [B, 9 months]

This mother meant that she wasn't working in the way that her boss meant. But she certainly was working at being a mother. She felt exasperated with herself for losing her chance to make this clear. Mothers often catch themselves making self-deprecating comments like hers: "I haven't been able to do any real work lately," or "I'm only looking after my baby these days." Looking after a baby may feel like "something" at the time it is happening, but at other times mothers find it difficult to explain. It's hard to find the words to communicate what "looking after my baby" really means.

Unlike nearly everything else that we do, a woman can become a mother without any training, qualifications, or supervision. Once her baby is born, a mother can find she has become one of the most influential people on earth. True, her influence may affect the lives of only one or two new people if she compares her influence to, say, that of a celebrity or perhaps a schoolteacher. But a mother's influence is likely to be deeply felt and to last for a lifetime. Collectively, mothers ensure the continuity of civilized life from one generation to the next.

There are many books prescribing what a mother should achieve. There are autobiographies by mothers bewailing the difficulties of being a good mother. But there isn't much that explores what mothers do achieve. If there were, we should have more words or phrases to describe motherly achievements. The result is that many mothers do not recognize their own successes. A mother may feel exhausted and her home may look chaotic. Yet she can be doing wonderfully well as a mother.

Being a mother is more than a role or a job description. It doesn't even describe behavior. Mothers haven't got a monopoly on motherly behavior. Most people are capable of being motherly. However, there is a difference between being *like* a mother and being the mother herself.

The word "mother" describes a relationship. It often has to be squeezed into all the relationships the woman has already. She usually is already a wife or partner, friend, colleague, neighbor, daughter and sister, and perhaps already a stepmother, godmother, or aunt. Generally, a woman will have given birth to a baby before she can start to use the word "mother" to describe herself. However, once she bears or adopts a child, the relationship between them is forever. Perhaps either she or her child decides to reject the relationship. Yet to outsiders, this simply becomes part of the unfolding story of that relationship. In this external sense, it outlives the lives of the mother and child. It may continue through other people's memories and statistics long after both of them are dead. It is possible for another person of either sex and of almost any age to be "just like a mother" to someone else. But it is unlikely that those two people will be linked together for so long a time.

Mothers are all around us. We can walk past a mother and child in the street, seeing—and not seeing. How much of a relationship can we see? If the child appears to be "good," people sometimes call the mother "lucky" to have an "easy child." But having a child is not easy. Mothers who say their babies are easy mean this in a relative sense. Many mothers go to exhausting lengths to mother their children, sometimes squeezing in time for a child amid many other commitments. To call them lucky might be kindly meant, but it can sound dismissive, bordering on insulting.

Yet, as with any relationship, one cannot clearly see it working. One can see a mother engaged in action, but what we see may not reveal very much.

> I had to have a scan, so I was radioactive for four days, Friday to Monday. I was told immediately that the scan was negative, so that was a great relief. But I wasn't allowed to hold G for those four days, and I felt bereft. I'd set myself some work to do, painting the outside of our house, so I just got on with it. On Tuesday, I held her again, and I thought I'd be in raptures, but it wasn't like that. I just felt . . . complete. I'm so in love with G. [G, 2 months]

How much of this inner drama would an outsider see? A woman painting the outside of her house on Monday, and the same woman on Tuesday calmly holding her child—an outsider would see little of the powerful motherly relationship.

There doesn't seem to be a phrase to convey the intensity of what a mother feels. If she has returned to work, she often finds it hard to explain to people at work that she still feels she is an active mother, responsible for her child. People at work often assume that "out of sight is out of mind," but a child may frequently be on his mother's mind. If a woman has chosen to stay at home with her baby, she may worry that she isn't doing enough. People probably tell her: "You must be very busy, now you're a mother." But, with a baby, the pace of her life has probably slowed down. She can feel demoralized and believe she is not achieving anything, just when her slow pace enables her to be in step with her child.

The essentials of mothering are invisible. It's hard to explain them in words. Practical tasks are only part of it. They do not account for that strength of feeling that goes with bringing up one's own child. A mother can discover this suddenly when she has been looking after her baby all through a long day. In the evening, her husband comes home, and at last she can exchange news with another adult. He is the one person, the father of their child, whom she can expect to understand her. Perhaps he asks her something generous like: "How's your day been?" It has been a difficult day. Now she can share it, hope for some sympathy, and regain her energy. She tries to find something to tell, but this can be frustrating. The words she uses simply don't match the experience. If she is a single mother and her childless friends ask the question, answering it can be even harder.

> I'd been to the hospital with G that day, and I could tell F about it in about five minutes. I felt gutted. It had taken me all day to do it. [G, 2 months]

> I tell F about my day—and there's nothing to tell. B soiled three diapers and he stopped crying for half an hour. What's important about that? [B, 3 months]

My husband gets in from work and asks me what sort of a day I've had, and I tell him I took G to a café with my friend and her baby. I can see from his face that he thinks I've had a pretty easy day. And I can't explain that I *haven't*. When I go to the café, yes, I know it was nice to talk to my friend. But I couldn't relax and concentrate properly—and neither could she. We were both looking after our babies. [G, 3 months]

F comes home, and he's full of his day. And what can I say about mine? B's learned to open the oven door. It doesn't sound like anything, though I was really excited when he did it. But I couldn't expect F to be wild about it. [B, 10 months]

When a mother can't explain her day, she is very unlikely to say to herself: "Maybe the right words are missing." Who has the energy to be insightful at the end of a demanding day? No, a mother who has little to relate usually assumes that this is because there really is very little worth telling. If it felt important at the time, if she feels tired now, she supposes that this is because she must have blown up little events out of proportion. She let herself get excited over nothing much. She is tired from doing very little. Exchanging stories at the end of a day seems a uniquely human activity. People use the narrative to make sense of the day's events, and to state and solve problems. When a mother's story seems to shrivel in her own eyes as she tells it, she cannot use the telling to make sense of her actions for herself—let alone help her partner to understand.

Motherly achievements often go unseen. If there aren't words for them, how can we recognize them? For example, how could one explain what the mother was doing who took her two-month-old daughter to the hospital? Just planning the journey must have involved much thought. A mother of a two-month-old doesn't plan one successful journey. She plans several, in which she tries to cover and solve the most obvious things that could go wrong. And what about keeping a two-month-old from crying during the unavoidable waiting times in a busy hospital? The mother was bringing her intimate relationship with her child into a public place, over which she had little control, and where social norms applied. How does one explain the complexity of all this?

Perhaps the lack of words accounts for a stark sentence that I found in an American book on mothering: "Yet being a mommy is boring." The writers continue: "Many women find themselves frustrated, anxious and uncomfortable in the role. . . . They begin having doubts about themselves as persons and mothers."[3] It is easy to feel bored doing something that doesn't make sense. People like to understand what they are doing and why. A mother might well feel "frustrated, anxious and uncomfortable" if she doesn't.

Let us suppose that you and I teamed up together to find out more about how mothers begin. We locate a new mother and ask if we can talk to her about how she is getting along with her baby. We arrange to visit one Sunday evening, after she and her baby have spent some time together. When we arrive, she is holding her baby against her shoulder and looking distraught. Suppose we ask her how she is getting on. Almost certainly we would run into a difficulty. The mother would reinterpret our question. She is most aware of what she is *not* doing. She is troubled by the basic looking after herself and the housework she has not managed to do yet. She lists all the chores that lie ahead of her. Suppose we persevere and ask: "But if you didn't manage to have your shower or get yourself some lunch, what were you and your baby doing before we came?" Then our mother would be likely to say in reply: "Nothing," or "Nothing much," or even "I don't know where all the time's gone."

Nothing? Has the time simply "gone"? Even now, as we look at her, you and I can clearly see that she is being present for her baby. She has given up her shower and her lunch. She is devoting her time and energy to him. We are looking at a baby who is being generously mothered. But most people would find it hard to explain this. Our language can be very clear and precise about anything practical. A person who has "tidied up" has both the words and a tidy area to show for it. It is much harder to find a word that describes the giving-up-things mode of attention a mother is giving to her baby. Often there is no obvious visible change in the baby to confirm that she has made any difference.

We don't seem to have a problem when it comes to finding fault. We have plenty of words to describe what mothers do when they relate badly to their children. We could pack a small glossary with a depressing list of words and expressions: negligent, selfish, heartless, narcissistic, cold, uncaring, rejecting, irresponsible, unnatural, hostile, cruel, abusive, punitive, seductive, castrating, possessive, overprotective, interfering, controlling, domineering, overbearing, demanding, smothering, unable to let go, overinvolved, totally wrapped up in her baby, overidentified with her child, pushy, impervious, ambitious, overanxious, neurotic, hysterical, immature, inadequate, withdrawn, apathetic, depressed, indulgent, pampering, permissive, idealistic . . . You could probably carry on with this list.

These words are specific. They indicate ways in which a mother is thought to have related wrongly to her child. Usually she is wrong for doing too much or too little of something. For example, one mother might be labeled negligent, while another is called overprotective. But mothers need to protect their children. Not every mother overdoes or underdoes it. Those are two extremes. Logically, therefore, we need a third word that means "protecting her child the right amount." We could then use this word for all those mothers who were protecting their children well. Of course we might argue among ourselves about who these mothers were—but we still need a word to argue about.

This doesn't mean we shouldn't have the negative words and expressions. We need them. They help to pinpoint where a mother may be going wrong. The trouble is that we seem to have *only* this kind of negative vocabulary for mothers. For example, take the term "abusive mother": it doesn't seem to have an opposite. I have asked many mothers on different occasions whether they can think of any word that means the opposite of "abusive mother" to describe a mother who is relating very beneficially to her children. The response is usually a thoughtful silence.

No such word exists. Instead there is a much shorter collection of words that we use to indicate our approval of mothers. Examples are: warm, loving, wonderful, patient, understanding, kind, caring, nurturing, concerned, responsible, unselfish. Most of these words don't indicate anything good that she might have done. They describe the state of a mother's heart. The state of a mother's heart is invisible—and she herself may not be conscious of it. This means that when she does a number of motherly actions for her child, she has no word to describe the particular actions. We could walk into a room where a mother had just spent half an hour calming her distressed baby. We might apologize for disturbing her. She would probably reply: "It's all right; I wasn't doing anything special." But she was.

We live in an articulate society, continually questioning ourselves and each other. It is not fair to leave a new mother with a horrific collection of words to condemn her—and almost nothing in the way of praise for when she is doing something well. A whole vocabulary is missing to balance all the negative words and phrases.

The most motherly achievements are often written off as failures. "Worrying" is a good example. Most mothers worry. But what is a mother actually doing when she is worrying? If, for instance, her baby won't stop crying, she may do some energetic thinking. She can listen and watch him crying, putting aside her own assumptions. She can try to "enter into" how he feels. She may try to match up his behavior with explanations she has read. She may dredge up something she heard many years ago and had forgotten till this moment.

In other words, her thinking may be quick and wide-ranging and work on several levels. She may end up with a fairly clear idea of why her baby is crying. Then she checks out this idea with someone and they tell her that she "must stop worrying so much," as if all that careful thinking had been stupid. It is only too easy to feel crushed and stupid by this kind of remark. But that is because the word "worry" is normally used to suggest a pointless and repetitive way of thinking. A much more appreciative word is needed to honor intelligent motherly concern.

Mothers sometimes borrow words from the field of psychoanalysis, and perhaps they do this in an attempt to upgrade their experience. It's easy to hear a mother label her own actions as neurotic or obsessional, compulsive, phobic, or paranoid. For example, a mother may say she is being "paranoid" because she doesn't want her friend to visit her newborn, since her friend has just told her that she may be coming down with the flu. Or she might call herself "obsessional" because she keeps checking whether her baby is hungry. She might say she was "neurotic" because when her baby sleeps for a long time she suddenly panics that he might be ill or dying.

All these examples describe situations when the mother is being careful because she hasn't got enough experience to be able to assess risks accurately. She prefers the safer option. She may have read about Sudden Infant Death Syndrome (SIDS), or perhaps her baby was once ill when she thought he was asleep. Isn't she justified in feeling anxious after that? Many mothers have particular anxieties and frequently check that their fears have not become reality. This behavior is logical and is a good way for them to learn.

> I was worried about so many things at first. I was quite neurotic, I see that now. [B, 6 weeks]

> *First mother:* B stopped breathing and went floppy. I hung him upside down and patted him. I called and called to him. I dialed 911, and we went to the hospital. It was so sudden. One minute he was fine, and then . . . Now I feel as though I'm going *mad* because I'm continually checking that B's all right. I'm so afraid it will happen again. [B, 7 weeks]
>
> *Second mother:* That happened to me, and I can remember being just the same. [B, 9 months]

> I felt really neurotic because I kept wanting to check B. As soon as I had left his crib and satisfied myself that he was peacefully sleeping, I started to worry again. At first I tried to stop worrying, but it didn't work. Then, one evening, I told myself to stop fighting myself and to check as many times as I wanted to. I must have checked about thirty times, that first evening. I thought I was going crazy. But the evening after that, I noticed I was leaving longer gaps between checking. Now I've got the confidence to

know B's asleep. I still check several times, every evening. [B, about 3 months]

I got into a total sweaty panic state on the plane. I was thinking that I can swim, but B can't. [B, 7 months]

These psychoanalytic words were used by Freud to identify irrational behavior. To use them for the normal process of learning is therefore not helpful. Some motherly words would be much better. We could then save the psychoanalytic words to apply to those mothers who, for example, get truly stuck in baby-checking behavior and don't manage to learn from experience. These mothers may need a chance to talk about their fears to someone. But if the words are used generally for all mothers, this will dilute their meaning and we shall lose the useful distinction that they still have.

The only group of people who have recognized that there is a real shortfall of useful words to describe mothering seem to be psychology researchers and psychiatrists. They have coined several words. For example, "bonding" was invented by Marshall Klaus and John Kennell in the 1970s, and the word has caught on. But even they, when they thought about it, weren't completely happy with the gluey connotations of this word.[4] Another expression is "attachment parenting," which refers to a theory developed in Britain and the United States to explain how small children spontaneously relate to a reliable parent figure or substitute.[5] Then there are particular words like "entrainment," which has been defined as: "While the infant moves in rhythm to his mother's voice and thus may be said to be affected by her, his movements may reward the mother and stimulate her to continue."[6]

One difficulty is that as soon as a psychiatrist or researcher has invented a word, he then goes on to show how important it is for mothers and babies to do whatever his word describes. "We believe that every parent has a task to perform during the postpartum period," declare Klaus and Kennell.[7] It is they who define what the task is.[8] This kind of writing turns mothering into a minefield, with "experts" to guide mothers through the danger areas, instead of mothers guiding researchers and—most important—using their own language. Surely no mother ever invented pseudoscientific terms like bonding or attachment parenting or entrainment. Mothers talk about love.

Ordinary words can be so helpful. One word that has recently entered the English language in relation to childcare and has been useful to breastfeeding mothers is "positioning." This word was coined by two women health professionals in 1970.[9] It refers to the importance of holding the baby in the optimal position to reach his mother's breast. This may sound obvious, but it isn't. The position varies according to the height of the woman, the size and shape of her breasts, the size of her baby, and the chair or bed she is on. If the baby isn't in a good position, breastfeeding will fail—which is what frequently happens today. Mothers who hear the word might not know exactly what it means. But it alerts them to something they can ask about if they are worried about how to breastfeed. Many of the reasons why so many women thought they "couldn't" breastfeed become understandable once we can use this word.

Yet until a few decades ago there doesn't seem to have been any need for a word to explain this. The information must have been transmitted wordlessly. "In traditional societies," writes Jacqueline Vincent Priya, "all mothers breastfeed and there is an assumption that every mother can and will do so. In all the places I visited, I came across no one who had been unable to breastfeed or who knew of anyone who had failed to provide enough breastmilk for their baby. For girls growing up in such a society, breastfeeding is an everyday activity which they see going on around them and so they learn the techniques unconsciously from an early age."[10] Young children from breastfeeding families, boys as well as girls, put dolls or soft toys to their own nipples in the way they have seen so often. This suggests that, for millennia, women must have visually transmitted this precise and subtle information very successfully from one generation to the next. The achievement is awesome.

Perhaps up till now, mothers haven't needed precise words to describe mothering. Perhaps that explains why we haven't got many.[11] Women saw each other being mothers. The importance and value of what they were doing was obvious. A new mother today, struggling alone with her baby in her apartment, is no longer in this traditional world. On the other hand, she usually has a phone beside her and may have access to the Internet. Mothering is communicated by words as never before. If the words don't exist, communication is hampered.

> So few people will say: "Well done!" when you're a mother. It makes all the difference. [G, 8 months]

Mothers frequently report how a friendly smile from someone in the street or an appreciative remark helps them to feel supported and confident for the rest of the day. But the people who give smiles and appreciation are usually mothers themselves. If other people don't know what mothers can do, they are unlikely to realize that a mother is doing something good, even though they may be looking straight at her.

In the chapters that follow I have had to write out in "longhand" certain descriptions of what mothers do because there are no words or phrases that sum them up. But one could argue that this is making language seem too important. Do the right words ultimately matter? Isn't it enough if mothers do plenty of motherly things, even if they haven't got the right words to describe them?

I believe there is good reason for concern. A mother isn't living in a social vacuum. She isn't just struggling with her own self-esteem, as some people seem to think. A baby is more than her private enterprise. He is not her leisure-time hobby. She is bringing up a new member of our society. Each of us is a member of this interactive society. We can see this if, for example, we watch a mother whose baby starts crying in a slow-moving, hot, crowded bus. Isn't the mother aware of us? She probably glances up anxiously to see if we are disturbed or sits in defiant tension because she feels sure she knows the answer already. Our signals matter to her. Each of us is taking part, though perhaps at moments we haven't noticed, in the upbringing of the new generation.

But our participation is hampered. There are far too many negative words around, all making it easy for us to disparage someone who is struggling to do something difficult. Most work can be described by words that help us to recognize how well we are managing. Mothering is unique in enabling mothers to focus on how *badly* they are doing. Contrast the mother on the bus with a woman on the same bus who is making a fashion statement. This second woman can pick up a range of mixed reactions from other people's expressions. In contrast, the mother with the crying baby will be sensitive to our disapproval. But why shouldn't she too receive a spectrum of reactions? Surely mothers need a range of little signals to orient themselves. That doesn't mean that any mother will do exactly what we like, any more than the woman making her fashion statement will. But she certainly needs the possibility of our admiration to redress the balance.

How can anyone feel satisfied at the end of a day doing something as responsible as being a mother, without being able to explain to herself what she has done well? How can she discuss her day properly with other people if she can describe only her failures? This has a practical implication. If women perceive mothering as unsatisfying, will they enjoy doing it?

It seems that there are always some women who love being mothers whatever the difficulties, and others who hate it. In between are the majority who can turn either way. If there are plenty of words to support their career abilities, but only negative words to pick out their failures as mothers, won't these women feel reluctant to put their reputations on the line? Isn't it only too understandable if they prefer a career that offers them self-respect? Many mothers who have careers complain that they don't gain much financially because their earnings go into paying someone else to look after their babies. But at least these paid carers can then share the responsibility with them.

Historically, some mothers have always paid for child care, which generally took place within the home. Today, however, most mothers work away from their babies and therefore require baby carers. "You'd go mad if you stayed at home, just you and the baby," is what they often say. Surely there is some truth to this. It can feel mad to shoulder such a heavy responsibility with so little recognition from other people for doing daily, ordinary things well. We hear a great deal about the damage a mother can do to her child. But what about the good? Surely the good she does will last her child for his lifetime. Why is this said so rarely?

To sum up, the language we use is important. It transmits a picture of motherhood. At present, it transmits a distorted picture. Women are being misled into believing that they can succeed at their jobs, whereas being a mother is so difficult that success is impossible. A more honest picture would give heart to many women who might choose to look after their babies if they thought they had a chance of being good at it.

What Mothers Do is an attempt to draw a clearer picture. Our starting point will be to listen to what individual mothers say. Most of the statements that follow came from mothers who were sitting in a circle, cradling their babies or watching them play, at one of the variety of meetings I attend. The majority were first-time mothers, whose babies were small enough to bring to meetings. This is useful because the beginning of being a mother is the time when most of the larger questions are asked and decisions made. This is when a mother starts to build up her whole "system" that will become her mothering style. So these meetings are a good way to learn about mothers. But we also need to be aware of the times when they give a "fuzzy" picture because they haven't got precise words. We may also notice them doing more than they think they are doing.

The chapters that follow are arranged under topic headings. It may seem unnatural to select bits of conversation that relate to the topic of each chapter, rather than to reproduce complete conversations in their contexts. However, I have found it revealing to gather together similar statements that I have heard mothers make, sometimes years apart from each other. I have listed them in order of the age of the baby and hope this will be helpful.

We start with a chapter that, logically, needs to come near the beginning. But mothers would be unlikely to discuss it at the beginning of a meeting. It brings out strong feelings, and mothers like to sound each other out first.

two

"nothing prepares you"

Sitting in the safety of a circle, mothers (usually first-time ones) are clear that their lives have changed profoundly since they had their babies. The images they use are dramatic. "It's like being in a different country," "on another planet," "in a separate orbit," "in a parallel universe." They usually have to rock and cuddle their babies as they speak, because the babies tend to cry, perhaps sensing the strength of their mothers' feelings.

> I'm still recovering from the *shock*. After B was born, the midwives left me in this private room. They said: "Your baby really needs you. You must feed him!" But it was night, and there was nobody to show me what to do. [B, 2 weeks]

> I didn't know I'd feel like this. I'm hugely protective. *I* am keeping this baby alive. It's terrifying. [G, 2 weeks]

B was a complete stranger to me when he was born. I love him now—but it wasn't love at first sight by any means. Why didn't someone tell me how *hard* it would be? [B, 5 weeks]

I was in total shock after the birth. I didn't know how to breastfeed or change a diaper or anything. I kept getting "birth" flashbacks, and it took me weeks to get over that. [G, 6 weeks]

Before you have a baby, you have a vision of this happy couple, smiling and taking the baby for walks in the park—and it just hasn't turned out like that. F and I are still trying to get adjusted to the parents we have become. [B, 3 months]

Becoming a mother is like being hit by an earthquake. It's frightening. All your relationships are completely changed by it. [G, 4 months]

I had absolutely no frame of reference. [B, 5 months]

It was a shock the first time. You feel *shell*-shocked. It was different the second time round. I wasn't in that same state of shock. [B, 4 years; G, 1 year]

These are strong statements. The word that mothers keep repeating is "shock." Yet "shock" is an extraordinary word to use about becoming a mother. Motherhood is hardly a new phenomenon. Don't mothers know what to expect? Haven't they managed to pass *any* wisdom on to each other, through so many centuries?

However, as mothers continue to speak, it becomes clear that "shock" is the right word. In traditional cultures girls are given a share of motherly responsibilities when they are young.[1] In Western cultures, most women walk into this world of motherhood as adults, with little experience and little to support them.

In the past most women would expect to become mothers. Motherhood gave a woman entry into the "mainstream" of women's culture. Without a child, she would probably be on the periphery, a kind aunt helping family and friends with their children. Once her baby was born, a mother would expect to be at the center of this feminine culture.

But today the story is different. Many women are in full-time employment. A whole culture has grown up that supports this change. When a woman has a baby, it means taking a break from her work, and this means taking a break from a wide and supportive network of colleagues as well. Her office may hold a "going-away" party for her. Even though she may be taking a break only for a few months, she can feel entirely on her own. Far from joining the mainstream, she can feel as if she has left the mainstream behind her and is venturing forth on a solitary journey. She can feel lonely. Her new loneliness comes from having lost her old supportive circle without gaining a new one. She may discover networks of mothers that welcome her. But the point is that she has to seek them out. The supportive maternal culture is no longer ready and waiting for her.

First-time mothers usually collect information about babies. They pore over books and journals, watch videos, and go to preparation classes. These alert them to expect some surprises. "The less she anticipates this upheaval, the more of a shock it will be," wrote Dr. John Cobb in a book with the very significant title *Babyshock*.[2] But for many women, even though they have attended preparation classes, the reality feels excessive. Surely someone along the road should have stepped in to warn them.

They were prepared to expect a slight shock at having a baby, but what they actually experienced was a massive shock.

Why are mothers so overwhelmed with shock? In a sense, a woman can't prepare for meeting her baby. But she can be prepared to be surprised. That's what happens over erotic love. It's revealing to compare how differently women get ready for romance. We don't go to falling-in-love preparation classes. Rather, the enormity of falling in love is described in songs and poetry, as tragedy and comedy, so it is communicated on many different levels by one generation to the next. "Oh, she's in *love*," we say, and those two crucial words convey a wealth of meaning. We expect the person who is in love to be dreamy, moody, forgetful, unavailable for ordinary commitments, and wholly focused on the beloved person. We pick up warning signals from childhood that falling in love can be a dramatic event and that it has the power to overturn our lives, for better or for worse.

By contrast, the experience of turning into a mother is rarely the subject of songs or literature. There may be stories about unusual crises, but there isn't much popular culture to ease a mother into her new role. This is where traditional lullabies must have been helpful. A lullaby can transmit all kinds of useful information in both words and melody. A mother singing an old lullaby can feel connected to her own childhood, to her mother and grandmother, and come to feel that she belongs to a whole community of mothers. She can turn to the child in her arms and wonder if he will sing the same lullaby to the next generation of children. Today, however, mothers often say that they don't know any "real" lullabies. They invent or adapt songs (see pages 161–62). This surely must leave them with a sense of discontinuity. Lullabies can also encapsulate useful mothering experience. For example, this lullaby comes from a collection called *Weavers of the Songs: the Oral Poetry of Arab Women in Israel and the West Bank.*

> Ah alnamnam, ah alnamnam
> *I put him to sleep, but he does not sleep.*
> *I put him to sleep in the loft,*
> *For I fear the snake.*
> *Rock him, O my brother's wife,*
> *Perhaps your voice will put him to sleep.*[3]

This verse shows how a mother cannot get her baby to sleep, so she passes the baby to her brother's wife. There is a second verse, almost identical, except that it is sung by the brother's wife. Now she, the brother's wife, sings that *she* cannot get the baby to sleep either. So she passes the baby to Said's wife. We are not told who Said's wife is. No more of the lullaby has been printed. This is surely because we are to assume that Said's wife won't have a magic solution either. The words of the lullaby are meant to be repeated, with more women's names being added or perhaps the same women doing a second round.

This tells us about mothers who are muddling along. It shows how much time it can take to lull a baby to sleep. It teaches that the mother does not instinctively "know how," nor have the other women got some superior wisdom that she hasn't. It hints at the anxiety of what to do if *no one* can get the baby to sleep. It also makes listeners more appreciative of a sleeping baby, and makes them question whether it took a lot of singing and rocking to get there.

This kind of lullaby does even more. Even if a mother is on her own when she sings it, she can feel connected to a whole lifestyle, which is slow and repetitive. Patience, compassion, and perseverance are important. The aim is not a pinnacle of achievement but continuity for the road that stretches ahead. Many women today enter this lifestyle with the birth of their babies. It turns all their usual values upside down. Patience and compassion are often despised qualities in the competitive workplaces where many women were employed until their due dates. But being efficient, quick-thinking on the phone, and able to meet deadlines and to coordinate well with a lot of other competitive people—none of this is of much use for being with a new baby. Part of the shock is being uneducated for such a change of orientation.

In older, more traditional societies, mothers took their babies to work, or they were brought to them for breastfeeding. This gave other women a casual, sidelong insight into what it looked like to be a mother. It must have been a time-honored way of preparing women for motherhood. Today, however, work and mothering are segregated. The two worlds are not supposed to overlap. How then is a woman who wants to work till the end of her pregnancy going to pick up ideas about what motherhood is really like?

Up to a generation ago, preparation would begin through childhood play. Today, little girls are still given dolls, but not usually baby ones. However, under-fives seem spontaneously curious about how mothers look after babies. No adult needs to tell them to go and look. New mothers often report that when they are sitting feeding their babies in a play area, children (boys as well as girls) will frequently stop playing and hurry over to study what they are doing. A child will stand and watch for a few minutes. She may say a few words, such as: "Is that your baby? *My* mom's got a baby at home." Her words sound like polite conversation to excuse her watching. After a few minutes, the child runs back to her game again.

The whole learning process seems to work on a visual level, without words. It shows that children need to watch not only their own mothers but also a *variety* of different mothers. From watching, a child learns not just about the practicalities but about the mother's attitude as well. A little girl watching a mother feed her baby would take in not just that particular mother's method but also something of the mother's dignity, or perhaps her casual ease in what she does. Through watching, whole traditions seem to have been transmitted from one generation to the next, with little use of language.

Today, this can be more difficult. Most mothers now return to work within the first year of their child's birth, which is a relatively recent change.[4] Many children therefore spend a lot of their time not in families but in peer groups. A team of professional women may look after them. It then becomes harder for them to catch those essential glimpses of mothers with babies.

Never has any generation prepared its girls as casually for motherhood as ours. In the past, preparation was usually informal, yet it worked. Girls were put in charge of their younger siblings. Such girlhood preparation might have been restricting, yet it seems to have disappeared without anything new to replace it. In what other society do so many new mothers say that they cannot remember holding any baby before they held their own?

In the past, it was assumed that most girls would become mothers. They were educated at school with this end in view. At some stage during the twentieth century, the old assumption faded. Girls are no longer expected to become mothers. This has had a liberating effect on the outlook of girls, but almost certainly it conveys a negative impression about motherhood.

Historically, education was developed for an elite. The aim was to raise the aspirations of educated people to a realm beyond the menial. Some of this attitude has changed as education has expanded—but not completely. It is a deep-rooted idea, so the more children are educated, the more likely they are to pick up negative messages about doing menial tasks. These include practical child care. An Oxford graduate, now a mother, puts this precisely: "Had my education been a waste of time? It had been a jolly good one, but it had taught me to believe that I was too clever, too *achieving,* to spend my time on such dowdy household chores as sewing in [children's] nametapes. It had also convinced me that Real Women Don't Have Babies."[5]

Education supports us in becoming independent thinkers who question and challenge. Mothers today say they think independently. Some are single mothers by choice. Some are the principal wage earners in their marriages. They are proud of their independence. But this may have an unforeseen consequence. Might not a proudly independent mother find it harder to be patient with her dependent baby? Babies today seem to be rushed through babyhood. Mothers praise them for how many continuous hours they "do" at night (i.e., sleep), for learning to play with toys on their own, for not showing "stranger-anxiety," and so on.[6] Perhaps very independent mothers find it harder to understand the dependent needs of their babies.

There is another way in which years of education and work can influence a woman's expectations of motherhood. Being a mother is an ongoing relationship. Dana Breen realized this when she wrote a new preface to her book *Talking with Mothers.* She describes what she calls "the hurdle model," in which a person prepares to overcome a particular difficulty or hurdle. After that, life returns to normal. Becoming a mother, she argues, is not like that. A woman is changed by it, and life is not the same after the birth as before.[7] But why should Dana Breen have to make this point? Surely everyone knows that babies come to stay. However, when we consider how women—today's women—have lived before becoming mothers, we can't help noticing what a large part the "hurdle model" has played.

Education requires students to jump hurdles. There are now tests and examinations right through school and college. They require that a girl prepare thoroughly, demonstrate her knowledge during a short and intense period, and relax afterward. This pattern tends to be repeated at work. A large proportion of today's women work. The more demanding a woman's work, the more it becomes filled with hurdles. There are application forms and interviews, getting to work on time, proving one's competence, special presentations and promotions, defeating rivals, defending one's corner, applications to extend one's scope . . . and on it goes. For each hurdle, a woman prepares, gets herself into gear to do her best for a short and intense time, and expects to relax afterward.

It is only too understandable that a woman might apply the "hurdle model" to childbirth. It looks like a familiar situation, for which the familiar preparation is needed yet again. There are books, videos, sites on the Internet, and courses offering plenty of information to prepare her. She must study hard, aim for a "successful" birth, and then she can go home and relax. Once she has recovered, life will return to normal, as it always has done. It is difficult not to make this assumption, even if vaguely. How alarming, then, to return home with the baby and find there isn't even a moment to settle down to a video or to join her friends for a drink.

Once a baby is born, a woman's life is completely changed. "The strange thing about being pregnant and being a mother is that, although we know the one leads to the other, they are not part of the same psychological thing," wrote Nigella Lawson. "When one friend of mine, shortly after the labor, said that she knew she was pregnant, but why didn't anyone tell her she was going to have a baby, I knew exactly what she meant."[8] So do the mothers to whom I have read this passage.

New mothers sometimes look back on their preparation

classes and feel betrayed. Surely the classes were scant preparation for life with a baby. But the classes can provide only a modest amount of preparation. By the time a mother attends them, only a few months separate her from giving birth. Understandably, the birth concerns her. Prenatal classes respond to her need for information about childbirth. It's a practical, teachable subject. Mothers are receptive and eager to learn. They may listen selectively, screening out information for after the birth. But even if they don't, the degree of unpreparedness that most new mothers face today is surely greater than a course of prenatal classes could make up for.

> I went to lots of classes and read books. I thought I was informed. But nothing prepares you for this. I'm a teacher, and I'd have been all right if I'd given birth to a five-year-old in a classroom. The birth was fine, and I realize now that that's what I'd prepared for. I've never done anything as hard as this in my life. I feel de-skilled. I'm isolated and I'm lonely, and I keep feeling I'm doing the wrong things. It's hard—and it's hard for me to *say* that it's hard. [G, 5 weeks]

> I feel cheated. There was no preparation for a day with your baby after the birth. I used to panic every evening. [B, 6 weeks]

> It's such a shock after the birth. I mean, you prepare for the birth, and suddenly that's *it!* There's this huge open space afterward. [B, 2 months]

> I couldn't think beyond the birth. I was *terrified* of it. [B, 2 months]

> I was so well informed about pregnancy. But pregnancy's a snap compared to what comes after. [B, 3 months]

> Why does no one tell you? They tell you about birth, about high forceps, and ventuse, and C-sections. But nothing for afterward. I thought there was something wrong with G because she wanted to be carried everywhere for about two months. I couldn't put her down for a moment, not even to go to the bathroom. I mean, that might not happen to every mother, but it doesn't seem as rare as all that. Why does nobody tell you? [G, 4 months]

> I remember so clearly the exact moment when we came back from the hospital. B was in his car seat, and I put it down in the front room of our flat, where we've lived for years and years. And I thought: "Help! What am I supposed to do now? What do I do with this baby?" Everything, all the preparation, was for the birth. There was nothing for after. [B, 9 months]

Perhaps these statements sound dramatic. However, reality has *become* dramatic. Overnight, a mother finds herself in a new territory. The very trivia of everyday existence are changed. Looking after a baby means that situations that once seemed quite safe and ordinary now look pitted with unexpected dangers and risks. A baby depends on his mother's vigilance. Perhaps you pass a new mother on the street and she looks a bit dreamy. This must be a "safe" moment. If anything startles her, you can see her eyes immediately become alert. Even the most laid-back woman learns that as a mother she needs to be practical.

I feel as if I've climbed Mount *Everest* because I've done three different things today. They all took a lot of planning. [G, 5 weeks]

When F and I go for a walk [with herself carrying B in a baby carrier], and F tries to talk to me, I can't listen. I'm too busy saying to myself: "Watch that step there. There's a crack in the pavement just ahead. Help, a cyclist." That's all I'm able to think about. [B, 6 weeks]

Every morning I wake up and think where I'm planning to go with B, and try to work out the access to and from places, whether it's got steps and how to manage with the buggy. You just can't go to places like before. [B, 3 months]

Part of my personality is frivolous, whereas motherhood is very practical. [G, 4 months]

All this may help to explain why new mothers often feel completely cut off from their childless friends. They feel they have crossed a great divide. Looking back to the opposite side, they can see these friends in a state of ignorance they understand well.

My friends call and say: "Are you coming clubbing? It's going to be brilliant tonight." They have no idea. I mean, even if I wanted to go, what do they think I'd do about B? But I can remember being exactly the same as them myself. [B, 2 months]

I used to be the same as my friend is now. I used to think it was so *boring* being with a friend who had a baby. I mean, why did she have to keep interrupting us to look after her baby? [G, 4 months]

Long ago, a childless woman was expected to offer help if a friend of hers had a baby. Today women may feel released from these traditional pressures, but this new freedom leaves a woman lonely when she becomes a mother herself. Then she may find it hard to get the warmth and understanding of her old friends, just when she needs them most. An old friend is a valuable reminder of the mother's old self.

Her friends may not understand how profoundly she feels about her baby. He has become a new and vital person in her life. When a mother is pregnant, the baby can seem like her private affair, someone whom only she and her partner really know about. But once her baby is born, he has become a new member of the society that we share. Other people make comments about him, and a mother can feel deeply troubled by them.

> G was crying, and my friend said: "She's a little prima donna." I felt so offended. He doesn't have children. But he was categorizing my child. [G, 2 months]

> There was a little boy in the mother and baby group where we were, with sticking out ears. It didn't *matter.* He'd soon have enough hair to look like everyone else. But this other mother called out: "Oooh, what a lovely pair of *jug*-ears!" I saw the baby's mother draw close to him and she kept stroking and stroking the top of his little head, and you could just see how terribly hurt she felt. You do want your child to be accepted. [B, 11 months]

A new mother's sensitivity seems to be functional. She is learning to tune in to how other people react to her child. If there is a problem, she will take a lot of trouble to ease it. She is the person who links her child to our whole society. She often notices details that no one else does. That is her "job" as a mother. The flip side of her sensitivity, which she needs in order to be a competent mother, is a new tendency to become easily hurt.

She has known her baby for his entire life. Many women are completely unprepared for the powerful feelings this evokes. Many of them defined themselves as "working women" and expected to fit their babies into their established routines. They didn't anticipate feeling so close to their babies that they might not want to return to work. This affects their work arrangements.

Recently, employers have become more flexible toward mothers. Mothers can now take "maternity leave" or plan a "career break," but the assumption is that this is a short-term arrangement. Babies are regarded as an interruption to the normal flow of work. This can encourage a mother to see her employment as more important than having a baby. Mothers often report the shock of discovering that after childbirth their values reverse. For the first time, their employment, which meant a great deal to them before, can look *less* important than the baby.

> If I give up my job, my career will be finished. I've got a science Ph.D. and my job is in research. It took me years to reach this stage. Now I'll be out of date if I stop working. But I want to be with G. I don't really *care!* [G, 3 months]

> What gets me is having to make all these decisions before your child is born. You don't realize how you are going to

feel then. I made all these decisions about going back to work—and now I don't want to. I don't want to leave B. B might be fine with someone else, but it's much too soon for me. [B, 4 months]

I've changed in a way I never thought I would. I never thought I'd want to stay at home and look after a baby. I'm under contract to take maternity leave till B's nine months old. At nine months, he'll be starting to crawl and walk, and I just don't want to think about it. I don't want someone else there, looking after my child. I want to be sharing it and seeing my child develop, myself. [B, 6 months]

Before the births of their babies, many mothers may well think they are signing their names to a generous amount of maternity leave. At the end of that time, they are contracted to return to work. If they refuse, their contracts require them to repay their maternity leave money, which is probably long-since spent. Many mothers find they feel devastated when the time comes to return to work.

Employment arrangements are continuing to change. Mothers are often experienced workers, and in order to retain them employers will need to offer even more flexible options. But this hasn't happened yet. It is a tragedy that because women are unprepared for the warm love they are likely to feel for their babies, too many of them are contracted to return to work before they are ready, and their babies are deprived of their loving daytime care.

The rest of this book explores what mothers learn and how they manage. At some stage, almost unnoticed, they transform from being "new mothers" to being "more experienced." Despite the lack of preparation, mothers do find their way.

Having a baby—like dying—is one of the great transitions that we face for which there can be no rehearsal. But that doesn't mean there can be no preparation. At the very least, we can be prepared to be disoriented and shocked. This awareness can be helpful. It is when mothers exchange stories about the difficult weeks after childbirth that they start to feel stronger. If everyone else is finding it hard going, it puts personal troubles in a new perspective. We may be shocked when we first have babies, but at least we could recognize that, given how unprepared we are, this is only to be expected.

A woman in the first shock of love is expected to be dreamy and forgetful. A person bereaved is expected to feel lonely and tearful. Mothers may be given a "warming-up" period of a couple of weeks. After that, they are usually expected to be calm and capable. Would it not be much more realistic to expect new mothers to be unprepared, anxious, confused, and very emotional for at least the first six months? If we could accept that this beginning is the norm for most new mothers, we would be in a better position to be supportive and respectful.

A mother would still be left with the smaller, unavoidable shock that each baby brings. The most common emotion mothers report when they first set eyes on their babies is surprise. Perhaps it is similar to meeting a penpal with whom one has corresponded for nine months. One is bound to build up an impression—but the real person is different. The nine months were a preparation of a sort. But now the relationship has really begun.

three

"all the responsibility"

The birth of a new baby ought to be a manageable surprise to his mother, rather than a complete confidence shaker. She needs to be calm enough to enjoy him and to work out what he needs. There is no word for the process of getting to know an individual newborn baby. It's a considerable challenge. This is no nine-to-five research project, with a computer to collate results and a comfortable night's sleep between one day and the next. Suddenly the new mother learns that she cannot even hurry to the toilet without first thinking about the safety and well-being of her baby. If she runs a longed-for bath, will she hear him crying above the noise of the bathwater? If she rushes off to her job and delegates care to someone else, will that person really know how to look after him and at what point to telephone and consult her at work?

The sense of shock seems to be at its greatest while the relationship is getting started. The mother hasn't tuned in to her baby's "signals" yet; nor has her baby tuned in to hers. Mothers report not the ordinary surprises of the learning process but the alarm of having too little preparatory ground under their feet.

> I can remember, in the beginning, great *waves* of panic going through me at being a mother. [B, 6 weeks]

> I trained as a midwife, so I was used to holding babies, and washing them. But I remember looking at B, after we'd got home from the hospital, and seeing his dear little face and hands—and having a wee bit of a cry at the responsibility. You don't prepare for *that* as a midwife. [B, 6 weeks]

> I can't get used to that feeling: "The buck stops with you." My husband asks: "Shall I change B for *you*?" [B, 2 months]

> Nothing prepares you for the responsibility. I've had a very responsible job. I worked long hours, and I hardly spent any time at home. Suddenly that's where I was, all day long, all on my own, with a totally dependent baby. [G, 3 months]

> F and I are still not over the shock. We can't believe how much B has changed our lives—and how totally exhausted we feel. You are not used to all the responsibility, twenty-four hours around the clock. Losing my virginity meant nothing by comparison. Having a baby has changed my life. [G, 13 months]

The key word that mothers keep repeating is "responsibility." As a breastfeeding counselor, I sometimes have mothers telephone me with what they think are questions about breastfeeding. Then, while they are trying to explain their practical difficulties, they break down in shocked sobbing as they suddenly realize that their underlying dilemma is that they feel overwhelmed. Their responsibilities seem enormous—and they are not prepared for them.

The word "responsible" is related to "response"—and responding is exactly what a mother finds herself doing. She learns to *respond* to her baby. In most relationships, this is done through words. If a woman was expecting an unknown guest from abroad, she could ask about her guest's preferences. It may seem a very unfamiliar process to have to watch and listen to the nonverbal "signals" of her baby. Slowly it becomes easier. But at first it often means a whole new style of communicating.

A new mother has to relearn what to expect of her baby. No longer is he that lively, kicking, hiccupping being, stretching and trampolining around inside her. After birth, it can feel as if she's getting to know a different person.

> *First mother:* I felt almost at one with B when he was inside me. I knew his every movement. I felt I loved him so much. But when he was born, he looked at me as if he didn't know me. I felt I didn't know him. I remember I felt betrayed. [B, 3 weeks]
>
> *Second mother:* I had the opposite reaction. When I was pregnant, I could just forget about it. A girl at work said she couldn't concentrate anymore because she was so tuned in to the baby inside her. I thought: "I don't feel that. Maybe I'll be a bad mother and I won't be able to love my baby." I had no idea what I'd be like. But now B is born, I love him and think about him all the time. [B, 6 weeks]

Extended families tend to spread the responsibility. Some couples divide the responsibility as equally as possible between the two of them. However, before they return to work, the majority of mothers shoulder the heavy weight of responsibility themselves.

There are bookshelves of advice on how to look after a baby. The books are often beautifully written and illustrated. The difficulty is that they contradict each other. Often a mother cannot decide which of two opposite suggestions is "right." Both sides seem so adamant that only their view is the "right" one.

> *First mother*: I want someone to tell me what to do. I wish I had a map. I'm all at sea. There's no routine, and I never know what to do when, or if I'm doing it right. [B, 8 weeks]
>
> *Second mother*: If you ever find that map, will you show it to *me*? [B, 8 weeks]

> What is *my* way of being a mother? I look for role models and there are none. I have this continual dialogue going on in my head that I'm not doing it right. [G, 4 months]

> I'm reading two books with opposite views about whether to leave your baby to cry. I'm really confused. [B, 5 months]

> B's very unsettled at night. He likes me to lift him up and carry him about. People said nights would be easier after the first three months. I keep wondering what I am doing wrong. [B, 5 months]

> I'm going to write a book about motherhood and put in all the things that no one tells you. Like, when B was small,

I could easily have rushed out to a phone booth and rung in and said: "Sorry, folks, I can't cope. It's too hard." There were times when I thought I'd never get through. [B, 7 months]

These feelings of being lost and disoriented are not recent. Tolstoy describes them. In his novella *The Kreutzer Sonata*, completed in 1889, the chief character, Pozdnyshev, describes his wife as a mother:

> *Quite apart from all the talk about illnesses and their treatment, about the best methods of rearing children and educating them, she was surrounded on all sides by a great mass of divergent and constantly changing rules and regulations, both printed and spoken. Children should be fed like this, with this; no, not like that, not with that, but like this; how they should be dressed, what they should be given to drink, how they should be bathed, put to bed, taken out for walks, how to see they got enough fresh air—every week we (or rather she) discovered new rules affecting all this. As if it were only yesterday that children had started being brought into the world. And if the feeding method was wrong, if the bathing was done in the wrong way or at the wrong time, and the child fell ill, then it was all her fault, as she hadn't done what she was supposed to do.*[1]

Reading this description, we are in a world which most of us recognize: the world of experts. Tolstoy was thinking of medical authorities who would guide mothers on feeding and bathing their babies. Today mothers are also faced with "authorities" on their children's emotional and intellectual development. To a new mother, the opinion of the expert who has never met either her or her baby can matter more than her own ideas. She supposes her baby must be out of line because he does not do what the expert assured her was "normal" for a baby of that particular age.

It may sound strange, but the solution to this "problem" does not seem to be a super-expert, the last word on all the conflicting experts. Far from helping new mothers, the experts may undermine the confidence each mother needs to work out for herself what her baby wants. She needs some practical information on child care, without too many stone-cast "rules." Any childhood memories and experiences she can recall are likely to be extremely helpful to her. She needs medical information if her child is ill. Apart from that, and although it may seem extraordinary to our expert-and-hurdle-oriented outlook, a new mother doesn't usually need much more.

If she feels disoriented, this is not a problem requiring bookshelves of literature to put right. No, it is exactly the *right* state of mind for the teach-yourself process that lies ahead of her. Every time a woman has a baby she has something to learn, partly from her culture but mostly from the baby. If she really considered herself an expert, or if her ideas were set, she would find it very hard to adapt to her individual baby. Even after her first baby, she cannot sit back as an expert on all babies. Each child will be a little different and teach her something new. She needs to feel uncertain in order to be flexible. So, although it can seem so alarming, the "all-at-sea" feeling is appropriate. Uncertainty is a *good* starting point for a mother. Through uncertainty, she can begin to learn.

With a new baby, dozens of questions seem to rush toward a new mother. For most questions, she has absolutely no answer. The decision making starts almost before a mother is aware that she is making any decisions. Perhaps someone wheels over a crib in the hospital ward and suggests she puts her baby in it. Whether she lays the baby down in the crib or continues to hold him in her arms may seem a completely trivial choice. Yet it's important. Next time around she either repeats her choice or modifies it.

In this way she builds up her own system. She herself may hardly be aware of it, though her baby may already be starting to learn what to expect from her. It is a bit like knitting, when the first few rows don't look like anything much. Only much later can one see that they were the start of a pattern. So the mother doesn't have to keep restarting with the basics. She can use her early decisions as a foundation on which to build a working system. On a good day, a mother can feel pleased with what she has achieved. This helps her to feel more confident and less chaotic. But there are bound to be difficult days when there seems no order, no sense, and no predictability. A mother may long for a super-expert, then, to show her what to do. New mothers tend to swing emotionally up and down between confident days and confusing ones.

This stage of learning is not the popular idea of a mother. Paintings and photographs portray mothers with calm faces holding calm babies and looking eons beyond the slightest shadow of self-doubt. Many people find it very hard to tolerate a mother who is feeling uncertain. They perceive her as a person who has lost control, who cannot cope, and who needs help. People around her step in quickly, as if filling a vacuum, to supply the "missing" certainty. Some make suggestions; others give orders. This can be disheartening for a mother. It is hard to feel so uncertain. It is even harder if she thinks that other people have lost confidence in her. Instead of seeing her uncertainty as necessary, she disparages it as *un*motherly. It seems like a sign of her incompetence, demonstrating that she has failed to become a good mother from the very outset.

Rarely is it necessary to tell a mother what to do. It may demoralize her further, and it certainly does not help her to learn. A mother needs to feel safe enough to risk feeling uncertain. People who offer advice cannot know all the details of her situation. They also don't usually have to live with the long-term consequences of their advice. A mother needs time to "grow" into parenthood, together with her partner. She needs enough confidence to experiment and change her mind a few times. She needs to learn that some of her ideas work. The most uncertain and underconfident beginner can gradually turn herself into a unique mother.

The miracle is that mothers manage to survive at all in such an expert-ridden climate. After lonely periods of confusion, they suddenly discover that they are starting to understand their babies. As their babies grow, so does their confidence.

> I'm learning to trust myself, rather than the books. After all, no one knows B better than I do, and even *I* don't know him that well. [B, 5 months]

> I haven't got a policy, and it's no good just doing what people tell you. It's a matter of juggling to see what works with this particular baby at this very moment. [B, 5 months]

> The hardest thing to admit to myself, and I *still* find it hard, even now, is that I *do* know really. I'm the sort of person who will always rush to a book to tell me what to do. But with B, I do know. It's simple. When he cries, I pick him up. And often we have such lovely times together. [B, 6 months]

> Every time I put a "should" onto what B is doing, from what I've read or something someone told me, it puts a negative on it. Then I think B is wrong and I "lose" B. And when I do that, I'm not listening to him anymore. [B, 6 months]

> I used to be like a leaf in the wind. I'd read something and think: "Yes, must try that." Then I'd read something that took the opposite view and I'd think: "Yes, *that's* the right way." But now I've discovered that my mood correlated with what I read. The more I read, the more miserable I felt. B wasn't like the babies in the books. It was difficult to believe I could just go with B. [B, 14 months]

Having a second baby can show a woman just how much she has learned:

> It's only when you have a second one that you realize how much you've learned from the first. I thought I'd be as scared as the first time. But I'm not. I'm thinking: "Hang on! You've been here before. You can do this." [B, 2 years; G, 4 months]

The mother who longed for a map to show her where to go had this to say when she had a second child:

> There *isn't* a map. I know that now. It's different for everyone. It seems important for every mother to do things her way, and for other people not to judge. I can remember everyone judging me, so I thought I'd got things wrong. [B, 4 years; B, 6 months]

The message that comes through clearly is that when mothers feel very uncertain they can be easily intimidated by "expert" advice. When you are listening to a mother, it can often sound as though there are three people in her home: herself, her baby, and whichever "baby expert" she is trying to follow. Expertise is invaluable in exceptional circumstances. But mothers can be pressured into supposing that they need someone to tell them how to run their everyday lives. While it is true that everyday life with a new baby can be unnerving, it can also be an opportunity to learn. Once they start learning, mothers find they can feel more relaxed.

> I saw a woman in a shop with a newborn, and I felt so glad I'd got beyond that. I really *know* B now. He's a little person. He's not a stranger anymore. [B, 2 months]

> Being a mother is all about feeling your way. That's not part of the dominant culture, which is all about planning and controlling. [B, 3 months]

> At first I felt as if G was made of bone china—you know, too precious to put down. I kept carrying her for the first three months, because *nowhere* seemed good enough to put her down on. I've got over that now. It seems funny, looking back. I don't know when that feeling went or where it's gone. [G, 5 months]

Part of the weight of the mother's responsibility is that no one can completely take her place. She remains responsible whether she has gone to work or left someone else in charge.

> I was longing for some time to myself, and I made F take charge of B. I drove down to the end of our road, and

> then—it was so weird—I just had to *jump* out of our car and phone home from a phone booth! F answered. I couldn't hear B crying, so I said to F in a frantic voice: "Where's *B*? What are you *doing*?" F said, in amazement: "B's just lying quietly beside me." I could tell from his voice that he thought I was exaggerating how hard it is, looking after B. [B, 2 months]

The father has his own responsible relationship with his child. However, neither parent here seemed to appreciate how different it is for the mother. The mother isn't just "looking after" her child. She is responsible for him even in her absence.

This affects her in all kinds of ways. For example, she can easily forget about herself in the urgent need to look after her baby. The early weeks are tiring, and she is often short of sleep. She can't always be calm and smiling. More troubled feelings may come as a surprise.

> I once picked up G violently, and I surprised myself because I didn't know I was going to. I suppose all your concentration goes to the baby, and you lose touch with yourself. [G, 3 months]

It helps to feel safe enough to explore these unexpected feelings. Two mothers who felt at ease with each other and with me had the following conversation:

> *First mother*: I feel ashamed of what I'm going to say. It may make me sound like a terrible woman. I used to have these really strong images flash through my head, images of throwing my baby out of the window, or even holding his head down in his bathwater. I'm aware that I have the

power to do that. They were like hallucinations. I used to keep having them, and it's only very recently that they've stopped. I don't know why they've stopped. In fact, I've only just realized that they have. [B, 5 months]

Second mother: I can relate to what you said about hallucinations. I used to have them too. Could it be to somehow help you prepare for the things you mustn't do?

Me: What do you yourself think?

Second mother: I think it's a sort of preparation. [G, 5 months]

I live on the second floor. Every day, when I carry G down the steps I have these awful visions of what could happen if I fell. [G, 4 months]

In my mind, G has died a thousand times. [G, 7 months]

These nightmares and virtual hallucinations sound like a kind of "in-house" preparation, but it is easy to see how one could interpret them differently. A mother might think that she really wanted to harm her child. Freud stated that people may not be conscious of their feelings; this hypothesis might lead one to believe that a mother who thought about drowning her baby was expressing an "unconscious wish."

Mothers who are starting to recognize their responsibilities also recognize their enormous power. A mother can choose to use her power for good or evil, for life or death. It can be difficult to make responsible decisions for good and for life, not for oneself but on behalf of a baby, and it becomes even more difficult when a mother is alone and short of sleep. It makes sense to recognize that she might often feel afraid that in a tired and irritable moment she might endanger her baby, either by taking insufficient care or by venting her irritability and frustrations with her own affairs onto her baby. The vivid scenarios that mothers report sound like an effective warning system. Perhaps these mothers are preparing themselves to make absolutely sure that, however tired and irritable they feel, they will be alert enough to keep their babies safe.

Nadia and Daniel Stern confirm this from their own observations of mothers:

> *Most new mothers fear that the baby will die or be hurt through carelessness or inadequacy. Have you never worried that the baby will fall from the changing table onto its head when you are not looking; or that the baby will slip out of your wet and soapy hands and drown in the bath? Or maybe he'll bang his head on the tub when you take him out, or get tangled up in the blankets or get caught under a pillow and suffocate?*

They voice several more possible fears that a new mother might have, and conclude:

> *These are the natural fears that keep new mothers vigilant, the better to protect their babies and at the same time to help themselves internalise and absorb their new responsibilities.*[2]

Some useful research could be done here. If a research study could demonstrate that many tired mothers experience these involuntary visions of harming their babies but show no signs of *actually* wanting to harm them, mothers could feel reassured by this information. It is frightening enough to experience these visions. If they are more like a warning to a mother—just that—then she can better understand herself. On the other hand, if a mother is told that her fear *must* be hiding her unconscious wish, the statement acts like a noose and cannot be invalidated. (The more a mother protests, the more she can be claimed to be "unconscious" and "in denial" of her destructive wishes.)

Some mothers, however, do struggle with ideas of wanting to destroy their babies. These thoughts are often *conscious.* They do not prepare mothers to protect their babies. Mothers who think like this are continually afraid that their thoughts and feelings might escalate out of control. They feel they might suddenly do something to endanger their babies' safety. It isn't easy to distinguish between the first group of mothers and the second. Perhaps there is some overlap. Mothers in the first group learn how to protect their babies. Slowly they become calmer. Mothers in the second group are not learning and remain anxious. Ambivalent feelings toward babies are further discussed on pages 87–88 and 192–210. These mothers sometimes feel calmer once their babies become children who can talk (see page 212).

As a baby develops, his mother starts to get more confident. At least some of the basics are now familiar to her. But then new questions appear on the horizon. A mother's new self-assurance may sound impressive—but it is usually tentative. A chance remark can start a mother reviewing her ideas. In my experience, even the most confident-sounding mother is quick to question herself. The whole of the first year may prove a steep climb.

> My friend does everything differently from me. She leaves her baby to cry, but I get a tight feeling in my stomach and I have to pick B up. I feel more confident about what I'm doing now, so I didn't feel I had to defend myself while she was there. But the *instant* she left and I closed

the door behind her, I started to think that she was right and I was doing everything wrong! [B, 8 months]

I liked explaining things to G. Then my mother gave me a copy of Dr. Spock. He says that too many explanations can confuse a child. That made me start listening to the way I talk to G. *Was* I confusing her? It's silly because now I've become really self-conscious and can't remember my old way of talking to her. [G, 10 months]

I feel confident on some days. Then some little thing I read or hear really throws me, and I lose my confidence all over again. [G, 12 months]

Mothers often imagine that they will eventually reach a stage of complete confidence. But perhaps such a stage is unattainable. To their credit, many mothers seem to continue to question their mothering choices for the rest of their lives. This self-questioning would be unbearable if it wasn't for surprising moments when mothers realize that, after all, they are not *totally* responsible for their children. Babies are dependent—but also strongly independent young people.

You don't need to rattle things in their faces. B likes a calm time, just sitting and watching our cat. [B, 4 months]

They let you know what they need. If you look, they show you. You don't have to think of everything yourself. I found it quite liberating when I realized that. [B, 5 months]

> You don't need to teach G to be curious, because she really *is*. And you don't need to stimulate her or teach her to play or anything. She does it all! [G, 6 months]

> I put B in a swing and pushed him for a while from the back. Then I walked around to see his face, to see if he was enjoying it. And I saw this really thoughtful little face. He was *thinking*. I could see he was thinking his own thoughts, though he hasn't got words, so it must be preverbal. He's *not* an extension of me. He's *him*. I feel so . . . The first year wasn't easy, I must be honest. But this makes it all worthwhile. I can see his intelligence burning like a little fire that grows and grows. [B, 15 months]

These early signs of her baby's independence can reassure a mother that what may feel like total responsibility is a delicately changing balance. The heavy weight will not be hers forever.

four

"being instantly interruptible"

This subject deserves a chapter to itself because it concerns one of the most difficult things that mothers learn to do. A mother may do it twenty times a day, yet she may be unaware of it. She may notice herself doing something before it—and after it. But something in between goes unseen. Although I have listened carefully to what mothers have told me for so many years, I have no quotations to offer for this chapter. If I prompt with a leading question, mothers usually agree that this is something they do. But they don't seem to regard it as anything special.

Imagine the mother of a young baby in her kitchen. The baby is asleep in the room next door. The mother is hurrying around, doing four things at once: tidying a surface, making a sandwich, trying to listen to the radio, which is on very low so that she can hear her baby if he wakes, and jotting down a shopping list because whenever she manages to go shopping with her baby she invariably forgets to buy something important.

Doing four things at once while the baby is asleep is a whole art that the mother has just learned. Not a moment will be wasted. Suddenly a loud wail of distress comes from the room next door. The mother stops tidying the surface. She may snatch up the sandwich to take with her, turn off the radio, and tell herself not to forget the item she was just going to add to her shopping list. Then she hurries to see to her baby.

It is this nameless act—when a mother puts down a whole myriad of threads of her personal existence as soon as her baby cries—that deserves some word to acknowledge it. Not all mothers respond. Some balk at being interrupted. Others respond but with exasperation, so the child gets a mixed blessing. But mothers who do manage to respond in a more generous way, at least some of the time, will confirm that it can be trying. Just when a mother is in mid-activity, her baby invariably wakes up and cries for her.

The mother can feel as if she has lost all control over her own life. "The strange thing about being B's mother is that B now calls all the shots," wrote one mother to me. Yet her son hasn't got the power to call those shots. No baby has. If babies really did have such power, their mothers' readiness to be interrupted would not be so admirable. Who likes being interrupted? Mothers who respond aren't usually afraid that their babies cannot wait. Most babies could probably hold out for a few moments while their mothers finished something. But the relationship might suffer. Mothers learn that their babies become distressed if they do not respond quickly. Seen like this, a mother's choice makes sense. She wants her baby to learn that he can trust her. She is in control of her own decision to respond, even when this interrupts her.

At first each outburst of crying is a surprise, but mothers gradually learn to be prepared even before their babies cry. They are "on call." A mother starts an activity knowing that she may be interrupted at any moment. While she is still new to all this, the sudden interruptions are comparable to turning off a computer without saving all the work first. Slowly a mother learns to spend a few seconds in "saving" whatever she was doing. This means noticing how she is putting everything down and reminding herself what she needs to do next in such a way that she can resume what she was engaged in with minimal trouble. All those complex little threads will be picked up later.

While the mother is feeding or comforting her baby, her thoughts are usually free to prepare her for resuming her activities. Leaving work half done is a feature of life with a small baby. Once her baby needs her, the mother may have to spend long periods looking after him, with the washing up half done and bits of the evening meal started. She may sit quietly with her baby yet be busy in her imagination, finishing off several activities in her thoughts. There may be a frustrating stop-go progress through these activities that continues all day. But once her baby is in a deep sleep, all that thinking has prepared her. If she has energy left, her use of time will be very efficient.

Though it has no name, at least this process has been described. Tillie Olsen mentions it, in arguing how difficult it is for a mother to write novels:

> *More than any other human relationship, overwhelmingly more, motherhood means being instantly interruptible, responsive, responsible. Children need one* now. . . . *The very fact that these are real needs, that one feels them as one's own (love, not duty);* that there is no one else responsible for these needs, *gives them primacy.*[1]

Being needed "now" is not easy. As Tillie Olsen says, no other relationship is like being a mother. A professional child carer has time off. A relative of an ill person may be in a more comparable situation. But one can usually reassure an ill person if he or she is no longer an infant. An older person, even though ill, can usually understand the call of "Just coming!" A young baby, on the other hand, will cry and cry, as if he believes his mother is never coming back.

Because human beings are good at adapting, some mothers become adept at being "on call." They find that after all they can make rough predictions and provisional plans. Gradually, being prepared to be interrupted becomes the norm. Then mothers find it much more difficult to cope with the old method of doing one task at a time and getting it all finished.

A mother may feel she has become stupid because she cannot focus on a single issue for very long the way that she used to. Her partner may also voice exasperation when he is trying to develop one idea in depth or tell her a complicated anecdote, and he can see that she keeps interrupting her attentiveness. It is hard for her to explain that undivided concentration seems a luxury to her now. Even if her baby is sound asleep, she will automatically interrupt whatever she is doing to look or listen, to make sure the baby is *still* all right. It is not a sign of disrespect for her partner. It is a sign that she is learning to become a reliable and competent mother of their child.

Can anyone really get used to these frequent sudden interruptions? Don't mothers resent their babies for interrupting them? Mothers record that their first response is often annoyance. It is revealing to check for how long they feel annoyed. What do they feel at the moment when they actually get to their babies and see their hot, crying faces? Facing her child, a mother can see how much she was needed. Her baby's distressed face makes this clear. So the interruption seems worthwhile. Some mothers—not all—describe those moments as times when they have felt a great flow of compassion and tenderness for their babies. This has overcome their earlier annoyance. It has provided the energy to attend to the baby without feeling resentful or that they were under their babies' control.

Slowly the baby develops. His mother finds that he becomes less distressed if he has to wait a few moments while she finishes what she is doing. Almost imperceptibly, fewer of his cries have that urgent pitch. In the end it becomes rare. But the reasons for it are usually then more serious. For the rest of her life, her child may suddenly turn to her and expect her immediate attention.

This prompt reaction of mothers is no trivial act. It must be one of the reasons for human survival. We surely owe our own lives to the countless hardworking mothers before us who responded to the cries of our infant ancestors. The health of a small baby can deteriorate suddenly, and then he needs his mother at his side. So her habitual promptness was, is, and will continue to be important.

But this is not the only value of what the mother does. A baby is not necessarily ill when he cries for her. Yet the mother's prompt response conveys something vital to her child about their relationship. We shall understand it better if we try to put ourselves in the baby's place.

We have all been infants ourselves, yet it isn't easy to recall how we felt. Once it was we who lay so small, inexperienced, and helpless. Once it was we who cried because our lives depended on it. We had lost our life-in-the-womb, where we had been protected from hunger, bright light, noise, and sudden changes in temperature. Birth brought us into an exciting world but one with a host of bodily discomforts. We felt the ache of hunger or suddenly were suffering from gas. Sounds were much louder, no longer mitigated by water. Most of all, we had lost the independence of movement that we had known in the womb.

After birth, we might wave our arms and legs, but the amniotic fluid had gone and the lightweight air just slipped past our hands and feet without helping us to move. Perhaps we would wake up in dazzling light, so different from the dappled darkness of the womb. It was too bright to see. We could not even raise our bodies to look around us. In our distress we cried, and a few moments later our mother was at our side.

If our mother came, it meant that she had responded to us when we felt most vulnerable. That gave us a reassurance we hadn't had in the womb. In the womb, we had been alone—unless we were one of a multiple pregnancy. Once born, we discovered time and again that we could trust an adult person to come to our side.

It is true that several people can take turns to respond to a crying baby. It need not always be the mother. Yet there is an advantage when it continues to be the same person, although this isn't always practicable. We might get closer to the baby's situation if we imagine being ill in the hospital. If we are totally dependent on those who nurse us, the changes of nurse can be disturbing. No sooner have we achieved some rapport with one nurse than the shift changes, and we have to use our precious energy to start all over again, building up a rapport with someone else. Babies seem to be in this position.

It may seem a trivial act for the mother to put down her longed-for sandwich, keep her frustration under control, and go to see to her baby, but it has important consequences. Her baby learns from it that he can call for help from another person no matter how busy she is. He learns it slowly, through repetition. We recognize that he has learned it because this makes sense of his behavior. At first he cries with a desperate sound, as if he has forgotten how quickly his mother came only an hour ago. Months later, his cry sounds loud but less desperate, more like a call which he means her to answer.[2] Now he seems to *expect* her to come promptly and to feel upset if she doesn't. However, if she comes a great deal later than usual, he is often in a state of distress. This makes sense if we consider that from his point of view, his expectation of a trustworthy mother who came when he cried appeared to have been betrayed. It may take longer to calm him. Once calm, however, he seems happy to trust his mother again. A few delayed responses on her part don't seem to make a difference.

Mothers sometimes fear that they will "spoil" their babies. They fear that their babies will manipulate them into coming "just for attention," and that they will grow into children who will expect their mothers to keep putting everything down for trifles. This doesn't seem to happen. If a baby is crying for attention, he seems to need it. If an older child has become manipulative, it is nearly always because he hasn't been able to get what he needs by more straightforward methods. Moreover, one can see how a baby who has been given attention when he cried for it develops into a generous child, who is sensitive to the feelings of other people.

It is important to repeat that nothing in this book is a prescription. Not all mothers choose to be instantly interruptible. Those who do may not do it every time. It fits some mothers' systems and not those of others. It's an example of a valuable act that has no name. Because it has no name, it is overlooked.

Mothers hardly notice when they do it. But we could be more aware of this wonderful act and observe how often mothers are doing this.

five

the power of comfort

Human comfort is one of the finest strengths that we offer each other. It can be casually given, by a touch, a smile, a few words, or even by silence. Yet it's very effective. It doesn't usually alter the source of our troubles, but it strengthens us so we feel better able to confront them.

Many mothers comfort their babies when they cry. This often goes unnoticed. The mother of a baby who cries a lot usually receives pity for being disturbed. She will be perceived as "unlucky" because her baby needs her so much. Her new ability to comfort is frequently overlooked. This chapter is not meant to pressure anyone into comforting but to increase our sensitivity to those who do.

Comfort seems to work cumulatively, which means that it is hardest to give at the beginning. Newborns, especially, seem to live mostly in the present moment. When they cry, it sounds intensely in the present, and that makes it hard to deal with. Any of us can cry "like a baby," but however hard we cry we can eventually get back our adult perspective and it calms us. A newborn, on the other hand, hasn't discovered this yet.

The immediacy of a baby's cry is powerful. This has a practical advantage. A baby needs to be able to alert his mother, since his daily—and nightly—survival depends on her. Which one of us would waken from the depths of sleep, night after night, if our babies didn't insist on it? So we rouse ourselves, remember that we are mothers and become alert. The crying demands that we do something about it.

The literature on crying babies tends to focus on technique. However, responding to a crying baby involves more than technique. Underlying what a mother does is her philosophy of human nature. She may hardly be aware of it, but it affects the many quick decisions she has to make. Her basic choice is either to see her baby as good, in which case she trusts him, or alternatively to see him as the product of evil human nature, or of original sin, which requires her to train him. This makes a great difference.

The mother who trusts her baby will pick him up and hold him close. The mother who sees her baby's crying as a cue for training will keep a distance. It can help if a mother who responds one way can appreciate that a mother doing the opposite is not ignorant or shortsighted. It's simply that the two mothers do not share the same basic philosophy. Once they recognize this, mothers can still reach out to one another in understanding. Not all mothers have a clear-cut philosophy. Some aren't sure what they believe. They try first one way and then another. Mothers who are undecided may find this chapter useful in clarifying some of the issues involved.

The mother who is training her baby usually gets much quicker results than the one who trusts hers. The trained baby will soon learn the consistent rules that his mother has laid down. This means that his mother's life will be more predictable and ordered. She may *feel* very different from the woman she was a year ago, but her lifestyle will have returned to something like the way it was. By contrast, the mother who trusts her baby can feel thrown into chaos. Days and nights have lost their shape. Nothing seems predictable. We shall track this second group of mothers because comforting plays an important part in their lives. Yet they are frequently compared unfavorably with the first group. Compared with a mother who trains her baby, a mother who comforts appears to be "doing nothing."

Many new mothers work at demanding jobs until just before their babies are due. This means that just before they take maternity leave, many of them feel bound to prove that they can still be tough, competent, and competitive. In a large number of jobs, feelings are regarded as a hindrance, and a woman finds it easier if she can set her emotions to one side while she is working. However, a crying baby can reform his mother in an instant. He looks distressed and sounds frightened and helpless. Hard though this may be, it can have a heart-melting effect on her. She may suffer greatly in her concern for her baby. And it shows. Her face, her gestures, and her voice all soften and grow more tender and gentle. Her expression becomes alert and watchful. She feels warmly compassionate toward her baby. Her compassion then expands. She starts to notice first other babies, then other mothers, and eventually all kinds of vulnerable people.

> When G cries, it's a high cry of pain. I'm a complete lettuce leaf. I hold her and I cry too. [G, 2 months]

> I think: "Oh, please, *please,* stop." But she can't help it. [G, 2 months]

> *First mother:* B was crying at the mother and baby class. Nothing I did quieted him. I felt terrible. I thought all the mothers must have come to the class for a bit of peace and quiet, and *my* baby was stopping them. [B, 2 months]
>
> *Second mother:* I was there and I'll tell you how I felt. There were tears dropping down *my* cheeks too, not for B but for you. I knew so exactly how you must be feeling. [B, 3 months]

> I was watching a baby on television crying and crying for its mother. I knew it was hungry. And I noticed my palms got sweaty, my heart pounded, and my boobs were burning as if they wanted to burst out with milk right across the room. Before I had B, it would have passed right by me. [B, 3 months]

It's not only first-time mothers who feel this compassion. A distressed baby can upset an experienced mother too.

> B was different from my other three children. He used to cry every afternoon, especially after the older ones came back from school. It was terrible. I felt absolutely terrible, even though I'm an experienced mother. Even though I'm sitting here telling you all how terrible I felt when B cried, that isn't anything *like* as terrible as I felt when he did it. [B, fourth child, 3 months]

Nor is it the result of a woman's lack of familiarity with babies. Women who have worked as pediatricians, midwives, maternity nurses, and nannies frequently say how much of that familiarity becomes irrelevant once they have babies of their own.

> I've worked in a nursery for six years. I thought: "You are so used to babies, you won't find it difficult. No problem." But it's quite different being a mother. Nothing prepared me for the higher anxiety level when G cries. I am so *new!* [G, 2 weeks]

> I've cried so much these last two months. I've been a nanny and I've got a degree in early childhood studies and I've had to advise parents. I know the "answers" to a lot of mothers' problems. But it's *completely different* now I've got a child of my own. [B, 2 months]

> I thought I'd be able to cope with G's crying. I can cope with *other* babies crying. I'm a midwife, and I'm used to it. But when G cried, she seemed to turn on a little switch at the back of my head. It was terrible. F and I used to feel so sorry for her. We both used to cry with her. I did, and I'm sure F did too. [G, 9 months]

It can feel strange to be so tearful and sensitive. It's sometimes written off as "just hormones." A mother may feel like hiding away from the rest of the world. But the world benefits from the sensitivity and compassion of mothers. A mother can find herself constantly noticing, outside her window, wrongs and injustices in the wider world. She seems to sense them more vividly since she has become a mother. Compassionate voices tend to sound gentle, though what they say can be disconcerting.

At first, every time a small baby cries, it sounds urgent. His mother usually starts by picking him up and putting him to her breast, or hurrying to prepare a bottle. A baby has a stomach about the size of a walnut, yet he has to double his birth-weight in about five months. An adult is "grown up" and has, by definition, finished growing. How can we remember how urgent being hungry used to feel? Without compassion, a mother might be exasperated at having to feed her baby so often. Surely babies are sensitive to the way they are given food. A compassionate mother can show that she is "for" her baby during those many moments of essential need.

Less commonly, a baby's cries are shrill and piercing. Clearly they aren't due to hunger. Immediately, his mother becomes alert. She scans him minutely and is quick to notice signs of high temperature, pallor, muscular limpness, problems in breathing, or a far-off look in his eyes. This alertness seems universal in mothers, yet there seems to be no word to describe it.

At other times a baby seems to be crying for no particular reason. It can't be hunger. It doesn't seem to be pain. Perhaps the doctor reassures the mother that her baby is not ill. People say he has "colic" or is "fretful." A baby may cry himself to exhaustion without anyone discovering why. When there is no obvious cause, there is no obvious solution to the crying. What can his mother do? It upsets her to hear her baby crying so much. She ought to be washing clothes and organizing supper. But she can't. She can't think of anything beyond it.

Mothers are quick to discover that babies respond to particular comforting actions. "Already by the second week," observed Judy Dunn in her book *Distress and Comfort,* "we find that the human voice is more effective at calming a crying baby than a rattle or a ball."[1] A mother's ability to provide comfort has been recorded since ancient times. "As a mother comforts her child," wrote the biblical prophet Isaiah, who lived in the eighth century B.C.[2] For centuries, people have noted how adults in extremes of pain or under torture would cry out for the comfort of their mothers. Even recent social research demonstrates that people feel calmed by a woman's smile and nod, whereas a man behaving in the same way arouses anxiety.[3]

How strange, then, that so *little* has been written about learning to comfort. No one supports the mother while she is learning how to comfort or celebrates her when she is able to give comfort. People ask mothers: "Is he sleeping through the night yet?" "Have you started him on solids yet?" "Has he got any teeth?" No one seems to ask: "Have you discovered what comforts him?" Yet the ability to sleep through the night or to digest solid food or to grow teeth has little to do with mothering. Babies reach these milestones when they are mature enough, whereas being able to comfort depends on a mother's ability.

Invariably, a mother starts from the uncertainty of *not* knowing how to comfort. Each new child is an unknown person. If she has several children, she discovers that she has to adapt to each child. The mother of twin girls remembered that she couldn't hold them both in the same way. "Rachel liked to bounce and Grace liked to sway," she observed.[4] A mother of twin boys commented that one was comforted by being swaddled, while the other liked to move freely. It takes time to work all this out.

Imagine a toddler falling down in a playground and starting to cry. "He needs his mom," everyone agrees, and they lift him, sobbing, into his mother's arms. He is wailing. Huge hot tears roll down his flushed cheeks. His mother rocks him for a moment and strokes his back, and the child starts to relax and calm down. "Better now?" asks his mother, simultaneously checking him for injury. He gives a wavering smile, then a steadier one, and nods his head. Off he goes to continue playing. This wonderful transformation took only a few minutes. Whatever did his mother do?

It is clearly not the first time she has comforted him. The whole process depends on both mother and child recalling earlier times. Yet if you could rewind an imaginary video right back to the start, when the toddler was just newborn, and if you studied the images closely, you would be unlikely to see the mother comforting the child so efficiently. She would probably be in that difficult but important state of motherly uncertainty. Her baby is crying and distressed—and she simply does not know what to do.

> G cries in the evening from nine o'clock till midnight. She gets so hoarse she can hardly cry. It's terrible. We feel so helpless. We pass her from one of us to the other, and neither of us can do anything with her. [G, 6 weeks]

> When B's crying, I feel as if it's forever. I feel desperate. When he's *not* crying, I know that of course he won't always be like that. But when he *is,* I lose all sense of the future. [B, 4 months]

When a mother loses her sense of the future, this is because she is caught up in the immediacy of her baby's urgent crying. Living in the present, without much sense of past and future, can feel unfiltered, chaotic, and very intense. But it can help a mother to "reach" her crying baby. This is something that many new mothers find themselves doing. They are then in a position to help their babies to calm down. I have watched mothers choose comforting methods that were perfect for their babies (such as sitting down to breastfeed, swinging them, rocking, patting, stroking, jingling a set of keys, whistling, humming, repeating their babies' names) and at the same time trying to keep conversations going with other mothers—without a trace of awareness that they were doing something wonderful.

I have searched the literature for accounts of comforting, but there is extraordinarily little available. Several studies have been written on "soothing."[5] But this seems to mean helping the baby to stop crying. Comforting goes further. The mother is not just trying to change her baby's behavior. She feels compassionate toward his distress, and she wishes she could help. The word "com*fort*" derives from the Latin *fortitudo,* which means "strength." Mothers use their compassion to find ways of helping to restore their babies to a sense of strength.

Because I can't find a published description, I shall offer a tentative account of my own. It is meant to describe what I have seen mothers do. It is not meant to tell any mother what she "should" do. A mother who does it differently may well have noticed all kinds of details that I have overlooked.

The mother's first response is to acknowledge that her baby is distressed and that she is needed. She puts down whatever she was doing and gives single-minded attention to her baby. This in itself is quite a feat. Mothers quickly learn to do several tasks at once, so the change is considerable. Her baby now has her complete attention. As we saw in chapter 4, there is no word to refer to this vital act.

An essential part of the comforting process is her assessment of how bad things are. A baby cannot do this for himself. If we think ourselves back into childhood, we may remember times when we thought our grazed knees were a major disaster. But our mothers responded calmly, suggesting that grazed knees were perfectly normal. It seems likely that babies pick up cues like these. The mother's assessment serves to "contain" the situation. Even a very excitable mother usually calms down enough to make her appraisal. Her appraisal steadies her and gives her a base.

Then the rest of the world seems to draw back, leaving the mother in a twosome with her distressed baby. She could easily enter into his distress, but instead she seems to try to bring her baby to her calmer state. She doesn't do this by becoming still or silent. The ancient Greek philosopher Plato was puzzled that mothers who were trying to calm their babies gave them "not quiet, but motion, for they rock them constantly in their arms; and instead of silence they use a kind of crooning noise."[6] It is fascinating that mothers do the same today. "It is by no means easy to work out exactly how a calming technique is working," wrote Judy Dunn in *Distress and Comfort*.[7] This is probably because it isn't only a technique. The mother has to reach a calmer state herself to help to "bring her baby back" from an escalating state of panic.

The last phase of the comforting process seems to be a reorientation toward the world to help the baby move from the safe twosome back into the troublesome world again, but with more strength. The comforting may not have solved the problem or even stopped the baby from crying. But the mother can hear that the urgency has gone. She may say something like: "You *were* upset." "What a shame you got a fright!" "Would you like to breastfeed now?" This creates a bridge back to ordinary life and closes the phase of comforting.

An important part of the mother's comforting depends on her seeing her baby's distress as reasonable. This enables her to treat him with respect. She may not understand why he is crying, but she trusts him. She is not trying to deny his upset or to get rid of a "meaningless noise" for her own peace of mind. She feels truly sorry for him and wants to help him.

> At first, when B cried and I knew he was fed and I'd changed his diaper, I was like: "What's the matter, what's the matter?" It's very hard to accept that it may be a headache or a tummy ache, and you can't make it better for them. All you can do is this [rocking B], and hope it passes. [B, 4 weeks]

People say: "He's got a terrible temper." But he cries for a reason. [B, 4 months]

A friend came to visit, and I apologized because G wasn't in a very good mood. Usually she's very cheerful with me. And then I thought: "*Why* should I apologize? Why should G always be happy and smiling? I don't expect it of her. I accept her however she is." [G, 7 months]

One mother said her baby's crying "made" her pick him up. I asked her if she had any choice in the matter. She stroked the top of her baby's head and spoke with much feeling:

I've got no choice but to pick him up when he cries. No, that's not true. I *have* choices. I could put him in a nursery all day or leave him to cry. But I think it's like an insurance. You can't replace this year. I expect life can give him some knocks. I just hope that if he has a secure start he will feel nice and strong for dealing with life's difficulties later on. [B, 7 months]

This last is confirmed by a warm statement in *The Womanly Art of Breastfeeding* by La Leche League International: "Our suggestion to the mother of a fussy baby is: Don't let your baby cry alone. The comfort and security extended by your loving arms is never wasted. Love begets love."[8]

After the trial and error of the early weeks, there often comes a stage when both mother and baby suddenly seem to emerge into the sunshine. Everything has become more familiar. It is hard to recall that there was ever a time when the mother was tearful, confused, and bewildered.

G still wakes up at night absolutely screaming and obviously in some kind of pain, but now I know I'll be able to comfort her. I put her in her sling and walk up and down, and then it's all right. [G, 3 months]

There's her tired crying, that's sticking out her lower lip. And there's crying for food. Or crying to be picked up—and bored crying, I'm starting to recognize *that* now. [G, 3 months]

[One mother laid her crying daughter down on a mat in front of her and commented:] It goes against my instincts. I feel I should cuddle or feed her. But G definitely prefers lying on her own. Don't you, G? She'll soon calm down. [G, 3 months] [I timed it, and G had stopped crying and was smiling within three minutes.]

G cried for the first three months of her life. No crying now is as hard as that time. I used to stand up for hours, swaying her in my arms. Now I catch myself standing and swaying even when she's not with me! [G, 4 months]

Now when G cries, I know exactly what it's about. It's usually when she gets an idea into her head and she's cross with me if I don't go along with it. Or if I'm too slow. [G, 5 months]

I've learned that there are times to let B cry. Adults sometimes come back from the office and just want to unwind. Crying is B's way of unwinding. [B, 6 months]

> Just once, when B was crying, nothing was working. I thought: "What shall I do if I can't comfort him?" It was a moment of real panic. It's very important to me that I can really read him now, and I know what to do. [B, 6 months]

Once a mother starts to be able to "read" her child, she feels more relaxed. A much easier relationship can develop between them. The mother doesn't need to jump up every time her baby cries:

> I'm getting tougher. Today G was crying, and I thought: "Come off it! I know you can wait." [G, 4 months]

Mothers may enjoy some relaxed moments, but it is important to keep reminding ourselves that they arose, and could only arise, from the uncertainty of the early days. This is very underappreciated. Most people underestimate how much a "comforting" mother has done. One mother observed:

> G is very calm. She plays and hardly looks round to see if I'm there; she *knows* I'm there. People say she has a calm nature, but I don't believe that. It's not nature, it's what you do for them. [G, 11 months]

After the first year, the child needs comforting for fewer but more serious situations. When an older child is hurt or ill, his mother will often realize that she is developing more ways of giving comfort:

> One night G was really ill. I tried everything, but nothing seemed to help. In the end all I could do was hold her.

> Different holds seemed to comfort her at different moments. [G, 14 months]

Although the giving of comfort is so strongly associated with mothers, not all mothers give it. As we saw, some mothers have a different philosophy. They believe that comfort will "spoil" the child for life, and that mothers who comfort are "making a rod for their own backs." The whole process of comforting irritates them, and they don't always keep their irritation to themselves. Many mothers who choose to comfort their babies seem to have disapproving friends or relatives who provide advice from the "need to train" school of thought.

> When B won't stop crying, you get advice from all sides, oh, do this, do that. But I *can't*. I can't leave B crying, like they want. It's a pitiful noise, and I can't ignore it. [B, 4 weeks]

> When G cries during mealtimes, my in-laws [with whom she lived] always say: "Finish your *own* meal first." It makes me feel furious inside. [G, 2 months]

> People say you should leave your baby to cry. But for how long? When you're brushing your teeth, a few seconds of B's crying can seem like an hour. He seems to want to be carried all the time. I've hardly got time to do up a zip. But I don't like to leave him crying. [B, 3 months]

> People ask if she's good, meaning does she cry a lot. My mother's already called her a tyrant—and G's only twelve weeks old! [G, 3 months]

> G was crying, and my mother told me not to pick her up. But I did. I always do. I see it as meeting her needs. As I was lifting her up, my mother said: "Just look at her face!" I looked, and G had stopped crying. She was smiling. To me, it was a smile of happiness because she knew I was responding to her needs. But I could tell that my mother saw it as a smile of *victory,* that G had got me to do what she wanted. [G, 8 months]

Sometimes mothers realize that they themselves must have gone uncomforted when they were babies, and this seems to play an important part in strengthening their own determination to comfort their babies.

> My mom is always saying to me: "Let G cry! It won't do her any harm." But I can't bear the sound of her crying. And I'm thinking: "I bet that's what she did to me. She left me to cry." I feel so . . . [She indicated a choked sensation of her throat.] [G, 5 weeks]

> B screamed the other night. He didn't want food and he didn't want sleep. He wanted that nameless thing that mothers give, comfort, I suppose. It was scary. My mom died when I was a child. I find it hard to be needed. [B, 3 months]

> I feel I was abandoned as a child. Not literally. My mother used to put me to bed at night, and that was it. I think I just cried for a bit and then gave up. I'm not sure. I feel I did, but my mother can't remember. Only I'm left with the feelings of being abandoned, inside. [B, 4 months]

> I get in a rage when B cries, and I can't do anything about it. I know I was left to cry as a baby, and I feel this anger welling up inside me when I want to walk away and leave him when he cries. I feel so helpless. [B, 6 months]

Perhaps those with sad memories have more reason to talk about them. Few mothers mention happy memories. Just one mother described happy memories to me—though only when I questioned her. Her story will have to represent many similar but untold stories.

This mother assured me that her two-month-old baby never cried. I was surprised to hear that. During the course of a meeting we both attended, I noticed that he did cry several times. He was disabled in one foot, and this kept frustrating him. His mother was quick to comfort him whenever he cried. I asked her about it afterward, and she replied that she hardly noticed that sort of crying. It didn't "count." She herself was the youngest of seven children. "My brothers and sisters were so quick at cheering me up," she said, "that they used to make me cry on purpose, to see which of them was the quickest to make me laugh after!" She smiled at the memory, and I thought that it must have given her the confidence to feel she could comfort her son.

This is only a small and random collection of stories. However, it indicates that some mothers closely link their own reactions to their babies' crying with how their families had reacted to them as babies. Once they had made these links, these mothers realized why their reactions felt so strong. Making sense of themselves helped them to reach a calmer state in which they could attend to their babies.

Books that were written for mothers about fifty years ago advised them to put their personal feelings aside when looking after their babies, but today mothers may be encouraged to take their feelings into account. This new approach derives from the understanding gained from psychotherapy and counseling. One result is the more honest admission of feelings that a mother fifty years earlier might not have dared to think about, let alone voice to other mothers. It is, however, clear from these accounts that by recognizing their feelings, mothers felt able to do something about them:

> When G cries, I can't bear it, and I start to think I'm doing everything wrong. And I'm sure she picks up the tensions in me and cries even more. So I sit down and talk to myself, and try to feel less tense. [G, 8 weeks]

> I felt an inadequate mother. I felt it was all much, much too much for me. I lay down on the floor and had a three-year-old tantrum. I beat my fists on the floor really hard for about fifty seconds. F had B in a different room. After that, I could take B again. [B, 3 months]

> B was crying at night, and I didn't know what to do. F was sound asleep next door, managing to sleep right through it. Nothing I did was working. You can feel totally helpless. I was afraid I'd do the wrong thing. So I put B down, went to the toilet, and just had a cry myself. I felt I could cope the better for it. [B, 6 months]

> G was crying and I was crying, and I was at the end of my tether. I put her down in her crib and shut the door, and then I went into the kitchen, shut the door, and smashed an old plate. I had to throw it about five times because it *refused* to break. But then I felt much better. I was so afraid I'd do something to G. [G, 6 months]

Sharing these lonely moments was comforting for the mothers. Each found she received a great deal of warm understanding from her listeners. She received their undivided attention (babies permitting), the recognition of how hard it is to keep steady on these occasions, and compassion. Each mother could then return to her difficult situation with more strength. She herself had reached out for the marvel of human comfort and received it.

Some mothers, however, describe a confusing response when their babies cry. In those moments, their compassion for their babies seems to have ebbed out of their own reach. Instead, they experience a dull emptiness and a collapse of energy, or sometimes a surge of overwhelming rage and hatred, with fantasies of destroying the babies they thought they loved so much. A mother in this state finds it hard to believe that she has such negative feelings toward her own baby. It seems irrational and can give her the sense of losing control and going crazy. For many mothers, these feelings seem like a state they can get into if their babies cry for long enough, one that they are thankful to get out of afterward. It is not a comfortable state to stay in.

> I don't think women talk about what being a mother is really like. I didn't realize myself. Sometimes when G cries, I could throw her out, over the balcony. And yet . . . and yet . . . that's only a bit of me. One part. [G, 5 months]

Many mothers report moments like this. Some writers claim that all mothers, if they were honest, would admit to them.[9] However, this kind of universal claim must be speculative. Very little seems true of all mothers. It is more likely that some mothers do not experience these ambivalent feelings, not even for a fleeting moment, just as there are mothers who describe times when their feelings are definitely ambivalent.

A mother who has strongly ambivalent feelings usually finds that the sound of her baby crying affects her profoundly. She feels swept away by the intensity of the crying, and at first feels she would *do* anything and *give* everything for him to be content. At the same time, she seems to experience her baby's crying in a particular way. She hears in it very negative, critical messages about her own worth as a mother. His crying sounds accusing, as if he is attacking her, and filled with despair. She also expects more of her baby than he might be able to deliver. Babies cannot usually stop crying to order.

This starts a difficult cycle, which mothers find hard to get out of. Because the mother feels accused by the baby's crying, her attention becomes focused not on her baby but on herself. What has she done wrong? What is her baby accusing her of? These questions make it hard for her to fine-tune to her crying baby and to focus on comforting him. "We tirelessly examine our techniques, consult our textbooks, and search our souls for the reasons [for a baby's problems]," writes the Australian writer Susan Maushart, in *The Mask of Motherhood.*[10] Significantly, it doesn't occur to Ms. Maushart to look to her actual *baby* for the reasons. Yet the most tireless examination of her techniques, her textbooks, and her soul are unlikely to enlighten her. It is a search in the wrong direction.

Understandably, a mother can then feel less confident than ever. She tries to put things right by making enormous efforts to do things that she has heard will calm a crying baby. But because she hasn't given enough attention to her particular baby, she may not have discovered what her baby prefers. Her efforts may be misplaced. Then, if he still does not calm down, this seems to "prove" to her that she really is an ineffectual mother. She feels rejected, hurt, and bewildered. She is giving so much energy to calming him. Yet even now, he is not pleased with her. Does he want more of her? Can he really be so greedy and insatiable? He must be an absolute monster. She feels in a vulnerable no-win position. If she stops giving, then surely she has failed as a mother, and other people will think of her as a failure. But if she keeps on giving, she will be consumed by the "needs" of her baby. There will be nothing left of her. Either way seems a dead end.

This is the moment when she tends to rage at her baby. She has lost all sense that her baby's crying might be about something, and that she might be able to console him if she knew more about him. Her whole focus is not on the baby but on herself. This is not because she is a self-centered woman, in the usual sense of this expression. It seems to be the opposite. She doesn't seem to have a steady sense of herself. She can't withdraw to the toilet to cry or throw a plate to recover her sense of herself. Her sense of who she is feels shaky and threatened. She feels stuck in the groove of believing that, to please her baby, she is required to give, give, give until she drops. If her baby keeps crying, she therefore believes she must keep on giving. In her eyes, that is what "better" mothers manage to do, and it maddens her.

Her baby now seems like a heartless master with her as his slave. She feels she has no power and no rights. The more she feels controlled by her baby, the more often her feelings of hatred toward him are likely to erupt. She has lost touch with her own agency, her own responsibility for what she does. She may, for instance, hurry to pick up her baby when he cries, but the baby could not actually make her do this. Her act is her choice. Because she is not recognizing her power to choose, she misses a precious opportunity to feel pleased with herself for her motherly care. She also finds it hard to recognize that it does not make her a "bad mother" if she chooses to set limits on what she gives her baby, when she gives it, and for how long.

Some mothers find that it helps to acknowledge that they have ambivalent feelings, rather than struggling not to have them. They then feel calmer and more able to continue mothering. A few mothers find ways out of this cycle. One mother discovered that her own mother was unexpectedly helpful in showing her an alternative way:

> When B wouldn't sleep, I used to go up and down the stairs every day, up and down, and he cried and cried. Eventually I went back to my mom. I felt I didn't love B anymore. She picked him up, and I saw how she held him. I could tell that his crying was going *through* her, that it didn't go *into* her the way it went into me. And I thought: "Well, I could do that." That night he was lying in a crib, and I just wanted to pick him up and hug him. I loved him again. [B, 6 months]

Another mother found that looking at her baby helped her through difficult times:

> I've got very little patience, and I was always afraid I was going to turn into one of those women who batter babies. But now I find that when things get frustrating, it draws us *more* together. I look into G's eyes, and I see another human being there. Then I know we are in this together. [G, 8 weeks]

It can be especially hard when a baby cries a lot. Some researchers believe that this is crucial. They claim that if a mother cannot calm her baby, she will feel ineffectual as a mother. "We argue," write two American psychologists, "that if a mother has previously been unsuccessful in controlling her infant's crying, a state of helplessness will ensue."[11] Like so much research, this may well be true of some mothers. But people can be brilliantly resourceful. Such a sweeping claim does not do justice to the hard work some mothers put in, who manage to cope with babies who cry a lot. If these mothers are lucky, they receive sympathy from other people. But surely they deserve much more than sympathy. They deserve our admiration.

To take a single example, there was one mother whose baby girl cried all day and every day (but fortunately slept at night) for almost three months. I remember that every time I telephoned this mother, whatever the time of day, I could always hear her baby crying loudly as she picked up the phone. She talked frankly, both then and after it was over, about how desperate she felt. Yet she didn't mention any anger toward her daughter at all. One day I brought along to a meeting two paperbacks on the subject of crying babies. I asked her what she thought of them, and she replied:

> Even the covers look heartless to me. I definitely don't feel like picking them up, and certainly not opening either of them. You'd think babies had only just been invented. We don't seem to have any solutions. They've conquered heart transplants but not colic. That's where my anger lies. It's not her fault that G had to cry. I know she'd have liked to stop as much as anyone. I used to try very hard not to let out my frustration on her. I used to look at the wall behind her, or at the door, when I felt desperate. [G, 4 months]

One could argue, as some people have, that mothers bury their ambivalence and are unconscious of it. Maybe so. However, one can't bury everything. We would expect to discover little signs of the cycle of feeling accused by the baby. But this mother clearly felt differently. Like the previous mother, she was able to see her daughter as a human being. Even though she didn't know the reason why her baby was crying, she accepted that "G had to cry." She didn't seem to be blaming either herself or her daughter for her daughter's crying. She regarded herself as a beginner.

Logically, then, this mother's anger was directed at more experienced people who failed to help her—to the producers of books on crying babies with heartless-looking covers and to doctors who hadn't sufficiently researched crying babies. She also realized that her baby was an easy target for her own frustrations and devised a method of diverting her feelings. She was under more pressure than most mothers, and she chose to respond in resourceful ways. Apart from that, her account of herself did not seem out of the ordinary.

Her whole manner of holding and talking to her baby daughter looked very tender and comforting, and she also evoked the strong compassion of other mothers on her behalf. One mother confided to me: "I've been thinking about M and her crying baby all week. I couldn't get out of my mind how much she'd been through." [G, 11 months]. So, after her baby had calmed down enough for them both to come to meetings, the mother received much appreciation and comfort from other mothers.

Not everyone expects to be comforted. People who have been schooled into never making a fuss or never to "burden" other people with their troubles tend to withdraw when they feel unhappy. They feel safer alone, where they can "lick their own wounds," as the saying goes, to comfort themselves. There are also impersonal ways of getting comfort. A person can find it in drink, eating, smoking, drugs, computer games, or other lone activities. These are often repetitive and addictive. Another way of managing distress is to tell oneself: "It doesn't matter." "It's no big deal." "I don't mind at all." If this is a denial of a person's true feelings, the person may feel calm but at the price of shutting down a level of ordinary human sensitivity. A whole dimension of potential human contact is missing for people in this position.

This is important because it goes against a recent approach to crying babies. Psychology researchers now claim that it is important for babies to learn how to stop crying by themselves.[12] Fortunately, many parents still prefer to comfort their babies. If they didn't, we might find ourselves living in a society of very solitary people, who had learned to control their distress rather than to find strength through sharing it.

A comforted baby is in an exciting position. He has not been taught not to make a fuss. He fusses, receives comfort, and values it. Slowly he grows to rely on it. This is a huge transition. In the womb, where he spent nine long months, he may have learned how to turn skillfully in the amniotic fluid, only to find that the umbilical cord had suddenly twisted around his neck. There was no one to untwist it. He may have explored an interesting niche of the womb, only to find his head wedged fast so that he could not move it. There was no one to help, no one to enable him to feel strong again. As far as the baby knows, he has to depend on himself. Newborns have a special self-sufficient look. Learning to trust their mothers must represent an enormous shift of outlook.

After the birth, it usually takes several months before the baby trusts that his mother will come to comfort him. The process takes time. Slowly mother and baby fine-tune to each other. The mother learns that her baby responds to this or that particular comforting action; the baby learns to expect a whole series of little actions; and his mother recognizes from his cry when he expects them. A relationship of mutual trust develops and extends into childhood. A toddler can begin to remember that he has been comforted before, even though his knee still shows an impressive bruise. Slowly he begins to distinguish the trivial from the serious and to manage the trivial pains by himself. The older child, who is in more serious pain, can still fall back on the familiar voice, touch, and smell of his mother, and these seem to have extraordinary power. Out of all the chaos, anxiety, and uncertainty of the early moments has emerged the mother's ability to give enduring comfort.

This does not mean that every mother comforts her child every time. Most mothers are only too aware of times when they failed, when they weren't there, or when they were there but didn't realize their child was distressed about something. They were impatient when, with hindsight, they wish they had offered comfort. No mother is perfect. Yet as far as we can tell, enough mothers provide enough comfort for comfort to be associated with motherhood. The comforted child learns from his mother a way of dealing with suffering. Suffering comes with life. No one can avoid it. However, people can both receive and give comfort, and so help each other to grow strong enough to bear it.

"Children are certain cares but uncertain comforts," warns an old English proverb.[13] This warning may help us not to make tacit and one-sided bargains with our small children. Yet some children do comfort. Whether children who were rarely comforted as babies nevertheless grow up to give comfort is not clear. But mothers who learned to comfort their babies report that their babies definitely developed their own ways of giving comfort.

> We went to visit my tutor, and while we were there her husband turned up to ask for a divorce. The whole atmosphere was tense; it was as if someone had *died*. G was incredible. She kept reaching out her hand to people and smiling at them, so they had to smile back at her. My tutor's children were older, and G changed the whole

atmosphere. Everyone said they were so glad she was there, and I think she gave of her best. Next day I noticed that she was tired, and she slept for most of the day. She had really given of her*self*. [G, 7 months]

I told B I wanted to talk to him and I said: "Today, when I smacked your hand, I made a wrong decision. I'm sorry. I sometimes get it wrong, and you actually suffer for it." I was saying this to appease my own conscience. I didn't think that B would understand. But B got up on his knees and kissed me on the mouth. It was as if to say: "I heard you. It's OK. Don't worry." [B, 12 months]

B had whooping cough, not badly, but he keeps waking up at night, so I've had very little sleep. One day I was sitting with my head in my hands, and I was crying, and B came and laid the side of his head in my lap. It felt as if he was saying: "I know how you feel." [B, 13 months]

G comforts me as much as I comfort her. She pats me on the back when I'm upset, the way I used to pat her when she was crying with gas. It's so sweet. [G, 22 months]

The child may be young, but the warmth of his gestures often has the power to provide real comfort. His comforting can't be put down to expediency. He is not calculating a return but returning something that he has already received. He has learned from his mother just how good human comfort can be.

six

"I get nothing done all day"

Most people agree that being a mother is very hard work. But what exactly is a mother's work? On this question there is less agreement. People often talk as though "mothering" is quite different from all the work a mother is supposed to do.

For example, imagine a mother rinsing out some baby clothes. She knows her baby is asleep but might wake up at any moment. Sure enough, a few minutes later, the baby cries, so she grabs a towel for her hands and goes quickly to pick him up. He seems upset, so she cuddles him. She wonders whether he has had a bad dream, so she starts singing a nonsense song that he usually enjoys to cheer him up. Which of all these activities was her work?

Most people would say that rinsing baby clothes meant that she was working, whereas picking up her baby meant that she had to spend a lot of time not working. Mothers frequently describe a painful sense of "failure" about exactly those moments when, if we look closer, we notice that they were mothering their babies. The reverse is also true. When a mother is rushing around, busy with household tasks that may be concrete and visible but are surely much more peripheral to the work of being a mother, both she and other people are likely to say she is "managing to get her work done."

Today a mother can feel very lonely. A great many people are unaware of what she is doing. This is not because motherhood has changed. The essentials of being a mother appear to be changeless. But the world around the mother is always changing. Mothers can't, however, withdraw to a social vacuum. Being a mother is both a private and a social role. Each mother builds a bridge that links her individual child to the social world that we all share. If her bridge is a good one, her child will be able to use it to reach the wider world. The bridge is based on their relationship together. If she can relate well to her child, then her child has a good chance of growing into a person who will relate well to us. Our whole society depends on the way each mother relates to her child. This *is* her motherly work.

Most mothers are acutely sensitive as to whether people around them approve of their children. The most casual response of another person can affect a mother for a whole day. But how can people communicate their reactions in a responsible manner if they literally do not notice what the mother does when she is mothering her child? It's not that they don't care. Most people have strong views on how they want a child to be brought up. It's more that when they look at a mother sitting quietly with her baby, they cannot see much going on. It's not most people's idea of doing a mother's work.

It's easier to show this lack of understanding if we think of a slightly older child, just beyond babyhood. We might notice a mother and toddler in a supermarket, for example. The mother is relating to her toddler in several ways simultaneously. She is guiding him into the kind of behavior that she considers appropriate for his age in a public place. She is also demonstrating specific "supermarket behavior," which includes not knocking things off the shelves and not filling up the basket with everything at hand but choosing items and paying for them. She is showing him her personal values when shopping, such as calculating prices or prioritizing speed, and demonstrating how she relates to the checkout staff. She usually isn't teaching as such but sharing her world with him, and it's very demanding. Everything takes twice as long, and she has to keep switching her attention from the adult shopping world to the child world of her little companion. If a misunderstanding arises, it will be her job to mediate between the two worlds.

But now we come to the lack of understanding. If we asked our mother in the supermarket what she was doing, she would almost certainly reply: "My shopping." If we asked other shoppers and the checkout staff what they thought the mother was doing, most of them would answer: "She was doing her shopping." Yet the mother was doing ever so much more than that. She was doing two jobs, not just one. The second job comes silently under the umbrella of the first. It has no separate name. When a child reaches nursery-school age, teachers talk about the importance of "socialization." However, just when a mother is gradually and effectively socializing her child and doing a lot more besides—it counts for nothing because everyone simply perceives her as "shopping."

If the mother's activity is limited to "shopping," then her child's company looks like an impediment. He slows her down and distracts her from getting everything done in her usual competent way. But if we recognized that all this was part of her work, we could redefine her task as: "mothering *and* shopping." That would give her child a legitimate place in her actions. It would also explain why a mother can feel so exhausted and irritable at the end of a shopping trip. Two jobs are harder than one. It is even harder if she overlooks the second and sees herself as accomplishing only the first. Instead of being pleased that she has combined two jobs reasonably well, she usually ends up being annoyed with herself for apparently doing one job badly.

A further example of this lack of understanding happens only too often once mother and child have come home. When the mother unpacks her shopping, she can see the result of her efforts. But looking down at her toddler, she can't observe much change. She has tried to be patient with him, but he looks cross and tired, and is probably hungry. Where has all her mothering gone? As one mother complained:

> When you're at work, you know what you've done all day. You've done *x* number of phone calls and written so many letters, and you've got something to show for it. Now when I look down at B at the end of a day, and it's been such hard work, I think: "Where's the difference? Show me where all that mothering went!" [B, 2 months]

It hasn't disappeared, but it's hard to recognize. It is there, in front of her. Her child may indeed be cross. When he is cross, this may be *because* she has been mothering him well. He is not annoyed with her but *to* her. The difference is crucial yet easy to misunderstand. A cross child trusts his mother and has expectations of her. He asks more of her than of other people because she is close to him and seems to understand him. He often has the utmost confidence that his all-knowing mother will put things right for him. "A baby who cries a lot may do so because he or she has a close relationship with the mother," observed two perceptive researchers at a London hospital.[1] But this is the opposite of a widely held cultural assumption. The assumption is that a crying baby and a cross toddler are signs of *poor* relationships. So, unfortunately, most mothers do not take it as a compliment to themselves when their small children cry or get cross. Children's crossness, which can often indicate how much the children trust their mothers, is usually misunderstood, both by mothers and by anyone else within earshot, as clear evidence of maternal failure.

> G seems to save her screaming fits for me. When other people are around, she's entertained and happy. But when it's just us, she won't let me put her down, not even for a minute. [G, 7 months]

> F would love to comfort G. He'd love to take her to the next room and give me a break. He's like that. But when G's upset, it's *me* she wants. [G, 7 months]

> F took G out for the whole afternoon, and they came back tired, but they'd obviously had a whale of a time. F said G didn't cry once the whole time. Then he handed her over to me and even before I'd got her, her mouth was open and she was bawling. It's because I'm her *mom.* I'm the one person she can be honest to. She shares her real feelings with me. She knows I understand her. With F, she's on her good behavior! [G, about 18 months]

Babies don't usually confirm how well a mother is doing. It would be reassuring for his mother if her tiny baby would sit up, just once in a while, and say: "Cheer up, Mom! You're relating *brilliantly* to me!" But babies can't oblige. A mother can easily feel lonely and unappreciated in those difficult early weeks.

Most of the mothers quoted in this chapter were on maternity leave at the time of speaking. But not all mothers take maternity leave. In the descriptions that follow, mothers mention long stretches of time spent with their babies. These may not ring true for mothers whose mothering time with their babies is limited to evenings and weekends. There is no perfect way to bring up a baby, and these descriptions are not meant to suggest that every mother should put in long stretches of time. However, listening to what these mothers say may be useful to all mothers. Other aspects of the relationship are surely as familiar to employed mothers as to those at home. At the very least, a mother is responsible for her child. However she delegates this responsibility, she remains the final port of call. Through her, her baby does not face the world alone.

Time spent in being directly responsible for a small baby may be productive. But mothers don't feel as if it is. Especially at first, it is a huge "culture shock."

> When I worked, I had goals; I achieved them and moved on. At home, there is nothing I have to do. So I do nothing. I feel so inept by the end of a day, when all I've done is to get my clothes on. [B, about 2 months]

> All of a sudden, *Woman's Hour* comes round [on the radio] again, and you think: "What am I doing?" Clock time doesn't mean anything anymore. [G, 2 months]

> I trained as a lawyer. In the job I had before having G, I used to have to account for every quarter of an hour. Now a quarter of an hour just goes, and I haven't achieved anything at all. [G, 3 months]

> I am a woman who likes to get things *done*. [B, 3 months]

Women with employed partners know only too well how important the employment has become. Their partners are now breadwinning for the family. Money is an obvious result, and so partners are clearly "doing something." Many a mother has compared her day unfavorably with her partner's. As she sees it, her partner comes home in the evening and may at this hour be much more patient and playful with the baby than she is. In her eyes, he already seems more worthy because he is a money earner, and now he even appears to be the better parent. Her own efforts in looking after their baby all day can feel more like surviving the hours than the achievement it really is, on its own terms.

The father coming home in the evening may long to be part of the new family. But he needs an evening update. This can be frustrating for both parents. As we saw in chapter 1, the words are missing that would enable a mother to convey the significance of daily events. The mother may be intently aware of difficult days when the rhythm seems to have "gone wrong" between herself and her baby, whereas the next day all is sunshine again, but this is hard to explain. A person can say: "I had a dreadful day at work," and even without knowing the details, we know approximately what this means. Whereas "I had a dreadful day with B" may communicate nothing at all.

> I've been feeling really depressed. Partly it's the weather. But partly I'm just not getting anything done. I'm with B all day, and I think: "Where's my life?" [B, 4 months]

> The day goes by, and my mothering just happens. I can't see myself doing something special. [B, 4 months]

> I spend hours just gazing at B. I don't know what I'm thinking. My home is in chaos. Time just goes. [B, 4 months]

> I have this critical voice that keeps telling me I'm not doing enough. Especially if I'm just lying in bed with B [breastfeeding him] all morning. I suppose lying in bed sounds like being unemployed or being a student. I don't associate it with being a mother. [B, 5 months]

> I met my employer while I was out in the street with B, showing him the cherry blossom. He said hello and asked when I was coming back, and I felt sure he was thinking what a silly mother I was, doing meaningless things with my baby. [B, 19 months]

The words that mothers repeat in this kind of conversation are "not doing anything" or "getting nothing done" or "doing nothing." This is how they *keep* describing their experience. We need to listen carefully and to ask ourselves what "doing nothing" means. I used to assume that it meant the absence of "doing something." But listening to what mothers say, it sounds as though doing nothing is an experience in itself.

For a start, a mother's pre-baby freedom of action is either gone or, if she goes out to work, much curtailed. No longer can she enjoy unrestricted "bliss of movement," a phrase Tillie Olsen chose to describe time spent away from her home and from the needs of her children.[2] Time with her baby can mean sitting quietly for hours at a time. She can feel set apart from the busyness of ordinary life, and this can be disorienting. For example, the morning light may suggest breakfast to a mother, but her baby wants her attention, so she does not manage the breakfast "marker" of the day. If no one else is around, it does not even seem to matter. The day moves on, but her personal day feels motionless. This disoriented feeling is so strong that it may continue even at times when her baby does not need her.

> When B finally falls asleep at night, I don't know what to do. I sit there, thinking: "What should I do now? *Now* what?" [B, 2 months]

> When a friend comes and takes B, it's my time for me for a whole hour. Sometimes I just sit there and just be. Afterward I think: "Why didn't I do this and that and catch up on a few things?" [B, 9 months]

In some religions, such as Tibetan Buddhism, the experience of nothingness is one of the most difficult levels to be sought. However, the very act of seeking it must make a difference. Opening oneself to the ego-less sense of nothingness then represents a distinct and desirable change from the seeker's present state. Paradoxically, this must turn it into "something." By contrast, when a mother dismisses the way she uses her time as "getting nothing done," she is unable to see what she does as part of a desirable and significant change. Because she cannot see any change, she can easily feel that her motherly action (or inaction) of being with her baby has no value.

This contrasts the popular view of mothers as "busy." A "busy mother" is almost a cliché. The term suggests plenty of visible and useful actions. But life with a baby during his first six months outside the womb may not be active at all. Often it is slow. A mother can't touch a fast-forward button when her baby is breastfeeding, for example. He sucks, stops, gazes at her face for a while, continues sucking, closes his eyes and drowses off, still sucking, but wakes up in a flash to carry on sucking if she so much as stirs. Busy? Even her thoughts may seem sluggish and slow. Later she may have to get busy cleaning up, tidying, and making phone calls. But these actions are more loosely connected to being a mother. They are about taking care of herself, the rest of her family, and the home. She will have to do most of these actions when her baby finally falls asleep.

All this time, she is being *with* her baby. It is this invisible relationship that feels like doing nothing. She is refraining from busying herself with a long list of tasks and instead is slowing down her life to match the pace of his. For anyone used to the energetic speed of city life, the contrast is enormous. She almost has to loosen her active conscious mode and sink into something older and simpler in order to get close to the world of her baby. It isn't easy. Yet here is the very source of the momentous relationship between the two of them. Far from doing nothing, she is doing everything.

How does a mother start a new relationship? Recent researchers seem to agree about its first stage. Donald Winnicott, the psychoanalyst, coined the expression "primary maternal preoccupation" which sounds very similar to Daniel Stern's later "maternal attunement"[3] and Klaus and Kennell's "maternal sensitive period."[4] All three seem to be naming the same process. All three have tried to describe it. This in itself is extremely helpful. However, as psychoanalysts, psychiatrists, and psychologists, they then go on to name all kinds of deviations from a good relationship.

Winnicott and Stern especially give many accounts of what they see as failures of the relationship. Klaus and Kennell are concerned with general patterns. None of them seems to spend much time explaining what happens in a wide variety of particular relationships that are starting to unfold well. They also give the impression that they are describing a short-term state that a mother goes through for a matter of weeks after her baby's birth. Yet many mothers have described being in this sensitive state for at least the first year of their children's lives.

How do mothers describe the beginning of getting to know

their babies? They usually sound hesitant. Even a mother of many children will preface her wealth of observations with a remark like: "Obviously I can only speak from my own experience." Perhaps precisely because they speak with humility and describe only what they have experienced themselves, they can show us how to avoid grandiose theories about good and bad relationships. Through their observations, we can start to build up fragments of a picture of the great variety of good human relationships.

What, then, do mothers tell us? What are they doing at the very start? They may say they aren't doing anything. However, when we listen to them, it becomes clear that there are two ways in which they feel they are getting nothing done. One is when the baby is asleep in the mother's arms but she knows that the moment she puts him down he will wake up and cry. So she decides it's better to stay where she is while he has a good sleep. Often she seems to fall into a mindless daze. Almost, she has forgotten about her baby. Mothers often blame themselves for having long daydreamy periods. However, with a new baby, privacy can be a luxury. The mother can't always take a break from her baby when she needs it. Being absent in her thoughts seems a good way to restore her energy.

> Sometimes, for a few moments, I forget she exists. Once I was in a store, and G was in her stroller. I was leafing through some magazines and got absorbed in them. I suddenly came to and thought: "Hey, I've got a *baby!*" I felt I could have just paid for a magazine and walked off without her! [G, 4 months]

> When B was very small, I remember F holding him so that I could take a shower. It was the first time I had really been by myself. I really relaxed in the shower. Then

> I heard a baby crying. It didn't seem to be anything to do with me. I felt so guilty when I realized that it was B. I was enjoying the shower so much that I had forgotten that B was my baby. [B, 13 months]

A mother may need a break because she has spent an intense period on a much more focused way of "doing nothing." This second sort is the process of studying her baby minutely to get to know who he is. In order to do this, she has to get herself into a receptive, openminded, unprejudiced state. All her senses are alert. This can be very tiring, so it's understandable that mothers also need recovery interludes from such intense moments. As we shall see in chapter 7, most people keep sane by alternating work and leisure settings. Mothers appear to cope by alternating reality and imagination. After daydreaming, they can "come back," feeling refreshed. Far from doing nothing, they are having an absolutely essential rest.

At first, there is a great deal to learn and perhaps to unlearn too. Many mothers describe a period of chaos in the early weeks, which they find extremely frightening. By chaos, they mean that they cannot perceive much pattern or logic in what their babies appear to be doing. They are responsible for newborns whom they do not understand. Mothers tend to focus on the unpredictability of each day. They usually voice it as a failure of theirs. I've lost count of all the mothers who have cried:

> B [or G] and I have got absolutely *no* routine at the moment. I don't know where we've gone wrong.

Maternal panic is understandable. As we saw in chapter 2, in a more traditional society a woman would have been prepared beforehand with a number of "dummy runs," helping to care for other babies before her own. She would have seen many mothers around her caring for babies. She could have acquired a large mental database of information from which she could draw. But mothers today often start without these advantages. Days and nights meander on; everything feels chaotic. It is only too easy for a mother to feel she has failed. If only she could realize that she *hasn't.* The period of chaos may be a necessary part of starting this new relationship. It connects to the sense of uncertainty discussed on pages 51–56.

When a mother is in the midst of the chaotic period, she can look in astonishment at other mothers who have come through it. How can anyone with a baby appear so calm? The calmer mothers who have now moved beyond this early period of chaos can be generous in reassuring and encouraging the ones who are still struggling:

> *First mother:* I'm so tired. B didn't sleep at all last night. I was sitting for hours, watching the clock, watching two o'clock change into three o'clock, thinking: "*When* can I sleep?" [B, 4 weeks]
>
> [This evoked a chorus of sympathetic protest from the mothers in the group who had babies ranging in age from two months to eleven months:] Put the *clock* away! Don't look at it! You'll just make yourself miserable for nothing. It all sorts out later. You'll catch up on sleep in the end. Honestly, you will. Don't worry!

> I was feeling so upset, thinking I was doing everything wrong, that I decided to go for a walk. And I was glad I did. I met an angel from heaven! [The angel turned out to be none other than the once-clock-watching mother. But it was five months later, and she was now able to give

reassurance, in her turn.] She told me that she'd been through all that upset herself. She said I shouldn't let other people's criticisms get to me, because I knew my child better than they did. I went back home, and I was glad I'd been for that walk, because my energy levels were high again. [B, 4 months]

After a while, the sense of chaos comes and goes:

I look calm now. You'd never guess that I'd been screaming at my husband over the telephone just an hour or so ago: "I can't *cope*. There's no rou*tine*. It's all a *mess*. I'm a *fail*ure!" [G, 6 months]

Slowly these mothers discover that the overwhelming extent of the chaos decreases. They are learning about their babies, and simultaneously their babies are learning about them. This differs from the more conscious learning we saw in chapter 5, in which a mother responds to the urgent sound of her baby crying. Now her learning seems less focused. Mothers report no particular goal or aim. They sit quietly for long stretches of time because this seems to keep their babies contented. It may feel like doing nothing at the time. But afterward mothers realize that they have learned a great deal. It is often called "instinctive knowledge" or "intuitive knowledge" when the mother has acquired it. Perhaps this is because it is usually nonverbal and therefore *like* instinct and intuition. But instinct and intuition are quick reactions, whereas maternal understanding grows slowly.

People ask when I'm coming back to work. But I *am* working. I'm thinking about B all the time. I can't think about anything else. It's too difficult. [B, 4 months]

> I have to spend most of the day being, not doing. I have to let things go that I'd like to do, but I'm being B's mother. It doesn't mean that I'm not me, but I'm learning to be in the present. [B, 6 months]

If a mother spends long periods with her baby, little bits of pattern suddenly "click." For example, her baby may be very irritable in the evening and start crying. At first, the mother cannot think why. Nothing seems to have provoked it. Nothing has changed from the previous moment, before the crying started. It often takes weeks to realize that her baby is overloaded with excitement. A sensible baby should say: "I've had enough. Give me a break, and help me get to sleep now, Mom!" But babies' curiosity is very strong. They get into a state in which they can neither assimilate any more nor bear to turn away. Hence the crying. Once a mother recognizes this state, it all makes sense. Her relief is enormous. She also feels the excitement of having cracked some letters of a code. Deciding what to do is much less of a problem. She usually experiments with several ideas. But now she feels back in control.

Some interesting research has been done on how parents "interact" with small babies. Researchers have tried to separate each kind of interaction. Visual, verbal, holding, touching, affectionate, and caretaking behaviors have been carefully observed.[5] This may leave the impression that a mother ought to keep *doing* things with her baby. But this would be exhausting for both of them. They are often together in quiet and more inactive ways, yet very aware of each other. You can sit talking to a breastfeeding mother, for example, and she *looks* relaxed, as though she is doing nothing. After all, the food for her baby is created inside her. She doesn't have to busy herself to prepare it. While her baby is breastfeeding, she seems able to take part fully in the conversation with you. But she has an inner alertness, which does not show. Her arms are sensitive to any change in her baby. A mother holding her baby can almost hear him through her arms. She alternates listening to you with regular checking to learn how her baby is.

> I used to feel slighted when I was talking to a mother, because the moment her child said something, she would turn her face from me to her child. I'd think: "Oh, you think I'm boring." But now I'm a mother myself, I tell people I can understand how they feel. I explain to them that I'm interested in what they are saying. But with one part of my mind, I have *got* to look after B. [B, 9 months]

Gradually, as she learns how to make her baby more comfortable, she finds ways that suit her too. Both parties need accommodating. That is the secret of their relationship. They are two very different people, yet they need to find ways of being at ease together. The mother learns to be together with her baby and to get on with her own life too. One mother, a trained cook, discovered that she could make a kind of agreement with her small daughter.

> People keep telling me that I need a break from G. But I don't. She's great company. She likes what I like. The other day I absolutely *had* to fry a fish, so I told G and showed her the fish, and she seemed to know it was important. I put her in her chair, and she sat and watched me, and I actually finished it. Then I thought that since she was sitting there, being so good, perhaps I could cook something

more. But she immediately squirmed in her chair, as if to say: "You said *fish,* nothing else." [G, 5 months]

Each relationship is an original creation. Mothers sometimes borrow ideas from each other. But no one has the recipe for perfection. It would be ridiculous to suggest that every mother cooking fish should let her baby watch, for example. The whole point is that the mother finds a way for both of them to enjoy themselves. If the relationship works well, the mother finds that her everyday activities actually become more fun with her passionately curious baby to share them with. For her baby, the most mundane activity is exciting and new. A mother may crumple up a brown paper bag to throw it away, only to notice her baby staring, eyes round with curiosity, to see what that crackly sound was. Everyday life takes on a new excitement.

These relaxed moments are offset by tense ones, when the mother feels out of step with her baby. She feels she has been thrown back into chaos again. It can affect her mood for the whole day. For example, a baby may suddenly outgrow his midmorning sleep. One fine day he is wide awake, with a lot of energy. This may sound like a small change, but the mother has already started expending her energy, assuming that she would have some free time when her baby fell asleep. She would have paced herself differently had she known that she wouldn't have this break. Now she feels tired and irritable at the change.

Some mothers complain that they feel permanently out of step with their babies. The easy relationship seems to be working for everyone else except them. This is usually when the mother describes having high expectations of herself, and she also tends to demand more of her baby than he can deliver. She speaks as though she is driving them both up a ladder without a top. Some mothers in this predicament have found it helpful to compare notes with other mothers. They have said that this calms them and helps them to relax their self-expectations. They start to understand their babies better when they are expecting less, not more.

External circumstances can make this stage of mothering difficult. Some mothers feel depressed by their homes, or their precarious finances, or their relationship with the baby's father. There may be illness and death in the family or political disturbances that they cannot escape. It can be very hard for a mother to set aside her anxiety in order to relax and put in all the work of learning to know her baby.

The miracle is that, despite the difficulties and lack of social understanding, mothers do manage to make their way out of the early chaos. The journey from chaos to order seems to be the normal way that people learn. It seems to be a feature of human intelligence to be able to perceive meaningful patterns of behavior in apparently random actions.[6] Just how mothers perceive these patterns, and what they are, might be the subject for another book. Here we are trying to establish *that* they perceive the patterns and are not sitting "doing nothing."

A mother may start by doubting that there could be any meaning whatsoever in her baby's behavior. It is hard to listen to a mother who is in this state of chaos. I myself have sometimes worried whether a very distressed mother will really find her way. But she does. It is a marvelous achievement. Every new, unique, complex human baby is a challenge to our understanding. A guideline that helped with one baby often proves ineffectual with another. Yet if a baby seems unwell, even during the first few weeks, health professionals will ask the mother: "Is he behaving like his usual self?" They have discovered that they can rely on mothers, even at this early stage, to have collected a host of minute and detailed observations of what their babies are usually like.

If there is no mother or caretaking person, then the baby hasn't got anyone to make sense of him or communicate with him. Studies of children in deprived orphanages, such as those in Romania, show how impoverished a child can be when this maternal care is missing. The children's responses are reduced; they protect themselves with repetitive comforting behavior and often seem too discouraged to trust people. These studies alone should alert us to the tremendous achievement that so many mothers accomplish, almost unnoticed, in our midst.

There comes a moment, after the early period of chaos, when the two of them seem to come through from chaos to understanding. The change is unmistakable.

> I've been doing nothing, just pottering around with G all week, and I love it. She's so nice to be with, and I understand her so much better now. [G, 4 months]

> I can read B now. I know when he is too tired and cross, or when he feels bored. I know when he's a bit interested and a bit hungry, and those two feelings conflict. I really understand him. [B, 6 months]

> I recognize her signals, like some little squeals mean: "Give me that hairbrush back! I want to bite it!" [G, 7 months]

> I really like being with B, and I think he likes being with me. [B, 1 year]

Mothers who find it completely impossible to sit still, "doing nothing," may be comforted to learn that those mothers who do also demand to be up and busy again.

> When B's asleep, I get ten things done, where I got one done before. I feel guilty sitting down and enjoying a cup of tea. I feel I must do something. [B, 4 months]

> One day I just *had* to clean the kitchen floor. I told F he absolutely had to hold B so I could do it. It wasn't because it was so dirty. It was because at least then I could see something I'd done. I can look after B all day, and he doesn't seem any different. [B, 7 months]

It is important to repeat that there is no single blueprint for being a good mother. Some mothers develop very different relationships with their babies, in which the slow "doing nothing" has no place. This chapter is not written to unsettle their confidence in their own chosen style but rather to support those mothers who keep berating themselves for "getting nothing done."

If these mothers are fascinated by their babies, babies amply return the compliment. The relationship starts to flower.

> It's two-way. He stares up at my face, just wondering at me. I get as much as I give. [B, 3 months]

> I can't put G down for a second. She just wants me to carry her all the time. If one more person says it must be teething, I'll scream. There's not a tooth in sight. I have to keep reminding myself that G is intelligent. I mean, why would anyone keep wanting to be picked up so they can look at me? [Pause] I suppose I just can't believe it. [G, 7 months]

Yet this is not a sentimental relationship. If mothers spend stretches of time with their babies, the babies see their mothers in all moods.

> *First mother:* I say "Hello!" when he cries, and I say it in my "sweet" voice, and he just looks at me, and I'm sure he knows. He knows I'm not in a sweet mood. [B, 7 weeks]
>
> *Second mother:* Yes, I know. You meet this big-eyed look. I mean, I just couldn't *lie* to him. Sometimes I go to him, and I don't feel so good, and I just can't lie about it. I'd hate to deceive him. [B, 4 months]

> B doesn't get a picture of an idealized mother. If you are with your child all day, he sees you when you don't feel like talking or when you're down or crying. He sees all of it. [B, 9 months]

This reciprocal studying of the other person shows that mother and baby realize they need to learn about each other. They do not automatically know what the other one is like.

> In the beginning, it was cuddling. It was a cuddly relationship. It depended on me physically holding B. Quite strongly but not too tight. I'd sit like that for hours. Sometimes I could feel myself losing myself, as if I were all B and had entered his consciousness. It seems really strange to remember that now. [B, 8 months]

The mother's "as if" safeguard is crucial. One could "lose" oneself in a film or a novel in a similar way. It's an attempt to make sense of a different world. One can open a novel, aware of sitting on a particular chair and perhaps of having limited time for reading. Details of the novel then "draw one in." At a certain stage, one gives oneself permission to forget temporarily about the chair and the time limit. But on a deeper level, we anchor ourselves and can return to ourselves. We are not Elizabeth Bennet or Darcy. It was as if we were, for a short time. It brought us closer to understanding them. Mothers seem to describe a similar process.

Until I became a mother myself, I had no idea how much there was to learn about each baby. Years earlier, as a student, I had read Winnicott's popular book *The Child, the Family and the Outside World.* I wasn't sure what to think about it then, so I stored my copy "for when I have children." Then, when I had my first baby, I felt that I had lost my bearings in a strange new world. One day I suddenly thought of Winnicott's book. I remember the excitement of finding it again, with my new baby still tiny enough for me to hold her in one arm, and his book in the other. The first paragraph gave me a slight jolt, as if something didn't sound quite right. Yet Winnicott's friendly and conversational style had me racing through the first chapters without stopping. Then I made myself return to the first paragraph. I had to read each phrase separately before I could identify the one that troubled me. The whole sentence is: "I am a man, and so I can never really know what it is like to see wrapped up over there in the cot a bit of my own self, a bit of me living an independent life, yet at the same time dependent and gradually becoming a person."[7] The phrase that had startled me was "a bit of my own self."

I turned from the book to the baby in my other arm and back to the first page again. *Was* my baby "a bit of my own self"? No. That was my whole difficulty. She was completely different. Nor was she "gradually becoming a person." She looked and felt like a real person already. She so obviously had her own thoughts and her own way of seeing things. She continually challenged me. Though she was so new, I was compelled to relate to her not as a "baby" but with the respect one feels for a fellow person, equal to oneself.

Mothers and babies behave, from the start, as if they recognize each other as separate people. Mothers may give the appearance of effortless togetherness. They may describe themselves and their babies as "we," for example in a sentence like: "We've had a really nice day together." The whole point of this kind of sentence is that it describes two different people who are learning to understand each other and to get along. The mother's use of "we" does not deny her baby's separateness but affirms that they have found a way to be together nevertheless.

Some mothers say they tell their babies little sequences of the day's events. Most babies make attentive listeners. Their eyes open wide, and they pant with excitement. Not every mother uses words during the first year. Some mothers say that talking to a baby makes them feel self-conscious and silly. The mother who made the agreement about frying her fish was one of these. She made her contract by using a minimum of words and relying mostly on gestures. Words are not essential in this kind of exchange. The important actions are the attending to each other and taking turns.

Even though communication is thought to be important, this early stage of it can still feel like "doing nothing." It's spontaneous and fun. But years later, at school, her child will be building on the mother's early work. This maternal groundwork is surely fundamental, even though it was probably undervalued as "nothing" at the time.

As the mother learns to communicate with her baby, another dimension of their relationship comes into focus. This is the moral relationship between the two. Once it was regarded as a vital part of being a mother. It used to be discussed within a religious framework. Now that organized religion has declined, this whole area seems to be an embarrassment. It is not a comfortable subject. For a start, mother and baby do not relate as physical equals. We have only to step back for a moment to see that the mother is by far the larger, stronger, and more experienced of the two. So their moral relationship must be seen in the context of a stronger person relating to a weaker one.

The moral relationship between a mother and her baby is a large and complex subject. Only a small part of it relates to this chapter. It provides another important area of being a mother that is rarely discussed. Silence turns it into "nothing." Yet it is an intrinsic part of a mother's daily experience. She may ask herself frequently whether she is being a good mother. Other people may challenge her with their views on the best way to bring up her baby. Sometimes a total stranger may walk up to her in the street and ask: "Is he a good baby?" "Morality" and "being judgmental" are unpopular concepts today. Mothers may not always be aware how often they are thinking about moral questions. Yet they are sure to be doing so.

How to be a good mother can seem a bit abstract during pregnancy. Expectant mothers may be given plenty of advice by their family, friends, and professionals on the best way to take care of themselves for the benefit of their unborn babies. Expectant mothers sometimes complain that they don't understand what all the fuss is about. However, once a mother can see and hold her baby, it doesn't seem fussy at all. By a miracle, her body has just given birth to a completely new person. How awesome that this miracle of new life has been entrusted to her! New mothers report their passionate desire to do the best they can for their babies. Being a mother is not enough in itself: most of us resolve, there and then, to become *good* mothers.

Translating goodness into daily actions is a different matter. There is rarely time to take stock. A mother is beset with moments of choice. They may seem so trivial that the mother's decision looks pragmatic. It is easy to overlook the moral dimension. She herself often complains that she doesn't feel like a person with free will anymore. How can she have choices? Surely the shoe is on the other foot. Her strong-willed baby is making all the choices. Isn't she almost tied to him, like slave to master, hurrying to his side when he needs her? Far from having choices, she has lost her old freedom to plan her day. Yet she is using her power to choose. The ultimate choice over what she does remains hers, every time. She is the stronger party. Every time her baby wants something and she provides it, she has chosen to use her adult power in a humane way. She is overlooking all the little moments of choice.

Typically, she has to choose in mid-action. Trivial-sounding questions turn up, thick and fast. Babies often seem to fall asleep just when the mother has an appointment to be somewhere else. Should she wake him up or miss the appointment? He won't come to any physical harm if she wakes him. But his sleep looks deep, and it seems an act of great selfishness to rouse him. She weighs his interests and hers, in moral as well as in pragmatic terms.

> I feel a bit like a nun, in the nice meaning of the word. I keep the telly off because I think it wouldn't be good for B to keep it on. I could so easily not bother to do things like this. But I'm glad I do them. [B, 4 weeks]

> I keep weighing what's good for her and what's good for me. Everything is hard to decide. [G, 5 months]

> I've got all these questions running around in my head, such as am I giving B enough attention? Am I neglecting him while I get on with things? And we're *always* late! Am I damaging him by always hurrying on his little shoes so that we can try to be somewhere on time? [B, 6 months]

> It's hard to know how far we should let our babies take risks. If we were men, we'd say we were at the cutting edge of science, and be patting ourselves on the back for it. But we're women, so we just keep beating ourselves up with guilt. [G, 13 months]

There is also the complex balancing of sibling interests or, perhaps, the needs of a pet. Whom should the mother care for first, and on what grounds?

> I think one of our cats has become clinically depressed since G was born. He just won't get out of his basket all day. He wants my attention. It's awful. The cats were my babies for all those years before we had G. [G, 3 months]

> It's hard when both children want me at the same time. [G, 5 years; B, 3 months]

These examples are moral, because the mother is weighing the best way to act. Far from getting nothing done, she is wielding enormous power. How easy it would be to abuse so much power. How impossible it is to always use it well. Often her choices are made in the chaos of the moment. At first they may not be consistent. She experiments, thinks it over, and sometimes changes her mind. But slowly a recognizable pattern emerges. Slowly a mother's small choices start to connect up with each other. From this, her baby gets his first taste of justice.

One person who recognized the enormous moral power of mothers was Plato—but he was quick to recognize that such power was far too precious to be left in women's hands. In his last work, *Laws,* he was considering the best way to organize human society, and therefore what kinds of laws would be needed to preserve this best possible social organization. He worked out what kinds of citizens would be required to run his ideal society, and this led him to ask what kind of babyhood they would need to give them the best possible preparation for their adult responsibilities. His arguments are still thought-provoking today. He was in no doubt that adults were influenced by their childhoods. He even thought that the amount of exercise that a pregnant woman took would affect her child.

Plato then went on to ask himself those questions that mothers know so well. Should a crying baby be picked up and soothed or strictly disciplined? Should babies be stimulated with special delights or kept calm? Should boys and girls be treated differently and, if so, from what age? Each question, he was sure, had an ideal answer, which would have a strong influence in forming the character of the child. The ideal answer could be encoded in law. But, reflected Plato, mothers and nursemaids might not obey such laws. He suspected that they would laugh at them. "Why," he wrote, "the ridicule we should be sure to incur!"[8] So, in his system, the father of each household was to be responsible for ensuring that every child was brought up according to the laws.

Fortunately for all of us, this totalitarian system remains Plato's dream. Mothers still have their moral power. This doesn't mean their power is unlimited. The mother shares it with the baby's father. Discussing questions together can be very helpful. Family and friends also influence the couple. As we saw at the beginning of this chapter, mothers tend to be sensitive to what other people think of their children. Then there are state procedures that can intervene if a mother seems to be ill-treating or neglecting her child. However, apart from all this, mothers have been left to their own devices. A mother can create her own unique moral system within her own home.

The greater challenge is usually not from adults but from her baby. Babies are not empty vessels into which a mother can pour her own values. Mothers can be astonished at how strongly babies assert their own values, right from the start.

> G's got a will over how I carry her. She likes to be over my shoulder. But when we went to the consulate to get my passport, we were arguing like mad because I just couldn't carry her that way. [G, 6 weeks]

> B can voice his own opinions now. [B, 4 months]

> G's so determined. If she wants something, her eyes get this intent look, and *nothing* will deflect her. [G, 6 months]

> You cannot control another human being. That's what I've come to realize. I can't force B to eat a special bit of food, for example, even if it's for his own good. [B, 12 months]

A great deal has been published about the moral education—or lack of it—of children. Babies are sensitive. They seem to pick up moral cues from an early age. If a mother treats her baby with respect, her baby tends to respond in kind—not instantly, but once he becomes old enough. So a mother has a more subtle power. She is teaching by example. This means that she need not focus on her baby's behavior as much as think carefully about her own.

This is not as straightforward as it may sound. Life with a baby can be frustrating, and there isn't always a third party to witness their exchange. It is only too easy for a mother to act out of frustration, to excuse herself from wrong and to blame the baby. The temptation is obviously very great. To their credit, some mothers report outbursts of irritation with their babies, followed by regret.

> *Mother:* I talk out loud to B. That way, I can hear what I'm doing. If I do something wrong, I always tell him so.
>
> *Me:* Do you ever apologize if you find you were in the wrong?
>
> *Mother:* Oh, I do, I *do,* I'm *always* apologizing. I hope when he's older he'll realize that that's the right thing to do. [B, 8 months]

Babies seem to study adults minutely to learn the rules of the adult world. If a mother apologizes to her baby when she has done wrong, he learns from his earliest days that she takes the moral dimension seriously. His mother doesn't have to sit down and convince him of its importance. He has long studied what she does in relation to himself. Conversely, some mothers exonerate themselves yet reproach their children for the same offenses. It is then easy for the child to conclude that ordinary moral rules are really "just for children."

When the child begins to crawl, he often develops a way of checking his mother's face before trying anything new. He looks to her for both pragmatic and moral guidelines. However, if a mother does not see herself as doing anything of value, she could easily overlook this opportunity. A stage on from that is when he points to things. His mother obliges with its name, and again there is a chance for her to say something about it. "Newspaper. Careful, don't squash it! Mommy and Daddy like it smooth."

Soon the child is piecing together phrases and sentences. Gradually he becomes able to challenge her moral rules with a host of questions, most of which start with "Why?" It is important to see that her child is challenging details. He is questioning particular rules. In doing so, he is showing that he has accepted the principle that there should be *some* rules to ensure that family members act kindly, fairly, and decently to each other. Mothers don't have to teach every rule. Just a few rules teach children what they need. They are learning the importance of justice itself.

Justice is an ancient human concept. The most primitive societies have codes of good and bad behavior, and appropriate rewards and punishments for it. This enables us to live together in complex, many-dimensional social groups, in which the majority of us respect each other's persons and property. We move from one setting to another, and we continually make those little shifts of adaptation. We learn social codes of behavior for different settings and develop our personal codes. We have to learn when to accept social codes and when to protest at their unfairness. So, ahead of the small baby lies the whole vast and complex social world.

Who can predict the future of a small baby? He may become an adult wielding great responsibility or, alternatively, find himself in a society where his rights are curtailed and he is oppressed. In such circumstances, his early experiences with his mother, and the memory of how she used her power in relating to him, may steady and support him in adult life. At critical moments, her moral influence may extend far beyond childhood, as Plato was sure it would.

When a mother sits quietly, being receptive to her baby, she may not be making any visible achievement. While we may continue to call this kind of relationship "getting nothing done all day," it is hard for the majority of mothers to recognize the remotest value in what they are doing. Rather, they feel valued only for the visible changes they achieve. Yet visible changes can be banal, as the sociologist Jessie Bernard pointed out: "Generations of children are protected, sheltered, nourished and socialised into human beings by the banal activities of diaper-changing, dish-washing, bandaging, and swing-pushing."[9]

This is not the way all mothers feel, but they still find their feelings difficult to justify. Some of those who recognize most clearly the importance of mothering are the ones working with young people who have missed being mothered. The irony is that these mothers generally have only a few months of maternity leave. When this leave is over, they are compelled for financial reasons—and despite their tears of grief—to leave their babies with professional carers while they go off to full-time jobs as remedial teachers, school psychologists, youth workers, staff at substance-abusers' rehabilitation units, or psychotherapists, to name but a few, all of which are concerned with the problems of young people who have not had appropriate attention from their parents. But in caring for them, they may find that their own children are shortchanged.

When children reach school age, their ability to relate is easier to see. Then teachers call it "socialization," but this is another way of materializing the overlooked and invisible value of relationships. If a child has enjoyed a real understanding with his mother, then his ignorance of how to use the school toilets or eat with knife and fork can be put right in a few minutes. He will extend his respect for his mother to his teacher, listen carefully, and take pride in learning. If the child has grown up at home in a battle zone in which his parents don't show him much respect and see no point in trying to understand him, he may well see his first task at school as being that of protecting himself from what he perceives as endless humiliating onslaughts by adults, rather than that of learning the niceties of school behavior.

When he grows into an adult, his plight is even clearer. Relationships have become a frequent problem. Adults spend hours of their leisure time in individual or couple counseling and therapy, group therapy, parenthood groups, and even training in "people skills" because it doesn't come naturally. For anyone who has listened to people talking in this kind of setting, a recurring theme is that the "client," as the person has now become, does not seem to have been respected by his mother in his early years. Understandably, the child has now grown into an adult who lacks the experience of a good early relationship. He may never have experienced the joys and pains of risking love for another person. He may not realize that, though it can be soothing to have things "my way," it can be more exciting to do things differently for love of another. Two people in a strong friendship or marriage can develop further than either of them would on their own. It is possible to learn all this as an adult, but how much easier it is to grow up with the experience.

We have all kinds of remedial systems to help us, yet we are continuing to undervalue the work that would ease the problem in the first place. If we keep referring to the slow periods of being a mother as "getting nothing done," then most mothers will continue to see what they are doing as "nothing."

seven

so tired I could die

The tiredness of a new mother is in a league of its own. It's easy to overhear exchanges like:

"How are you?"

"Tired!"

"So'm I. If you put me to bed, I'd sleep for a week."

"A *week?* All I want is four unbroken hours."

"I used to wonder what mothers meant when they said they were tired. Now I know."

"You get too tired to think of ideas that would help you be less tired."

"In the first few months, you really think: 'I am never going to get a proper sleep ever again.'"

"Your sense of humor goes when you're so tired. I can't *bear* people making jokes."

"You get things out of proportion. All your judgment just goes when you are that tired."

What makes the mother of a baby so tired? Mothers usually reply: "I need more sleep." A stretch of continuous sleep is a wonderful restorative, and mothers rarely get it. But this seems to be only part of the explanation. A big part of it seems to be that mothers think they *oughtn't* to be tired.

This is reflected in the way that mothers describe their tiredness. They aren't proud of it. They don't justify it as a worthwhile result of having a new baby. Their manner is confessional, as if they are somehow at fault. In a conversation about tiredness, it is usual to hear a mother say she feels "out of control" or that she has "no routine at the moment" or that she "can't crack this tiredness thing." A mother can sound more like a struggling business manager than the mother of a human baby. This is understandable because when she mentions her tiredness, she is usually given advice on how to feel less tired. No one praises her for being tired in a good cause. Tiredness therefore looks like a sign of bad management.

Mothers of first babies feel especially disoriented. They may have heard friends say that having a baby was tiring—but then, other people are always complaining. Before the baby's birth, the agenda didn't look too demanding. After all, don't babies sleep a lot? When they are awake, they just need feeding, help in bringing up their gas, and diaper changing, and all the time left over can be for play.

After the birth, the degree of tiredness can come as a rude shock. The mothers who talk to me tend to regard themselves as competent women. A few months earlier, many of them were giving all their energies to demanding jobs—for example, in teaching, health care, television, or business. They were used to stress at work and took pride in rising to difficult situations. Their self-images were positive.

Such self-images tend to fall away during the first months of being a mother. The change seems unbelievable.

The tiredness of an employed mother is relatively easy to explain, but what about the exhaustion of mothers who take maternity leave? They are at home, which is a place associated with free time and relaxation. How can a mother possibly complain of feeling tired at *home*? Here she has personal comforts. Here she is in charge. She doesn't have to worry about a work hierarchy, or deadlines, or being made redundant. Many mothers assume that life at home will be easy. Before the birth, they plan to liven up the easy pace (and to deal with the guilt of enjoying it) by decorating a room or starting a course of study. How can they then explain to their hardworking partners and friends that they feel so tired—when they've just spent an entire day at home?

Why is tiredness such a feature of mothering a baby?

At first, mothers often feel just a little more tired than usual. During the early weeks, many newborns spend a lot of the day asleep. Studies show that an average newborn sleeps for about sixteen hours of the twenty-four.[1] (Most of the babies I know are not so average!) A new mother expects to be tired then, and other people expect her to be. At this stage, night feeding seems the most tiring part. Apart from that, if her baby is sleeping so much, being a mother can seem relatively straightforward. A mother often thinks she has an "easy" baby and starts to resume some of her former activities. Then, just as she decides motherhood is much easier than people told her it would be, and just as the offers of help and the friendly phone calls of sympathy start thinning out, her baby seems to reach a new stage. Instead of falling asleep after every feeding he looks up and gazes around, alert and fascinated.

At this time, newborns are often especially lively at night.

Adults expect to wind down and sleep at night. Newborns seem to experience day and night differently. Many are overwhelmed by bright daylight and daytime noises. Then, just when their parents turn down the lights and talk in quiet voices, newborns appear more comfortable. They open their eyes, look around, and grow lively. The novelty of it can be fun for a while.

> I like nights. There's just me and B then, and I feel as if it's just me and him in the world. I don't begrudge the tiredness. It seems a small price to pay. [B, 6 weeks]

But the price increases. Most babies need to feed at night. They have small stomachs, which need to be refilled more often than adult ones, so they often wake up hungry. Many have a predictable time, often during the morning, when they prefer to sleep a bit longer. But this is probably when their mothers expect to be awake. In his book *Sleep Thieves*, Stanley Coren writes: "A new baby will result in 400 to 750 hours of [maternal] sleep lost in the first year."[2] This is mostly because mothers have to wake up to feed their babies at night, and don't like sleeping during the day.

Another difficulty is that adults and babies have different sleep rhythms. The adult sleep cycle is thought to be around eighty-five to ninety minutes. However, the baby's is a much shorter, fifty to sixty minutes.[3] So, when a baby wakes up comfortably after a one-hour complete cycle of sleep, it may be only two-thirds of the way through his mother's cycle. Instead of feeling refreshed, she wakes up feeling frustrated. She may complain about shortage of sleep because she doesn't realize that it is also the breaking into her sleep cycle that can leave her feeling so ragged.

Yet human beings are adaptable. We don't have to sleep the

exact number of sleep hours that we have lost. Nathaniel Kleitman in his groundbreaking book *Sleep and Wakefulness,* which was first published in 1939, describes a process that we now call "recovery sleep." For example, "after 3–4 days of sleep deprivation, a typical young subject sleeps approximately 12–14 hours and may sleep an hour longer than usual on the next night but not much more than that."[4]

Kleitman's experiments were done with volunteers who had to stay awake for continuous periods. Mothers tend to doze or drift into a light sleep. There is a shortage of information about them. The key word is usually "fatigue" in research literature. "Unfortunately, there is a dearth of research on fatigue," state the authors of one paper.[5]

A few studies have been carried out on fatigue suffered by doctors, military personnel, disaster workers, air-traffic controllers, pilots, and long-distance truck drivers. But they don't seem to have been done for new mothers. "A search of nursing and related journals from the past twenty years revealed a number of studies of fatigue in healthy and ill populations but few studies about fatigue during the childbearing period. . . . Fatigue during the childbearing period continues to be an understudied topic," conclude researchers Renee A. Milligan and Linda C. Pugh.[6] If mothers knew more, they could plan better.

An outsider might well ask what the problem is. Surely mothers, babies, and sleep have not changed since human beings began. Haven't mothers found methods of coping with tiredness during this time? The answer is that social patterns have changed. The solutions that used to help mothers are often not workable today.

To start with the obvious, electricity has opened up all kinds of after-dark activities that were not possible when oil lamps and candles were all there was. We have electric light, electric forms of heating, television, and computers at all hours. We must spend far more time active and awake than people did before electric light came to be generally used. Even before the baby's birth, parents may have been stretching their energies to the limit. When a baby is added to this precarious balancing of round-the-clock activity with minimal sleep, the scales tip toward parental exhaustion.

In addition, a baby doesn't necessarily drop off to sleep when he is tired. Modern life is not just stimulating for parents: it stimulates their baby too. This state of affairs may be familiar to the parents, but to their baby it is all new. The bright lights of an ordinary home, the amplified sounds of a television, and especially the quickness of his parents' voices and movements may be very exciting to the baby. The pace of life is particularly fast in cities. Even if parents realize this, they usually find it difficult to slow down. Mothers describe how, when their partners return home from work, the two of them start the evening meal, which means a lot of new sounds and smells for their baby. It can then be difficult for the baby, who is now wide awake, and keen to stay awake with curiosity and excitement, to calm down again and fall asleep.

Single mothers often report that getting their babies to sleep at night is not a problem because the evenings are so quiet. This is confirmed by mothers whose partners have gone to work abroad for a few weeks. These mothers first say that they don't know how they will manage at bedtime without the help of their partners—they then discover that it is easier because evenings are no longer so exciting. Some mothers, whose husbands and older children all return noisily home in the early evening, have found that their babies get overly excited and benefit from a nap earlier in the day.

A mother can be surprised at the contrast when she takes her baby from the city to rural places.

> We were on holiday in Spain. We lived in a lovely remote cottage by a wood, just F, B, and myself. We didn't do much because there wasn't much to do, and we completely slowed down. I discovered that B had a rhythm that I never noticed in London, because I'm always checking my watch and finding that it's time to do something that I'd planned. There's so much choice in London, and I love it. But in Spain, I realized how relaxing it was. We all had a rest when B did, and all felt like getting up at the same time. [B, 11 months]

> Even if you keep your own little room quiet, you can hear planes and helicopters and radios, and so much noise. Whereas in India [where the mother had just stayed with her husband's family in a remote village], the night is dark and quiet, and there was nothing for us to do except sleep. [B, 15 months]

In traditional societies, mothers' responsibilities are usually shared, and a mother's female relatives are expected to help her. But in modern societies these relatives are not usually available. They are more likely to be in full-time employment. The mother's mother, traditionally the first person a new mother would turn to, may well be at work all day and some years from retirement. If their mothers live close enough, new mothers may make special arrangements for childcare with them, but it is no longer an informal system that can be taken for granted.

Mothers who still live in traditional families report that the responsibilities are spread among their female relatives. Someone takes the baby while they sleep, and they get plenty of practical help. But, they are quick to add, there are strings attached.

These mothers have received a modern education. They have been taught to think independently—and they do. But their relatives usually expect them to follow family custom in caring for their babies, and grow offended if the mothers want to do things differently. So these mothers feel there is a price to pay for the help they receive. In other words, this time-honored traditional solution to maternal tiredness may not suit today's mothers, who take pride in making their own decisions.

Another change relates to the structure of work. Most modern work is organized in such a way that a mother cannot have her baby with her while she does it. The majority of mothers now return to work during their baby's first year. This means that they are virtually running two lives: one at work, though "on call" if their babies need them, and their free time, not relaxing like their non-parent colleagues but "catching up" with the needs of their babies. "Every study of working mothers," says the writer Melissa Benn, "shows that they are stretched to their limits of endurance."[7]

A further difficulty affects women whose work is intellectual. Never before have so many women received higher education. When these women become mothers, they report a drastic sense of change.

> "I can't concentrate on a *book*." [G, 6 weeks] [Said in alarm by a mother whose livelihood depended on reading.]

> My brain is a big part of my identity. It's gone totally *blunt*. I just have to let it go, and have faith that it will eventually come back. That's all I can say. [G, 3 months] [It may be reassuring to learn that, three years later, this mother's first book was published and received glowing reviews for the high quality of its scholarly research.]

I walk around in a brain-dead daze. [G, 6 months]

Recent studies endorse what these mothers are saying. "Sleep is of the brain, by the brain, for the brain," wrote J. Allan Hobson.[8] So it makes sense that women who have made academic careers will feel especially disoriented when they go short of sleep. It would surely help if they were prepared for this change and reassured that it is temporary. It's difficult enough looking after a baby—without the additional anxiety that one's brain might be permanently blunted.

There has also been a significant change in the place where babies sleep. In traditional societies, babies sleep beside their mothers. But today, in Western societies, babies are often "settled" in their own cribs to sleep and in their own separate rooms. This can be unexpectedly tiring for a mother. She has to get up at night and walk to another room each time her baby wakes up for a feeding. In addition, she surely sleeps less deeply if she needs to keep an ear open for her baby's cry or sounds from the baby monitor. Breastfeeding mothers often "rediscover" the relaxation of sleeping with their babies. Some of them learn to breastfeed almost in their sleep, hardly needing to rouse themselves.[9]

Some mothers report extreme distress at being woken by their babies during the night. It is surprising to learn how many of them once, as babies themselves, were trained to sleep through the night. Today sleep training can be more sensitive. But when these mothers were babies, their own mothers were advised to go out of earshot, leaving their babies to "cry it out." Perhaps not every sleep-trained baby turns into a distressed parent. But some do.

As mothers themselves, they seem to regard night as a time when they absolutely *must* sleep a certain number of hours—and there is an urgent pitch to these mothers' voices as they state exactly how many hours they want to sleep. At the same time, they describe feeling deeply distressed by the sound of their babies' nighttime crying. Perhaps it reactivates their own early shock of being trained to sleep without their parents at night. They have not retained conscious memories of crying. But when these mothers turn to their parents for suggestions for getting their babies to sleep at night, they are startled to hear about how they themselves had been left to cry.

> I was one of those babies who slept through the night. I *need* my eight hours. Now I'm lucky if it's five. It's torture. I feel absolutely *tortured* by it. [B, 4 months] [This mother learned from a family friend that she hadn't automatically fallen asleep as a baby but had been left to cry herself to sleep in a downstairs room.]

> By day I can manage, and I feel so happy and proud of the way I mother. But at night I become a different person. [In tears] When B won't get to sleep, I just get so desperate I can't cope at all. [B, 9 months]

So these mothers feel in conflict. They are distressed to hear their own babies crying at night and want to respond sensitively, but at the same time they seem to feel the pressure from their own rigid babyhood training to sleep through the night no matter what. Several mothers reported that what enabled them to cope was the help of their husbands at night. They seemed to have chosen spouses who had more flexible approaches to sleep than their own. It helped to have someone encouraging and comforting them while they voiced their deep sense of "wrong" at having to wake up at night.

Some research might be done in this field. How much

maternal distress at being up at night is the result of sleep training a whole generation? Human beings are adaptable. One of our strengths, on which our survival sometimes depends, is our ability to stay awake for exceptional periods and to recover sleep during safe moments later on. Sleep training may interfere with this ability. A baby can be trained to sleep for regular hours to suit social convenience. This may solve an immediate difficulty but make it harder for the baby to grow into an adaptable adult.

Part of the difficulty at night is not just the immediate tiredness. It's the mother's concern that she might not have enough energy for the long day ahead of her. Mothers tend to plan ahead.

> I think how will I manage to the end of today, and how will I manage to the end of the week? Then there'll be another Monday, another Tuesday, and another week, then there'll be another *year.* How will I manage all that? [G, 2 months]

> I wake up each morning, and I have to think of a day for two [people]. [G, 5 months]

Employed mothers seem especially aware of how tiring the hours can be.

> The nanny was sick, so I had to go home. I was exhausted after one hour of it. You can't even go and make yourself a cup of coffee. Work is so much easier. [G, 7 months]

Most people operate by having two separated "spheres" of activity. They travel to a workplace where a completely different style of behavior is required from that in "free time." Even people who work at home usually make a clear distinction between times when they are working and times when they are free. This difference can be very refreshing. By changing from one setting to the other, we can give ourselves a break from one set of circumstances, while we return, with renewed energy, to the other. If one setting has become problematic, we can discuss it and get some comfort in the other. But, often, after her child is born, a mother can find herself restricted to one "sphere" of activity. This takes some getting used to.

When a mother is having a difficult time with her baby, there may not be another completely separate setting where she can take stock and recover. She may not even be aware of her difficulty, because there isn't a word or expression to describe it. Many mothers say they feel "trapped" at home. Perhaps this feeling comes from no longer being able to operate through two separate settings. Some mothers return to work not just for the money but to "keep sane." It can be difficult to spend day and night in just one sphere of activity.

This may explain why tired mothers often react well to a crisis. A crisis is, by its nature, exceptional, so different rules apply. Even though this may be stressful, it can also be re-energizing. A number of tests on non-mothers have demonstrated that a subject may be deprived of sleep but nevertheless can perform well during an emergency. Mothers can do this par excellence. They describe drawing on extraordinary resources of energy, especially if their babies are ill.

> Without sleep, you feel terrible. I'm not saying it's nothing. But when B was ill and I really thought he might not make it, I didn't care *how* little sleep I had. [B, 7 months]

> You draw resources out of yourself somehow. When G was ill, I sat upright with her all night because that's

what she wanted. She screamed if I laid her down. [G, 10 months]

Ordinary life is less dramatic and more ongoing. A mother has to pace herself for continuity. In a crisis, life acquires a sudden "shape." Without a crisis, life with her baby can seem without shape. Day becomes night; weekday becomes weekend. Everything continues or needs doing all over again. Nothing is finally finished.

The odd thing is that mothers often don't realize that this is true of many mothers. For example, when a mother takes her baby out to the park or shopping, this can change the mood of them both. Once they are out, the baby seems interested, and the mother feels proud of her achievement in getting them both through the front door. She then feels less tired. This means that when other mothers look at her, they see a calm-looking mother with a happy baby. In the same way, when she is looking at them, she is almost sure to mistake their temporary calm for their permanent state. It won't occur to her that she is giving the impression of being a calm mother herself. Instead, she may well return home feeling discouraged because she seems to be the only mother who is finding it so tiring.

Having a baby seems such an ordinary event. In crowded London streets, and every time they turn on the television, mothers see people. Logic dictates that all these people must once have been babies—millions of them. Millions of mothers must have cared for them. Being a mother can't be so very difficult. Competent women like themselves ought to be able to handle it. Surely the world is not full of exhausted mothers. The conclusion seems obvious. They are failures. Their tiredness is proof of this.

It is revealing to compare their feelings with those of another group of tired people. Medical students and resident doctors, like mothers, suffer from broken sleep, but it affects their morale differently. "Medical students and residents [i.e., resident doctors] often recount their times without sleep like badges of honour, tangible symbols of their dedication to the profession and testimony, to all, that their sacrifice justifies the status of the profession."[10] In other words, medicine has status, and the sacrifice of sleep can seem justified for so worthy a cause. But what if the cause is a baby? A mother is not trained, nor has she passed competitive examinations to qualify. She is not paid a high salary for being a mother. She is not responsible for a ward of patients, just one small baby. She can feel demoralized and exhausted just from that, and the lowering of her morale greatly adds to her tiredness.

Perhaps this is why mothers can feel re-energized by talking to each other.

> I could give you so many examples of stupid things I've done when I'm tired. I've poured my coffee into my cereal, and once I took B several miles to a shop to change a skirt that wasn't right, and when I got there, I found that I'd left the skirt at home! [B, 4 months]

> All I want is sleep. All I think about now is sleep. [G, 5 months]

> G wakes up every hour and a half at night. I get so tired I can't move. I want to reach for a drink of water [after breastfeeding], but I'm too tired even to raise my arm. [G, 5 months]

It's an awful thing to say, but I find myself wishing I could pack G away for the night and take her out again next morning. I long for sleep. [G, 6 months]

When B won't sleep, I think I'm going to die. I know I won't really die. I just feel trapped. [B, 6 months]

During the day, it's hard to believe that how I feel at night can be real. I get so tired then that I feel I can't go on. It sounds terrible, but I've just *prayed* to God to let me pass away. [B, 6 months]

People who aren't mothers shouldn't be *allowed* to say they feel tired! [G, 6 months]

These are descriptions of *cumulative* tiredness. Not much is known about the effect it has on mothers. Perhaps the research done on doctors is the best available to give us some idea of how mothers are affected. Recent research on resident doctors showed that though they might have felt proud of being tired in a good cause, cumulative tiredness also affected them adversely. Amazingly, resident doctors were still able to perform well for short periods. But personal relationships suffered.[11] As we've seen, mothers, too, tend to respond well in an emergency. Like doctors, they can also snap at family and friends.

I screamed at F: "I don't care about *you*! I don't care about G. All I care about is getting twenty-four hours' sleep." [G, 6 months]

Although they voiced these strong feelings, none of the mothers quoted here had mental breakdowns or was unable to cope. Acknowledging how they felt clearly was a part of coping. Any mother who tried to sound "positive" when one mother was voicing how exhausted she felt (for example, by suggesting that this mother should count her blessings instead of complaining) would be politely told by other mothers, "You must be having an easier time." The majority of listening mothers are completely sympathetic to a tired mother's complaints. Most mothers recognize tiredness. It is an area of common ground.

Could a mother literally die from lack of sleep or even from interrupted sleep? This doesn't seem likely. She would be more likely to collapse in sleep first. There is, however, a more figurative sense in which a mother's references to death can make sense. When I looked through my notes, I was impressed by how often mothers said they felt as though they were dying. This sounded histrionic because although they were physically tired, they were very much alive. However, their words make sense if we hear them as statements not just about their bodies but about a whole way of life before the birth of their babies. It can feel like bereavement. Nothing is the same anymore. There is no way back to the old life. This truly has "died."

When a mother says she feels desperately tired, it often means that she hasn't yet acknowledged this. Her old way of life can still seem like the "real" one, and the baby can seem like a temporary aberration from it. If only she could "manage" the baby, then her life could return to the way it was before. As one mother expressed it:

> If you weren't so tired, if you had lots of energy, you'd be rushing around doing all sorts of things you think you have to do, or you like—and then you'd be too tired for *them,* wouldn't you? [B, 4 months]

Modern society is not organized to facilitate the transition women have to make when they become mothers. It's a momentous change. New mothers often cope by telling themselves to expect motherhood to be challenging at first, but then it will get easier. It certainly does get easier. But not automatically. It becomes easier when mothers take leave of their old lives and adjust to the new.

At one meeting several new mothers were describing how tired they were. Three mothers of older babies were also present. These older babies were aged between eight and fourteen months. Their mothers listened in silence to the new mothers. After a while, I asked the three whether they had been tired at first—"Sure!"—and whether they still felt so tired today—"Not anymore." I said that if they had solved the problem, could they suggest anything that the new mothers could do. All three answered in a spontaneous chorus: *"Live with it!"* Then each of them looked around at the other two, whom they hadn't met before this meeting. They could hardly believe that they'd all three come out with the identical words.

I asked for more details, and their replies were similar:

> You just adapt yourself. You *have* to.
>
> They can't change their sleep pattern to suit you, so you just have to change yours to fit in with them.
>
> I used to think I had to have nine hours' sleep every night. I really *had* to. Now, if I get six, I feel lucky. But I can cope now. Just to survive, I've had to. When G sleeps, even though I don't really like sleeping during the day, and I think I ought to be catching up on my work, I sleep

too. I make a point of letting things go and making sleep a priority.

Mothers find all kinds of solutions. Sleeping when her baby sleeps is not a panacea for every mother. It's just one example. The main change is one of attitude.

It's when you stop resisting and say "This is life for now" that it stops feeling so frustrating and so exhausting. But it's hard to hold on to." [B, 5 weeks]

I can only speak for myself. I don't know if it would help anyone else. B kept waking up at night and I was getting so tired. Then, somehow, I got my head around it. I thought: "If he wants to [breast]feed at night, that's what he wants. It's not for me to tell him not to." And then somehow I could do it and manage to find the energy. It wasn't so bad, once I'd made that decision. [B, 3 months]

F, B, and I get up every morning at eight. We have an hour and a half up, and then, at half-past nine, we all go to bed for a two-hour nap. We live with my in-laws, and I know they wouldn't approve, but they've gone out by then. At first, I was like: "This is getting nothing *done*. Where has my *life* gone?" But once I stopped feeling guilty about our nap and just accepted that this was how we were, it was much easier. [B, 8 months]

Helping their babies to sleep was then more of a technical question.

> When B seems to be sleepy, we lie down in bed and I put my eyes close to his, so he can see them closed, and then he closes his and he's asleep. [B, 2 months]

> I always leave an old T-shirt beside her that smells of me, and that seems to keep her asleep. [G, 4 months]

> B goes to sleep if I make really loud snoring noises. It shows how much *snoring* must go on in my home! [B, 6 months]

A big adjustment for some mothers was overcoming their reluctance to accept help. Many felt that they should be managing something as ordinary as a baby on their own.

> A friend came around and we had a nice chat. Just as she was going, I realized that I could have asked her to look after B for me. It was too late to ask her then, and I was annoyed with myself. Because I work, people see me as very capable. I'm not the sort of person they think of offering help to. My friend made me realize that I need to be more honest to my friends about what they can do for me. [B, 4 months]

> I felt terrible every day, worse than if I had jet-lag or a hangover. My mother-in-law came to stay for a few days, and she took B so I could catch up on sleep. I had two extra hours' sleep for two mornings and slept a bit in the afternoons. I also knew I could sleep for as long as I wanted because she loves having B. So then I caught up and I feel fine now. [B, 4 months]

One day I was desperate, so I phoned F at work and *ordered* him to come back and look after B so I could sleep. [B, 5 months]

F dances G to sleep against his shoulder. They have music, but G doesn't like baby tapes. She likes a particular jazz one. [G, 9 months]

For some mothers, methods such as sleep training, "controlled crying," or "self-comforting" hold the key. The whole philosophy of these methods does not appeal to me, although some mothers find it works for them. If the training doesn't work, or if it once did but the baby outgrows it, the baby can become very distressed. However, mothers often adopt a method because they are desperate for more structure, and their determination seems to help the method to work. They then feel back in control of their lives again.

There are always stories of other mothers and babies who manage so much better. A friend of mine told me her baby slept right through the night for ten hours. I felt so jealous and thought: "Why can't *B* do that?" That night he woke up, no different from usual, but I found I was really angry. I fed him and he fell asleep, but I was so angry that I stayed awake. And what I think about that night now is that I was fine when I didn't compare babies. One should never do that. I can manage perfectly well if I accept B as he is. [B, 5 months]

Employed mothers have to devise particular solutions for conserving energy. Often this involves cutting out former activities, such as taking home extra work or going for after-work drinks with colleagues. Many mothers say they have a much more economical attitude to work.

> People give me funny looks because I don't socialize after work anymore. As soon as it's five o'clock, I'm out of the door to get back to G. [G, 8 months]

One could add to these ways of conserving energy that mothers find. But this might leave the impression that tiredness is always solvable. Sometimes it isn't. Babies of around one year old are often active by day and wake frequently at night, for no obvious reason. Then a mother can feel desperate for sleep yet equally desperate to comfort her baby when he needs her at night. I have spoken to many mothers who have sacrificed their own sleep, waking up numerous times every night because their babies cried for them. It seems terrible that these hardworking women think of themselves as failures as a result. Surely a mother who has chosen to sacrifice her sleep deserves respect and admiration for her generous mothering.

As babies grow older, mothers often describe a recognizable pattern. An older baby can be very independent by day, but come night he wants his mother. Mothers tend to expect a more even development. Many assume that daytime independence will be matched by nighttime independence as well. So when a nine-month-old baby seems to want her more at night, his exhausted mother wails that she feels as if they are both "going backward." But they aren't. It's more like the swing of a pendulum: if it swings farther out, it will return farther back too.

Mothers often report their irritability, not with small babies, but with nine-month-olds and upward. This seems to be because they expected a difficult first six months, followed by an easier six. But children do not necessarily develop at this tidy pace. A nine-month-old may have an intense need for his mother's care. Many mothers find that it is at this stage that they really have to confront the change to their lives. Having a baby is not like taking an extended holiday from daily life. It *is* daily life. Once a mother has accepted this, she is able to look for more radical solutions to deal with her tiredness. She then feels calmer toward her child. Life is not a tug-of-war between conflicting needs. They are both on the same side. Life is slower yet seems more harmonious. Now a mother's love for her baby has room to flower.

> I seem to exhaust myself rushing around. I like to do something each day. But one day I gave in to the rhythm and did things G's way. We stayed at home, and I breastfed her for as long as she wanted. I felt really happy and glowing after. [G, 5 months]

> I feel as if I've crossed over a bridge. B still breastfeeds at night and everyone keeps telling me that I've got a problem. But this week I found a site on the Internet, and I've discovered that B is *typical.* He's just a normal baby. I used to count every feeding at night. Now I look at B and think: "You can feed as often as you need to." Now I've stopped worrying, I don't feel so tired. I gaze at B sucking and I'm full of love for him. [B, 6 months]

> I was looking for a file, and going frantic because I was so tired that my memory had gone and I couldn't remember where I'd put it. B was moaning and wanted me, so finally I took him into the study with me, because I was determined to find that file. But I didn't. Then I saw the way

> B was looking at me, you know, and I thought: "Hey, this is becoming stupid! What is important, a file or him?" So I went and picked him up and held him close to me and just relaxed. And straightaway into my head came a memory of where I'd put that file, and I knew where it was. [B, 7 months]

Mothers often wonder how they could ever manage with more than one child. Surely it will be twice as tiring with two? But often, with a second child, a mother can see that lack of sleep does not wholly explain her tiredness. With her second baby, she may be short of sleep and tired, but not like the first time. She and her first child have created the basis of a family system. Her first child will probably help her to "educate" the younger sibling. So it is nothing like the tremendous adjustment that she went through the first time.

When a mother complains to her family and friends that she feels so tired, they may long to help. They may point out things she does that they think cause her tiredness. They point these out to her, hoping to be helpful. Yet perhaps the help that a mother needs most is to be listened to. If she hasn't asked for advice, she may not need any.

Taking trouble over a baby is definitely tiring and sleep-depriving. But mothers could probably cope better if we all acknowledged how complex and difficult it can be. If a mother says she is short of sleep, this could be a sign not of her failure but of how well she may be mothering. I believe that the real, *dreadful* quality of maternal tiredness is the mother's sense of struggling against prevailing disrespect. The baby may tire her, but we, if we aren't careful, can exhaust her.

eight

what do babies seem to want?

Can we generalize about babies? Some people claim that they can't see the slightest difference between one baby and another. But those who see babies every day observe all kinds of differences, even at birth. So is it possible to say anything about all of them?

Babies are mysterious. Much of our understanding depends on what we offer them. We offer and wait to see how they respond. We can't offer everything, so there must be a great deal that we simply don't know about them. Inevitably our knowledge is limited. But at least we can make a straightforward start. Newborns make their feelings obvious. Through cries and body language, they signal unmistakably, "Bliss!" or "Not sure about this," or "Terrible!" Years ago this was our language too. As mothers, we suddenly find ourselves on the receiving end of this ancient language.

Mothers report that the obstacles to understanding are not the clear communications of their babies but their own expectations.

> When G was born, she didn't come with any user instructions. I read all the books I could lay my hands on and asked everyone I knew. It was only recently that I understood and I realized that I did really know what she wanted. My problem was that I didn't think she ought to want those things. She wasn't like the baby in the books. Now I'm learning to accept who G is and to feel all right about what she wants, so everything has become much easier. [G, 8 months]

Mothers inevitably start by being uncertain about what their babies want. Each baby surprises his mother with something new. I was once telephoned by a mother who asked me, as a breastfeeding counselor, to help her understand her baby's latest behavior. "None of my previous children acted like B," she said. I could hear quite a few children's voices chattering in the background, so I asked the mother how many children she had. "Ten," she replied, "but B is different from all the other nine." This experienced mother was humble enough to realize that she still had more to learn.

By the time the baby is only a few weeks old, his mother may proudly remark: "B has *always* preferred this to that." This sort of observation is different from the orderly research that a psychologist might do on a sample of babies. Motherly observations tend to be haphazard and particular. The advantage is that all those tiny details that mothers describe have been observed in a natural context, not in a special testing situation. Psychologists are sometimes skeptical about how much they can trust what mothers say: "a verbal report is often an extremely distorted sign of the essential quality the scientist wishes to know in its less disguised form," wrote Professor Jerome Kagan in the first chapter of his book *The Nature of the Child*.[1]

But aren't mothers scientific? In one way, mothers are compelled to become scientists of high integrity. A mother, like a researcher, may start out with a mostly open mind—though perhaps with one or two ideological axes to grind. However, having a baby is likely to make her get rid of those axes very quickly. Only too often she discovers that a cherished belief of hers does not work for her particular child. Like a good scientist, she then has to modify her ideas. If we listen to mothers talking, we have a fair chance of hearing examples of this because the subject comes up so often.

> I've had to drop all my set ideas about who G is. One moment she is quite calm. The next, she is a ball of fire. I hadn't expected that. [G, 2 months]

> I somehow had the illusion that I'd be able to put B in a backpack and travel everywhere. But that idea's gone out of the window. B gets overstimulated and whiney, so we have to come home. [B, 5 months]

> B pushes us out of bed now. He likes his own space. I had this image of him wanting us all the time—but he doesn't. [B, 13 months]

> I wish G would stop saying "No." She says it to everything I ask her. I keep thinking she shouldn't be saying it. In my culture, we hardly ever use the word. We say: "That might be difficult." [G, 16 months]

> I have this fixed picture in my mind of what G wants. But meanwhile she's not fixed. She's developing on. I find it hard to keep up with her. [G, 2 years]

In other words, a mother who listens to her baby's "signals" finds that she has to abandon her own expectations. She has a great deal to tell us about her individual baby. By listening to many mothers, we can also get a composite picture of what many babies seem to want. Obviously a composite picture is not a blueprint for any individual baby, but it can offer useful guidelines. To my surprise, I found that the picture gained from my own listening has a strikingly clear outline. The information I have gained from mothers has turned out to be basically consistent.

From mothers we learn that whatever babies want, they demand it passionately. And what do they most want? Among all the individual details, a pattern emerges from the accounts gathered for this chapter. It is unmistakable. Mothers describe how—more than entertainment, more than play, perhaps even more than safety, food, or comfort—babies want us to make room for them in our busy lives. They want us to welcome them, to allow them to listen to what we are saying and to be listened to, to share our good times and our bad, to be shown everything that we're up to and to be included in what we do, as proper people. They don't show much enthusiasm for being treated like "babies." They don't even seem to want a continuous diet of one hundred percent of our attention. Babies seem very interested in studying parents who are partly preoccupied with their adult concerns. In other words, babies want something from us that may be difficult but not impossible for us to supply.

Making room for a baby is a very adaptable goal. It doesn't depend on particular preconditions. Mothers adjust according to their circumstances. It makes light of all those divisions between one mother and another that sometimes cause so much dissension, such as whether she is employed or not, whether she breastfeeds or formula feeds,[2] or whether the baby sleeps with his parents or is trained to sleep in a crib at a particular time each evening. A healthy baby seems capable and intelligent enough to adapt to any combination of these possibilities. What babies want from us appears to be something more fundamental. It does not seem to be about the particulars of what we do but about the sense that they matter profoundly to us, and that we have given some thought to their interests as well as our own.

This is not the picture one always finds in parenting books. Sometimes babies are portrayed as demanding, greedy, or downright insatiable. It is true that a baby may want a huge amount of whatever is on offer. At a superficial glance, this might seem greedy. Nevertheless, the most enthusiastic baby does eventually reach a point of satisfaction. A baby can seem "too demanding" if a mother is listening to authorities who drown out the voice of her own baby. Only the baby can be sure of when he wants to eat and when he is ready to sleep. Mothers who study their babies find that their babies get hungry and sleepy not at clock intervals but according to their personal patterns. Mothers then report that their babies seem not insatiable but reasonable.

There doesn't seem to be a proper word to describe this process of deciphering what a baby wants. Yet, as we saw in chapter 3, it is basic to being a mother. Perhaps "tracking" will do for the moment. A new mother tries to track her baby's times of hunger, liveliness, and sleepiness. In turn, her baby tracks his mother to learn about her. Mothers notice that babies who are understood continue to communicate, whereas babies whose cries are dismissed as meaningless become quieter.[3] Not that understanding is always perfect on both sides. But sometimes there are moments of genuine rapport. The early basic exchanges over eating, waking, and sleeping prepare the way for the baby's later more complex wishes.

Over the years, it has been my privilege to hear mothers recounting the results of their detailed tracking. It is clearly difficult to do justice to this field, given the wealth of material. So I have chosen a few areas as a small sample of the data that mothers collect. It is not intended to be a balanced picture, but I hope it is an interesting one. I especially hope it includes enough maternal observation to challenge the stereotype of the greedy, self-absorbed baby.

Immediately after birth, a baby needs to learn how to survive. The most basic abilities, such as breathing, sucking, and swallowing without spluttering and choking, all need to be learned. Mothers report how babies develop and enjoy their physical achievements.

> B's very restless. He's longing to sit up. He wants me to prop him up all the time. If I lay him down, he gets furious. It's as if he's saying: "You can't do *that!* I'm not a *baby!*" [B, 4 months]

> Everything pleases him. He likes to stand up and he likes to make his leg muscles go stiff. [B, 5 months]

> B is nearly crawling, so I put him on the floor and felt like saying: "Go on, B, you *can* do it!" But then I saw he was perfecting other skills before crawling. He was clambering over things. And he is managing to get back into a sitting position after keeling over in nearly every direction. I was fascinated. I just sat back, watching in amazement. I was glad I hadn't urged him to crawl, because then I'd have missed out on all this. [B, 6 months]

> Have you noticed how relaxed babies are? G is always trying to do something new. If she can't do it, she just moves to something else. She doesn't . . . [M made a hand

> gesture of someone driving herself on.] And when she *does* succeed, she isn't even especially excited. It's as if she always knew she could. [G, 8 months]

Some people argue that young babies haven't got "wants." When they cry, it is from need. A strong proponent of this way of thinking was Sigmund Freud. He maintained that at this stage, babies are dominated by their uncivilized instincts. In his vivid way, Freud wrote: "If an infant could speak, he would no doubt pronounce the act of sucking at his mother's breast by far the most important in his life."[4] Babies have often been dismissed by much less thoughtful people than Freud with the claim that they are "only interested in food."

Do mothers confirm this? Mothers spend a lot of time feeding their babies and discussing how to feed them. One would expect them to corroborate Freud's theory. But they don't. From mothers, we get a different picture. Indeed, babies have to eat. They need to double their birth weight by about five months. Feeding is bound to be a major activity, and fortunately most babies enjoy it. But they seem to make room for a great deal else. From the earliest months, mothers recount:

> When I was pregnant I used to listen to a lovely cello piece every day, and I'd relax to it. Now, if I put it on, G instantly relaxes, even if she was crying before. [G, 3 weeks]

> B played with his baby gym. He suddenly realized how to concentrate and hit something. He did that for a whole hour. Then he fell asleep. He slept for so long that I was frightened. It was way past his time for a feeding. So I phoned the midwife and she came round. She said he

> was perfectly all right, just tired from so much playing! [B, 7 weeks]

> [One mother described a visit to a friend who had a blind baby. As she was leaving, her friend said: "My baby's smiling at you." The mother reflected:] I didn't think so, because her baby wasn't looking at me. But I'd forgotten that she was blind. I think, now, that she was smiling at the sounds of us talking. So it *was* me she was smiling at. [Her baby and her friend's were both about 3 months old.]

> I had a breast abscess, and my doctor advised me to change from breastfeeding to formula feeding. At first I thought it would change our whole relationship. I thought I wouldn't be special to G anymore. But I am. Our relationship isn't based on food. It's based on nurturing and understanding. I'm the one who really understands G. She makes it clear to me what she wants. [G, 4 months]

These mothers are not relating to little bundles of instincts. They are relating to complex people, young though they are. Looking after someone whom one perceives as a person is completely different from facilitating a bundle of instincts. A person awakens fellow feelings. These fellow feelings help parents to respond to their babies in ways that are demanding and often sleep-depriving. A sense of fellow feeling generates parental energy to do things because they feel right rather than because they are easy.

Most babies have a very simple message to get across to their mothers. The message is that they feel happiest when they are in their mothers' company. This sounds simple in theory. In practice, it can be quite frustrating. The baby seems to want to go everywhere the mother goes, so her entire daily life becomes a one-handed affair, while she holds her baby with her other hand. If she was holding a doll, it would seem absurd. But a proper person who evokes fellow feelings is a different matter. Mothers often talk about their babies with great respect, almost like one adult about another.

> G doesn't like to be left alone, so I take her to the bathroom with me. I've become expert at pulling down my pants with one hand, and she stands on my knee. [G, about 3 months]

> G sleeps with us and pulls my nose in the morning to wake me up! I can remember being a child myself, lying in my crib in the morning and feeling in limbo. I don't think babies feel alive unless someone else is there. [G, 8 months]

Babies learn hugely from spending time with their mothers.

> B keeps saying "Isss!" and I thought: "Where did *that* sound come from?" Then I realized that I say "This" a lot. It made me realize how much B is observing me and taking it all in. [B, 7 months]

> One evening I said to F: "What's the time?" I saw G immediately look at her wrist. Of course she hasn't got a watch. I was amazed at how much she must be noticing. [G, 15 months]

A mother told me she was returning home with her daughter, who was not quite two years old. The mother suddenly thought of something she wanted to try out on their piano. Her daughter seemed to walk very slowly, and by the time they got home the mother could hardly wait. She flung off her coat and sat down at the piano immediately. She expected her daughter to come and sit beside her, because the little girl usually wanted to do whatever her mother was doing. But her daughter went into the bedroom, and the mother could hear rummaging and rustling noises. Finally the little girl emerged, proudly wearing an ancient hat. She hurried to her mother, squeezed up on the piano seat, and started to play. The mother suddenly realized that although she had taken off her coat, she had forgotten to take off her own hat and was still wearing it at the piano. Her daughter must have noticed this and drawn the conclusion that hats were de rigueur for piano playing. Not for her to question why. If her mother wore a hat, so too must she.

There doesn't seem to be a word for what the mother is doing. It means: being available for her baby to observe. As a whole way of life, it requires considerable self-discipline from the mother. I hasten to add that this is not a prescription. It doesn't mean that every mother should make herself available to her baby all day to ensure the perfect relationship. These are examples to show how mothers who spend long periods of time with their babies are doing more than feeding them. They are building up many-sided relationships. Obviously a mother who is away from home during the day will find her own way of relating to her baby.

Babies today have a daunting amount to learn. They seem to learn continuously by studying people they love. They have all kinds of learning projects on the go. They do not only love, and they do not only learn. They combine the two. Doing this seems to be an important part of what they want.

A mother who notices how much her baby is learning may

not always realize how much he is learning about *her.* The two are in a close partnership. She sets certain rules, which she may hardly be aware of, about what is allowed and what is forbidden. She also has a stretch of patience, after which her tolerance snaps. A mother also indicates by her expression, her tone of voice, and her responses what her values are. Babies learn within the framework of all this.

One very early shared pleasure is the discovery of music. It usually starts with singing. Even mothers who do not normally sing a note nevertheless seem to sing to their babies. I have not yet found one mother who never sang anything at all. When I ask a mother whether she sings, the reply is usually: "Well, not as such." "Well, *you* mightn't call it singing, but B likes it!" "I just sing G silly things. I'd *die* if I thought anyone else was listening to me."

> It's for when B is a bit grizzly, like after his bath. I sing things like: "Now I'm putting *on* your sock, *on* your sock, *on* your sock." He likes that. [B, 3 months]

> I sing "The Teddy Bears' Picnic" and G sings back! [G, 3 months]

> I sing about everything I'm doing. I'd hate anyone to hear. They'd think I'd gone barmy. But B loves it and it allows me to do more things because he can hear where I am. [B, 3 months]

> When the radio's on, G holds out her hands to the loudspeaker and waves them around everywhere, as if she is trying to catch hold of the notes. [G, 6 months]

> This is B's drum. It's his *favorite* toy. [B, 14 months]

The desire for music seems to be innate. In London there are several local music groups set up for babies. A group of musicians, even if they are babies, can produce more varied sounds than one singing mother. However, it is exciting to discover that mothers start not by traveling to a special group at a set time but by singing songs as part of their daily lives.

Aristotle stated that "melody and rhythm are ours by nature," and he saw them as leading to the birth of poetry. He observed that from childhood on, men enjoy imitating and also take pleasure in making representations of things.[5] Poetry, he wrote, depends on our ability to perceive one thing as a representative of another.

Mothers' observations show that we can do this when we are very young. Before we can draw and before we can express the wonderful complexity of our ideas in sentences, we seem to be able to recognize that one thing is similar to another. The best example I have at present comes from a child of twenty-one months. He spun round a stuffed toy frog on his finger, so that the frog's four legs stretched out from its body horizontally as it spun. "*'Elicopter!*" he exclaimed, looking at his mother. "Yes, just like a helicopter," agreed his mother, and the boy looked satisfied.

This is especially reassuring in the light of recent reports that computer technology is killing off children's imaginations. Imagination seems to develop even before a child can experiment with a computer. From mothers we learn that babies develop the prerequisites to grow into musicians and poets before they are two years old.

Another whole field of interaction is that of jokes. Like appreciation of music and the pleasure in using imagination, a human appreciation of jokes seems to start when we are young. It is interesting to find that Freud, who wrote a fascinating book on jokes, stated categorically that "children are without a feeling for the comic."[6] He supported this position with reasons, but it is a pity that he thought it necessary to sound so certain. It is amazing to discover, by listening to mothers, just how soon babies acquire a sense of humor. We learn to laugh long, *long* before we can talk.

> F came into the room, and he'd just been washing his hair, so he had a red towel around his head. B looked very puzzled. Then F took off the towel, and B burst out laughing [i.e., in recognizing his father]. [B, 2 months]

> F plays with a glove puppet. He puts it on his hand and makes it talk in a silly voice. It's the first time I have heard B give a real belly laugh. He laughs so loud, it makes us laugh. [B, 7 months]

> B makes jokes, like he pretends to cough, and then he laughs at himself and expects us to laugh. [B, 14 months]

> G has her own jokes. The other day she took her little cotton hat and put it on the cat. Then she just stood there, laughing. If I hadn't happened to be looking, I would never have seen. Then she took the hat off the cat and went to do something else. [G, 15 months]

Another discovery is how early babies start to communicate. Our ability seems innate. Some books and articles suggest special methods that parents can use to stimulate their babies' responses. But do babies need elaborate methods? Mothers report that it is the babies themselves who initiate "conversations." Conversations grow up with language as one stage on a long continuum.

> *Mother:* B's just asked me to lift him up. *Me:* How did he do that? *Mother:* Arched his back. [B, 4 months]

> B used to shout, as if he'd just discovered his voice. But now he's vocalizing, with inflections. He says a whole "sentence" and then pauses before he carries on. [B, 7 months]

> I was thinking that food was a trip I put on B. Maybe he didn't really want it, because he never cried for it. I just always offer him my breast. But when I did the experiment [i.e., of not offering her breast], I realized that B didn't need to cry because he was giving me all these little signals, like little grunts, and I was picking them up. [B, 7 months]

> When G wants to get out of the bath, she points to the bath towel. Oh, and in the morning, she points to the curtains so I'll draw them and begin the day. But when she points to something and I don't understand her, she gets absolutely furious with me. She expects me to understand her. [G, 11 months]

> You can have a proper conversation with G. She's only three, but it isn't like talking to a child. She can tell you what she *really thinks*! [G, 3 years; B, 3 weeks]

This whole process depends on mothers (or other caretaking persons[7]) appreciating and exchanging these communications. Mothers become experienced at understanding what their own children are saying, while an outsider will listen in total perplexity. Yet to the mother, her child's communication is crystal clear.

So when talking to his mother, the child can feel confident of being a good communicator.

Babies don't just communicate what they want. They communicate just as passionately what they *don't* want. Early on, mothers learn to distinguish their babies' cries of fear and anger. At first a cry of fear seems to be an involuntary response. Only after several months do babies appear to learn that their mothers can understand them. After that, the cry of fear develops into a communication.

> *First mother*: One night G suddenly gave a huge scream of fear. *Me:* How could you tell it was fear? *Mother*: I *knew.* I could feel her fear in my whole body. [G, 6 weeks]
>
> *Second mother*: G screamed at night too. I thought she was hungry. It was only after that I thought she must be having a nightmare. She didn't wake up. [G, 2 months]

> A friend said "*Boo!*" B used to laugh and laugh. But now he's suddenly become more sensitive and he cried. [B, 8 months]

> I decided to be a bone-marrow donor. I was very relaxed and not at all afraid. I had G on my lap and I didn't think she'd notice. But when the nurse put the needle in, she absolutely screamed, as if she was in pain. She didn't want anyone to hurt *me*. [G, 13 months]

These mothers were understanding of their babies and sympathetic toward their fears. Other mothers are understanding but not necessarily sympathetic. One mother found that her eight-month-old daughter was showing signs of "stranger anxiety," which the mother found unacceptable. "I'm afraid it will turn into a habit, so it's got to be nipped in the bud," she said. She made her daughter spend time with strangers, which, she said, "cured it."

Many mothers were socialized themselves, as little girls, not to show anger. When their babies express anger, they report finding their babies' anger harder to deal with than their fears.

> I'm not good at expressing my anger. When G gets angry, I have to suppress a feeling of—well, my mother would say: "Go to your room, and don't come out till you feel better." She never listened to what I said. [G, 6 weeks]

> *First mother:* G gets really angry now, and sometimes there's nothing I can do to make things better. [G, 5 months]
>
> *Second mother:* But I've come to the conclusion that sometimes it's important to let them be angry and to put a sort of mental space around them. It's important to be there and not walk off. After all, it's not usually personal. Sometimes something has annoyed B and he is just cross. [B, 18 months]

Understandably, as babies learn to communicate, they are also capable of boredom, when their intelligence is not sufficiently challenged. A lot has been written on how to stimulate babies. Many mothers report how guilty they feel if they have spent a "lazy" day at home or when the main outing of the day was a functional one to the shops. But perhaps babies don't need a daily diet of stimulation and entertainment. They seem happy to observe and later play alongside their mothers, the two of them close together physically yet each absorbed in separate activities.

This development of separate play usually starts once the baby can sit up without keeling over. Then his two hands are free to explore. Mothers report that it doesn't take a lot to awaken the interest of a small baby. How many people have given an expensive toy to a baby, only to find that he is far more engrossed in the wrapping paper than its carefully chosen contents? The ability to play with toys seems to develop much later.

> G likes to explore a bag of rice. It's crackly and it feels bumpy. She quickly gets bored with commercial toys. [G, 5 months]

> G plays with a cereal box the size of herself. That's what she loves best. [G, 6 months]

> B's gone from "need" to "want." A tiny baby just needs things and can't wait. Now you can see that B sets his mind on something and he gets terribly upset if you take it away. As a baby, he wouldn't have noticed. [B, 7 months]

> If B wants something and I've put it away, he remembers exactly where I've put it, even hours later, and he stands and points to it. [B, 12 months]

> G's very determined. If she wants to hold a knife and I take it away from her and try to distract her, she *won't* be distracted. She gets really angry. It's the knife she wants, and only that will do. [G, 13 months]

The baby's growing delight in being able to act independently means that all kinds of conflicts of interest can start to arise. Misunderstandings occur. For example, a mother may offer to help her baby with something, only to find that he is deeply offended because he wanted to do whatever it was unaided. Meanwhile babies cannot understand why mothers have to brush their teeth and change their diapers, and especially why mothers take these activities so seriously. Most difficult of all to grasp are the differences between the mother's special "home" rules and her "out" rules. Mothers report head-on clashes of will until they find tactful ways of asserting their parental authority.

> We were in a store and B started pulling books off the shelves. At home he's allowed to, but I said: "You can't do that here." I put the books back, and he was *furious*. I tried to pick him up, but he made an eel of himself. I thought about it a lot afterward. I've got a sock drawer, and B likes to empty all the socks out. Then he makes a special noise and puts all the socks back in. I *think* he wanted to put the books back in the store. But they were for sale—he didn't understand that. [B, 11 months]

The task of a parent is to take on responsibility for the child, and slowly to hand back little bits that the parent judges the child can manage. Children are constantly begging for more independence, but this may sometimes be bravado. A mother may load even a small child with too much, too soon.[8] This seems especially true of sophisticated concepts such as expecting a child to remain in a room full of strange people while his mother dashes out for what she knows (but he doesn't) will be "only a minute"; or to require the child to wait patiently for "a turn" while seeing another child playing with a waited-for toy; or to "say sorry" for causing another person pain. A young child is still a newcomer to the complexities of social life. Mothers often miscalculate because they don't realize that a concept that they take for granted is actually made up of several completely new ideas that their children haven't understood yet.

As babies start to uncover some of the rules of life in all their complexity, they start to expect a certain logical consistency. They protest at what looks to them like unfairness. Often their anger is directed at something that has offended their sense of justice. Even before they can explain themselves, they get passionately upset if their mothers change their minds about something or appear to contradict themselves.

Perhaps this sheds some light on temper tantrums. They are often described as extra-strong bouts of temper. But this misses their characteristic element. The child is hysterical. Often he rejects offers of comfort. He may be sobbing something like: "'Nother swing! *Please,* Mommy! Please! Swing! 'Nother swing!" But is it just another turn on the swing that he wants? True, he sobs that it is. But maybe the situation is so complicated that he hasn't yet got the ability to explain himself.

Usually, when one asks, it turns out that the child feels misunderstood. He feels categorized as "bad" or "naughty" when he didn't intend to be anything of the kind. So the child on the swing may have had many turns already, and confidently asks for a fifth turn, when suddenly his mother says "*No!*" in a burst of exasperation. It is her tone of voice that has upset him, not the loss of the actual turn. Suddenly he senses that his mother has lost patience with him, for no reason that he can see. This feels unjust, yet too subtle for his simple vocabulary. A tantrum seems an understandable way of expressing his dilemma. If his mother misunderstands and thinks badly of him, this is a disaster, as he sees it. He is desperate to set the relationship right again. It is their usually good relationship that counts, and hardly ever the material object that appears to be causing all this passion.[9]

A mother who knows her child well can unravel the complexity of his distress. If his mother can explain the dilemma, the child calms down like magic. As mother and baby develop more understanding of each other, they can have periods of harmony together. It can look so natural that it can give the impression that being a mother is effortless. Yet the harmony depends on all the mother's earlier work.

Isn't this harmonious relationship a kind of friendship, even though the child is so much younger and less experienced? Aristotle, who wrote a detailed exploration of the nature of friendship, observed: "Parent seems by nature to feel it [i.e., friendship] for offspring and offspring for parent."[10] Mary Wollstonecraft, the great eighteenth-century early feminist, drew a similar conclusion.[11] This trusting friendship appears to be exactly what children themselves want of their parents.

Mothers who have reached this stage of friendship discover that it becomes especially important if they suddenly fall ill. They were amazed at how sensitive their babies were, even at a young age.

> I had the flu last week. I've always wondered how I could still be a mother if I was ill. But B seemed to know when I was really out of it. He just played quietly on the floor beside my bed and didn't demand my attention at all. [B, 11 months]

> [One mother who vomited several times every day during her second pregnancy found that her toddler preferred to be with her even then:] B always comes with me. He has his own little ritual. He likes to pick up a tissue and hold

> my hand while I'm standing by the toilet. Then we flush it and put down the cover, and he helps me to blow my nose. As soon as I can, I give him a little smile. [B, 12 months]

> I've been seriously ill for about a month. I've spent two weeks in bed. I thought B would be annoyed because we weren't going to the park and doing fun things. I was amazed at how adaptable he was. He seemed to understand that I couldn't go out, and now he's absolutely *delighted* to see me up again. [B, 15 months]

These mothers were tactful in the way they adjusted to being ill. I was impressed that none of them conveyed to her baby that he had become a burden to her.

Mothers don't usually report—because it happens so often—how pleased their babies are when they *do* feel understood. Their eyes light up, they laugh and slap their thighs, and they give every sign that this is a precious experience. They hugely enjoy being a part of our lives and communicating with us. Surely they are trying to tell us that we are giving them what they want.

nine

what is motherly love?

There are two ideas of motherly love in circulation, one old, one new. Both claim to be true.

The old view assumes a love that excludes hate. The new view advocates love with hate included. This means that if a mother says she hates her baby, the old view calls this a lapse of her love, whereas the new view says it is part of her love. Perhaps it sounds like a verbal quibble. However, motherly love is surely the very heart of mothering, and a new mother may well feel anxious. Is her love good enough for her baby? Some people expect her to be besotted with him, while others assure her that even loving mothers periodically hate their babies too.

Surprisingly little has been written about the old, traditional view of motherly love. It probably seemed too obvious to spell out. It was seen as unique, different from a father's love or the love of any other person for a child. It referred to the special relationship that a woman had with her baby, when she had borne him inside her, given birth to him, and nourished him, typically with her own milk. It meant a love that was wholehearted, warm, and strong enough to last. A mother's love meant a protective and moral force that was completely *for* the good of her child. People admired mothers for being able to put their children's interests before their own. Traditional motherly love has even been regarded as the gold standard for love itself. It was seen as not just tender but tough as well. If a child did wrong, his mother was expected to teach him to do better. This meant that she was to focus on the child's wrong deed yet without losing sight of her basic love. Motherly love was considered inviolable.

Throughout the whole turmoil of human history, this idea of motherly love seems to have survived in the background as a changeless constant. It has resurfaced in the most unlikely situations. It continues to flourish unexpectedly in societies that are not at all supportive to mothers. We can be sure of this, because motherly love is expressed by what mothers do. For centuries, people have painted and written about the outward signs of motherly love. From paintings and written sources, we get a clear and consistent picture.

For example, an Egyptian father, over three thousand years ago, wrote to his adult son:

> *Double the bread that thou givest to thy mother, and carry her as she carried [thee]. She had a heavy load in thee, and never left it to me. When thou wast born after thy months, she carried thee yet again about her neck, and for three years her breast was in thy mouth. She was not disgusted at thy dung, and said not: "What do I?"*[1]

This passage gives characteristic examples of what people have admired about mothers.

There has been criticism of mothers, too, when they weren't up to this high standard. Over the centuries, a number of poems and essays, usually by men, have been published, complaining, for example, that "modern" mothers sent their babies away to be wet-nursed. Good mothers, wrote these critics, often appealing to an earlier era, would demonstrate their love by breastfeeding their babies themselves. This was a recurring criticism of practice. The actual *idea* of motherly love was never questioned.

The first real challenges to this ancient idea started when great thinkers, such as Darwin and Freud, stated that people were basically out for their own survival. The old idea of motherly love didn't fit this theory. Freud specifically asked himself how a mother could possibly love her baby as devotedly as she did. He decided that the answer must be that she managed to transfer her original, self-centered narcissistic feelings (part of an earlier theory of his) onto her baby.[2] This redefines motherly love as a form of *self*-love. Later psychoanalysts thought motherly love arose when the baby seduced his mother with the appearance of a loving smile.[3] Other suggestions have been that it is a biological response, triggered by the hormones that flood the mother's body, especially if she is breastfeeding.[4]

There is also another, widely held view, which I found summarized in a children's book. *The Way Mothers Are* is a story about a kitten who keeps asking his mother why she loves him, even when he is naughty. "'So,' replies the mother cat finally, 'you don't think I love you just when you're good, and stop loving you when you are naughty, do you? That's not the way mothers are. I love you all the time, because you are mine.'"[5] In this view, motherly love is primarily about possession. All these ideas try to explain how a mother could sacrifice her own interests for those of her child.

Freud's question is a good one. How *do* mothers manage to

sustain their love, not so much when their children are naughty but on a daily basis, and also during all those times when they are ill? There is a whole genre of paintings, especially from northern Europe where winter nights are long, called *The Sick Child.* A feverish child lies in bed and, by the light of a candle, his mother keeps a constant vigil. How can she?

> *Mother:* B has been teething and won't be put down. It's been going on for two weeks. He cries all the time, and I keep holding him in different ways, first like *this,* then like *this.* I feel so helpless. Nothing I do makes it better for him. *Me:* What keeps you going, when it's so difficult? [M looked down at B. She gave a shy smile and said something.] *Me:* I didn't hear what you just said. *Mother* [just above a whisper]: Mother love, I suppose. [B, 7 months]

If motherly love can really sustain a mother, for hour after hour, through troubling times, is it based on real affection or determined by the mother's predisposition? By the time a woman becomes a mother, she is usually experienced at relationships. She knows a range of people. There are people whom she likes a lot more than others. Most mothers recognize from the start that their babies are people.[6]

This surely means that the love a mother gives her baby is not automatic but personal. It cannot be attributed entirely to hormones or to her reaction to her baby's smile or even to possession. Biology can explain some of it, but not all. If biology was all, then "love" would be the wrong word. We should be discussing an instinct. It is surely significant that all the major world languages refer to a mother's feelings as love. For it to be love, there has to be the possibility, or risk, that she could have found she did *not* love the child. Her love is therefore a passionate "*Yes!*" to her baby. If she loves this individual child, it is because she has chosen to. So the biological theories, challenging though they are, can still be absorbed into the traditional idea of motherly love. They seem to predispose but not predetermine a mother to love her child.

A more fundamental challenge to the traditional picture of motherly love developed during the twentieth century. (The following is a summary. An exploration with references will follow in the second part of this chapter.) For the first time, people have protested that the traditional picture leaves out a mother's negative feelings. Surely, they write, no mother can love her child unreservedly. The two of them are pitted against each other. The child is described as someone with unending demands, which could easily destroy his mother.

Traditional mothers, these writers claim, have been intimidated by social pressures. They were expected to conform to the demands of an impossibly high social ideal. They had to sublimate and crush their own needs, and give an appearance of submissive devotion to their children. So now these writers encourage mothers not to feel guilty if they fall short of these high ideals. A mother is urged to consider her own needs and to assert her independent identity. But she has to struggle for it against the demands of her child. That is why, even though she loves her child, she is expected to experience times when she genuinely hates her child too. She and he have interests that conflict. Her hate, then, is seen as an unavoidable part of her love. If, according to this outlook, she can acknowledge and accept her hate, she will be able to offer a more honest sort of love.

It is exciting when an old idea is suddenly challenged. The idea of motherly love must be one of the oldest there is. Now it is on trial, accused of hypocrisy. This charge ought to be examined. Motherly love deserves a fair trial in which prosecution can be weighed with defense. Up till now, however, only the prosecution's voice has been heard. No one has responded to this particular charge against motherly love.

Why don't individual mothers speak up if their experiences have been different? One reason may be that the mothers who do acknowledge their ambivalent feelings usually sound distressed. It might seem heartless of a mother to write that she feels differently. The mother quoted earlier was shy to acknowledge her love and would never have mentioned it if I hadn't questioned her. But a stronger reason is probably self-doubt. A mother might wonder if she is being naive to think she never hates her baby. Maybe these writers know more than she does. Maybe they will question her loving feelings and tell her that she is unconscious of her hatred because she has repressed it. How would she know, one way or the other?

The idea of "ambivalent" motherly love was first voiced, as we shall see, in a few books and newspaper columns. Now mothers are routinely taught at prenatal classes that they may experience times when they hate their babies. So how have they responded? Do they feel liberated by the new view? The short answer is that mothers differ. Certainly the new view hasn't eclipsed the old. The old traditional view is still with us.

Mothers often worry right through pregnancy that they might not be able to love their babies. Once their babies are born, however, many mothers find they fall in love with them in the traditional rather than the ambivalent way. Allowing for personal and cultural differences, mothers usually mention several precise feelings that give a recognizable "shape" to their love. These feelings seem universal. This doesn't mean they have necessarily been learned from their own mothers. Many mothers today clearly discover their love only when they experience it.

Listening to them, we discover that the relationship starts off with a built-in disparity. A newborn is likely to accept his mother whatever she does because she is the only mother he knows. Yet his mother may have fallen completely in love with her newborn. If only he could tell her that he feels the same. But the first months with a baby aren't like that at all. He seems preoccupied with the business of survival. Doesn't he realize she is a special person?

Soon he learns to recognize her and starts to depend on her, but he certainly seems to take her generous love and exhausting work for granted. After several weeks, he may be ready to give radiant smiles—but he smiles like this at nearly everyone. This can feel strange. It may be many months before he seems ready to show his mother how warmly and deeply he loves her. When he does, his love feels so genuine that his mother will probably decide on the spot that it was worth waiting for. Before then, there may have been times when she felt lonely and unsure of herself.

What this means is that a mother's love does not depend on an immediate return. In the beginning, it is one-way and very powerful. New mothers can be astonished at the sheer strength of their love. They describe a sensation of a huge and generous opening of the heart. Even though they may have felt they had already "given" their hearts to their partners, to their older children, or to a beloved pet, a new baby has the power to open an unexplored zone. This may sound frightening to someone who has not experienced it, yet mothers talk about their feelings with wonder and pride.

> Nights are hard. But then I gaze at her, and I'm totally in love. Time is suspended. [G, 2 weeks]

> One minute I'm thinking I'd willingly give my life for G. The next, I ask myself: "Do I really love her enough?" Then I think: "Hang on! If I'd give my *life,* I *must* love her enough." [G, 2 weeks]

> I spent the first few weeks being terrified that anything would happen to B. I cried a lot. I still do. I *couldn't* live without him now. [B, 2 months]

> I didn't like babies that much before I had G. I didn't look at them. I wasn't interested. I had no *idea* that I could feel so strongly for G. It took me by surprise. [G, 3 months]

> I had a terrible birth. I felt numb afterward. I only really started to fall in love with B when he was seven weeks old. Then it was just like falling in love with my husband. [B, 3 months]

> I'm so in *love* with G. I wasn't at first. I took a long time. [G, 7 months]

These kinds of statements don't sound as though mothers are parroting what is expected of them. They seem to describe feelings that went beyond their expectations. At first, it seems characteristic of mothers that they describe being utterly swept away with love for their babies, and seem to neglect themselves. Again, this might sound alarming to anyone who hasn't experienced it. But it seems like an emotional counterpart to the quantities of breastmilk with which most breastfeeding mothers are flooded. The breastmilk adjusts automatically after the first six weeks, and the mother takes a bit longer to learn how to balance her baby's interests with her own. But because the start was so generous, she now has a plentiful flow of love for her baby.

Although mothers give so much, they get back something, too, even at the beginning. A newborn is a stranger to the world. As his mother starts to make sense of his behavior, she relates to him as a person and he starts to respond as a person. His eyes grow huge with excitement when she talks to him. She can then feel not like "any mother" but like her child's "particular mother." Love seems to thrive on these personal exchanges.

Part of this universal "shape" of motherly love is the way mothers fall in love with their babies exactly as they are. This goes contrary to the theory of Dr. Brazelton, a professor of pediatrics, and Dr. Cramer, a professor of child psychiatry. They write: "All parents go through a more or less intense form of disappointment with their baby; this is a normal part of the parenting process."[7] This may be true of some parents, but no matter how many parents these two professors have met, it cannot entitle them to speak on behalf of all of them. However, since this is their dogmatic claim, only one counterexample is needed to disprove it. It is easy to find them. There are plenty of mothers who spontaneously report that they were completely satisfied with their newborns. I feel certain that had these mothers experienced a "form of disappointment," they would have mentioned it, because they could have used it to add extra drama to their stories.

> I went on a special diet to have a girl. There's an eighty-percent chance of success, apparently. I didn't want a boy. Then I had a scan, and I found out I was having a boy. But scans can be inaccurate, and I told myself it was a mistake. Of *course* I was having a girl. All through the labor, I "talked" to my baby as if it was a girl. When they said he was a boy and put him into my arms, it was a

shock. Then I looked at him—and suddenly I didn't mind if he was a boy or a girl or *what.* What a *beautiful* baby! He was *exactly* the baby I wanted! [B, 6 weeks]

B's perfect; he seems to have a real aura about him. Everything he does is wonderful, down to his little sighs. [B, 2 months]

Before G was born, I used to worry that I was so selfish that I couldn't love a baby if it wasn't perfect. But the other day, G was in the bath and I suddenly noticed that she hadn't got shoulders. F hasn't, and I thought: "Oh, *no!* G's got no shoulders just like F!" Then I thought: "But I still *love* her." I was really pleased because that proved that I *really* love her! [G, 8 months]

Being delighted with the baby she bore seems to be an important part of motherly love. Mothers often worry about giving birth to disabled babies. Could they still love a baby who wasn't physically perfect? Yet some mothers of disabled babies speak movingly of their feelings. They explain how they can separate their children from the disabilities. They love and respect their children as people and express anger if outsiders treat their children as less than people.[8]

Physical closeness seems to facilitate these feelings. While she is expecting her baby, a mother can feel him warm inside her. Once he is born, mothers describe an urgent need to maintain that warm physical contact.

I damaged my coccyx during the birth. But I love holding B. My husband and I both do. It's a lovely feeling. It seems to make everything all right. [B, 6 weeks]

> G is my buddy. Everywhere I go, she goes. [G, 3 months]

> The need to be with B is very physical. My arms *hurt* if I can't be with him. [B, 7 months]

Motherly love may suggest an image of a mother who is totally absorbed in her baby. However, you could be talking to a mother who is holding her baby and simultaneously looking interested in what you are saying and giving plenty of attention to you. Does this mean that she is ignoring her baby? Very unlikely. Most mothers, as we have seen, learn to "tune into" their babies' smallest signals. This mother can relax and give you so much attention because she can *feel* her baby in her arms. If her baby was elsewhere, even if you were holding him in *your* arms, she would be visibly more anxious and less able to concentrate. That huge relaxation that a mother feels when she is holding her baby is a characteristic marker of motherly love.

The biblical story of the Judgment of Solomon tells us just how strong these maternal physical feelings are. In this story, two women use exactly the same words to say that they are the mother of a newborn, and each claims that the other has let her own newborn die. In his wisdom, Solomon does not waste any time arguing with them. He says he will divide the surviving baby in two and give them half a baby each. This ruse divides not the baby but the mothers. The real mother instantly relinquishes her claim and begs Solomon to give the whole baby to the "wrong" mother. She has changed her mind for some reason. The ancient Hebrew text makes her reason clear, but English translators seem to have found the wording problematic. The all-male seventeenth-century committee of translators of the Authorized Version wrote that the mother is "moved in her bowels for her son." This misses the significance of the original. A literal translation of the Hebrew text tells us that the real mother *felt her womb grow hot*. After all, she had given birth only a few days earlier. She could not have found it easy to beg Solomon to give her child to a woman who had just let her own baby die. But the powerful sensation of her hot womb must have allowed her no hesitation. The interesting point of the story is that Solomon was clearly expecting this kind of maternal reaction from the true mother. In his wisdom, he understood what mothers were like. "She is the mother," he declares, and we are told that "all Israel" is awed by the wisdom of his judgment.[9]

Mothers feel *more* than a strong need to hold their own babies themselves. They also report feeling distressed when an uninvited person picks up their baby. They describe people asking, "Can I cuddle your baby?" or simply holding their arms out. It seems socially unacceptable to reply: "No, thanks, I want to hold my baby myself." This is one of those situations when a mother will label herself "possessive" or even "neurotic" for her strong reaction. But wanting to choose the moment when she thinks her baby can manage a new pair of arms is surely an understandable motherly response. Far from being possessive, the mother is simply being sensitive to the needs of her baby.

> It still upsets me to remember this. When B was two weeks old, I took him to visit my mother-in-law. F's first wife's mother was there, and she asked to hold B. I don't even *know* this woman. And then my mother-in-law said: "Of *course* you can hold him!" I didn't want her to, but how could I be the unkind one? B was asleep, and she held him for ages and ages. That's a *very* uncomfortable memory for me. [B, 12 months]

People keep touching G without asking me. Once this heavily made-up woman bent down and kissed G, and I was like [gesticulating panic] GET YOUR HANDS OFF MY BABY! [G, 5 months]

I remember being at a party and this woman wanted to hold G. I didn't dare say no. As soon as I'd handed her over, I wanted her back. I couldn't think of any acceptable way to ask for her. I felt so stupid because I kept following her around the room. In the end I said in this very unassertive voice: "Er, I think I need to have her back now." She gave G to me, but she said: "You really *should* allow yourself the occasional break now and again." I felt such a fool. [G, about 6 months]

It seems mean to say this, but when my mother-in-law has been holding B, he smells of her perfume. It's irrational, but I resent it. [B, about 6 months]

These are strong reactions. But they are important. Mother Teresa, who worked with social outcasts in Calcutta and took in abandoned newborns from rubbish heaps, used to say: "Being unwanted is the worst disease that any human being can ever experience."[10] This is confirmed by the moving words of an orphan who grew up in a Barnado's home and had never known his mother's love. He described what he felt he had missed: "A mother's love gives a child a sense of being. If love has never been there, then like me you just feel like flotsam floating in and out of other people's lives."[11] So the mother's strong physical feelings are surely vital parts of her love. Would a person feel like flotsam if his mother enjoyed holding him close?

This physically close motherly love is not in fashion at the time of this writing. It is common for a mother's relatives and health advisers to remark that mothers should create a "healthy" distance between themselves and their babies. This meshes neatly with the requirements of employers. However, although some mothers today find that they renew their energy if they take breaks from their babies, many mothers still explain that they don't want to. It is physical closeness they want, at least for most of the first year. This includes mothers who are contracted to return to work. They have to honor their contracts for financial reasons, but this can turn out to be a painful commitment.

> B's quite happy, but I don't like leaving him, even for two hours. It doesn't feel right. I'm so besotted with him. [B, 2 months]

> I don't want to leave G. I'm going back to work in five months, so F and I went to see a local nursery. Afterward I sat on a seat outside, and I couldn't stop *crying*. I felt as though they wanted to take her away from me the very next day. [G, 6 months]

> I laugh when I think of the sort of mother I *thought* I would be. I thought G would be in a nursery from three months, and I'd be back at work and going to parties on the weekend. [G, 11 months]

> I want to continue writing my dissertation for my degree. I found a nice person to look after B. But [in tears] I don't know what's the *matter* with me. I don't like handing B over, and he likes being with me. [B, 13 months]

Certainly not every mother feels this way. The interesting point is that, today, mothers who have a less physical relationship will generally be regarded as "normal," whereas mothers who relate closely to their babies are more likely to be seen as having a problem. These mothers are often told that if they are reluctant to leave their babies with someone else, it is only they who have "a problem" with it. Their babies will be happy to be left.

This is unlikely to be true. Few mothers would hesitate to enjoy some surplus time if they really believed their children would be happy. The mothers who don't like to leave their babies are, in my experience, almost always picking up signals that their babies are not yet ready to be left. True, the babies may seem cheerful for the actual time during which their mothers are absent, but only their mothers really discover at what cost. It is they who have to deal with the emotional consequences when the two of them are together again. Babies show certain feelings when they are relaxed with their mothers that they don't necessarily share with anyone else.

> Ten hours away from G is too long. I mean, it's too long for me, but that's not such a problem. It's *much* too long for her. After six hours, G is just *desperate* for me. She's enjoying herself, but she's desperate to . . . I don't know what. She buries her face in me, and breastfeeds, but it isn't just food she needs. [G, 12 months]

The dismissive comments of other people, then, can be especially trying for the mother. Instead of getting appreciation for her sensitivity to her child, she may find herself criticized for being "neurotic" at exactly the times when she is being motherly.

A great deal of what used to be regarded as typical warm

motherly behavior is frequently categorized today as "neurotic" or "unhealthy." At the same time, twentieth-century psychological studies have helped us to recognize how much children can suffer if their mothers abuse their love. A mother can be spasmodic in giving her child love, or seductive. She can dangle it like a carrot with impossible conditions attached or shower it only on her "favorite." She can hide it behind a casual, even mocking front. She can assure everyone that she loves her child "to bits" but be much more concerned to mold her child to other people's expectations than to respect the person he is.

Children can be hurt and confused by mixed messages, and this can affect their perception of love for a lifetime. The past century has enhanced our awareness of what can go wrong in mother-child relationships. Unfortunately, we seem to have ended up with too large a "bag" of relationships defined as damaging. Jumbled up inside it are all kinds of mother-child relationships that seem perfectly all right.

Is traditional motherly love really an impossible ideal? As a purely intellectual goal, it can sound so daunting. Does a mother have to hold her child all day and feel guilty if she has gone to work for a few hours? How can she know whether she is giving the "right" amount of the "right" thing? Mothers often question their feelings intellectually. Yet love appeals to the heart. Heartfelt feelings are *honest.* They are more simple and flowing, less weighed down by educated doubts.

Love still isn't easy. It can take courage to listen to one's heart. Nor can love turn anyone into a perfect mother. No such mother could possibly exist. Motherly love probably makes mothers more aware of being imperfect. Yet perfect love might be too strong a concoction for a little baby. The honest love we feel seems to work. Children seem to light up and glow when they are loved. They relax and unfold their life potential. Each new person seems capable of so much. Yet without their mothers' heartfelt love, it seems easier for it all to go sour.

Some people claim that time diminishes love. Mothers are often asked whether they are getting bored once the novelty of having their babies is over. For some mothers, this does seem to happen. They open up to their newborns in floods of tenderness. But then they seem to close the gates again. As their babies develop, these mothers relate to them in less tender, more brisk and irritable tones. Fortunately other mothers report that their love for their babies does not diminish. It deepens. This seems to be another universal feature of the pattern of motherly love. At its best, it is strong and lasts not for a few weeks but right through the mother's lifetime.

> I was thrilled at G's birth. At the same time, if someone had come in and said: "Ha, ha, only joking!" and taken G away . . . What am I saying? It's not . . . I *love* G, but I couldn't believe *then* that I'd really have a baby, that she was *mine.* If someone had said . . . It would be like two women pulling the arms of the same sweater in a shop. I wouldn't really have *minded,* the way I would now. [G, about 4 months]

> My love has grown. When B was a bump inside me, I was fond of him, and when he was born and so little and helpless, I loved him. But now he's more of a companion and I can share stuff with him; my love has expanded till it's quite huge. [B, 7 months]

> You don't feel as though you could possibly love them more than you do, and then something happens. I think our love deepens. It grows with your child. [G, 11 months]

> It's lovely. You don't get rational amounts of love and, with two [children], there's more love in the house than ever before. [G, 23 months; B, 6 weeks]

What happens when love grows? It doesn't become more showy. The mother of a small baby tends to kiss and stroke and cuddle him a lot. But as the baby grows, her love shows in an ongoing and continuous concern for him. Her senses are on constant alert.

> My reflexes have become very fast. You suddenly see B touching a vase of water that you didn't think he would be able to reach. [B, 9 months]

> B said his first six-word sentence today. My mind has to jump about to understand him and keep up with him. I get so tired, I keep falling asleep at about half-past eight, when he does. [B, 20 months]

Mothers learn to do several tasks at the same time as looking after their babies. Then they worry that their company might not be stimulating enough. They say how inadequate and upstaged they feel when their partner comes home or a visitor arrives and starts playing energetic bouncy games with the baby. This is characteristic of someone who hasn't got very long to spend with the baby. Babies can't be bounced and excited all day long. Mothers provide steady ongoing attention. They can easily underestimate the priceless value of their slower-paced love.

A lot of a mother's love goes into keeping her baby safe. She feels horribly aware of his vulnerability. There is so much to learn, and new situations keep arising.

> When G was little, I tripped while I was carrying her and nearly dropped her into the fire. In that split second, I discovered that I knew that I would do anything, absolutely *anything,* to make sure G was all right. Whereas normally I don't feel that. [G, 8 months]

There are many accounts of the extraordinary lengths mothers have gone to in order to protect their children.[12] But mothers have to cope with ordinary life too. It can be filled with trivia. Then mothers can feel irritated and frustrated—especially when they think they should be managing better. One mother said she would hear a "nagging or critical voice" that was never satisfied with anything she did. It helped her to identify it as coming from herself. Her baby didn't seem to be complaining.

Some mothers are articulate. They can explore their feelings without impulsively acting on them. Mothers who are less articulate might find this harder. But a less articulate mother may be just as sensitive in feeling. It is shocking to read bland statements by doctors about mothers, such as: "Any mother who claims never to have felt an urge to hit her child is either a liar or an angel."[13] One can only wonder why some members of the medical profession like to claim such absolute knowledge of mothers. Some mothers do say they have never felt this urge. There are no grounds for labeling them liars, and they certainly don't qualify as angels yet. They are ordinary women who were able to track their own reasons for being angry, rather than thinking that their baby was the cause of it.

Some mothers can trace their problematic feelings back to the way they had been brought up as girls. For example:

> *First mother:* When I was a child, my parents never hit me. But if I did anything wrong, they practiced the silent

> withholding of love. That was a very frightening thing for me. Now I'm terrified of passing it on. [G, 8 weeks]
>
> *Second mother:* I recognize that. I do that sometimes to B, even though he's so little. It's so quick, it's like a reflex. *Me:* So what do you do about it? *Second mother:* Well, once you recognize you're doing it, it's already different. But I say sorry. I say: "*Sorry,* darling, Mommy's just doing her silly old thing. She loves you really, she really does." [B, 7 months]

It was a huge help to both these mothers to recognize the childhood influence on their present feelings. Even if they caught themselves repeating patterns of behavior, at least they could make good afterward.

The whole relationship between mother and baby develops gradually. It depends on getting to know and understand the other person. This makes it possible for two very different people to share a life together. Understanding encourages trust, and trust helps the two of them to relax with each other. We are all complex and subtle individuals. It is surely a miracle every time one of these wonderful relationships evolves.

There is also a paradox about motherly love. A mother may feel she is doing everything "for the baby." But her new life benefits herself too. Mothers often say their love has taught them to become both more down-to-earth and more spiritual. The intensity of a mother's love can feel close to religious awe. She can feel overwhelmed with wonder as she gazes at her baby. Her love may lead her to a new appreciation of life itself. Mothers mention that they feel touched by something beyond themselves, something good and eternal, whole and central. Motherly love seems to combine extremes of giving a lot and receiving a lot.

However, not every mother experiences this. Some mothers

feel alarmed at the prospect of doing so much for their babies. Some of their feelings have already been described in chapter 5—when their babies cry, these mothers feel they are being swallowed up by their babies' needs. These same feelings greatly affect the way they love.

Mothers signal that they are in this position with four simple words: "I love G/B, but . . ." There is a cut-off point in the flow of their love. After that point, they no longer feel able to trust in the safety of a give/take exchange with their babies. It feels like all give. They pull back. Mother and baby then seem separated on opposite sides, each apparently feeling that they have to struggle against the other for what they want.

This is the dilemma that has been described by writers who use the psychoanalytic concept of "ambivalence" to challenge the traditional idea of motherly love. Several of their ideas seem to interlock, to form a whole outlook. The ideas have spread and have created a "climate of opinion," which has influenced mothers for at least one generation. I myself remember being affected by it. When one of my children was a few days old, I told my husband that I felt angry with our new baby. My husband asked "Why?" so I gave a reason. But it sounded a bit flimsy when I spoke it out loud. The truthful answer was that I believed mothers were *supposed* to feel angry. I felt obliged to feel anger toward my child to demonstrate that I was an up-to-date "honest" mother. It seems strange to remember that now.

Once I started reading, I realized where this idea had come from. There are several influential books and articles on ambivalent motherly love. More continue to be published, so I have rewritten this section several times, adding extra quotations. I have used published works rather than mothers' conversations, partly to be sure of having enough examples, and partly so that you can check these sources for yourself. There is more material than there is room to include here. Several common themes run through it.

If these new ideas are valid, then the old idea of motherly love needs revising. If the idea of ambivalence as a universal feature of motherly love is mistaken, then someone should spell out what its mistake is. I haven't read an exploratory study of this literature, so I'm going to take advantage of the subject of this chapter and attempt to investigate it here.

When a mother starts: "I love B/G, but . . ." the second part of this sentence is usually something like: "I've got to think of myself too," or "you've got to draw boundaries," or "there have to be certain limits." These limits allow a mother to withdraw. Her attention turns from her baby back onto herself. As a temporary shift, this can be helpful. It's probably an age-old way of dealing with an impasse, when a mother cannot fathom what her baby wants. She turns her baby into an exasperating "it," rolls her eyes to the heights of heaven, and heaves a huge sigh of sympathy with all long-suffering mothers.

After ten minutes of self-vindication, a mother may recover her energy and think something like: "I suppose B might be upset because I've been in such a hurry all morning." And he starts to make sense to her again. Making sense of another person is a vital part of human love. However, suppose a mother tries hard to make sense of her baby, but even then she can't? She can feel desperate. She may continue her search for meaning, or she may reach a watershed when she gives up. She concludes that her child's crying must be meaningless. She sees no further point in trying to look for a cause. Her goal then switches from trying to understand to trying to control.

Susan Johnson, an Australian writer, expresses this state of despair by addressing her baby in block capitals and with minimal punctuation:

> *WHY WON'T YOU STOP IT? STOP IT STOP IT STOP IT I'M DOING EVERYTHING I CAN EVERYTHING I KNOW I'M USING EVERY SINGLE PART OF MYSELF DOING THE BEST I CAN TRYING MY HARDEST GIVING YOU MY WHOLE LIFE AND STILL YOU WILL NOT COOPERATE WILL NOT SIMPLY LIE YOURSELF DOWN AND CLOSE YOUR EYES. WHAT DO YOU WANT FROM ME? WHERE DO YOU COME FROM, WHERE TIME AND SPACE AND ENERGY MEAN NOTHING TO YOU?*[14]

One senses her distress because she cannot understand her baby's continuous crying. As a mother myself, I know my heart goes out to someone who is completely exhausted and has run out of ideas to help her baby. But might there have been a reason why her baby wouldn't stop crying? There are clues in the book itself.

Two pages earlier, Susan Johnson gives a small but significant detail. She mentions that her baby "still fought at my breast." This suggests that she might not have held him in the best position for breastfeeding. Babies who are held at an uncomfortable angle struggle to get in a better position, and this has unfortunately been misdescribed as "fighting the breast." If a baby is in a poor position, he can't suck strongly, which means his mother's breast is not stimulated enough, which in turn means that she will not make enough milk.

Sure enough, a few pages later Susan Johnson mentions her concern that she is not producing enough milk. I know from working as a breastfeeding counselor how hard positioning can be. However, identifying the problem is a huge help. If a baby is not positioned well at the breast, it means that he has good reason for getting distressed. He no longer seems irrational. His mother may still be distraught because of the difficulties of positioning him well, but he makes sense to her again. This makes it easier for her to continue loving him.

Susan Johnson seemed to lose confidence that her baby could have a reason for crying. She drew what must have seemed to her the obvious conclusion: "In my experience small children are like ink on blotting paper, seeping out to the very edges of your life, leaving no white space whatsoever."[15] She was not the first to articulate this anxiety. In *Of Woman Born*, Adrienne Rich recalls that as a mother, her own needs were "always balanced against those of a child, and always losing."[16] Kate Figes, who wrote *Life After Birth,* declares: "A child's demands are limitless for they are inherently selfish and will inevitably find you nurturing as well as denying at times because all of their needs cannot and should not be fulfilled."[17] She also writes: "We co-exist with needs which often seem to contradict each other, for a child's demands are limitless. They would suck us dry if we let them."[18] Rachel Cusk, in *A Life's Work: On Becoming a Mother,* gives a visual description: "Five minutes later she [her baby] is crying again and I stare into the insatiable red cave of her mouth."[19]

This is the starting point for a whole approach to babies. In itself, the dilemma is not new. In the past, if mothers saw their babies as "insatiable" because their needs were not fully understood, they were encouraged to consider "insatiability" as naughty and sinful. As soon as their children were old enough, parents were expected to take vigorous action to teach them the virtues of patience and obedience. "Judicious" whipping must surely have been an outlet for maternal frustration, especially as it was perceived as being in so virtuous a cause.

Today's response is more sophisticated. Sigmund Freud opened up a new way of looking at mothers and babies. He spoke out for what he saw as the instinctual needs of young children.

This meant that their mothers had a different role. No longer were they wise women guiding their children up the ladder toward adult morality. Freud saw them as facilitators, learning from psychoanalysts what to do about their babies' instinctual development. A shift in the mother's position had begun.

This shift was taken a stage further by a British psychoanalyst. Dr. D. W. Winnicott was a hardworking pediatrician who was attracted to psychoanalysis. He had the misfortune to come under the influence of Melanie Klein. Melanie Klein recounted her interpretations of babies' behavior as if they were proven facts, and Dr. Winnicott, a childless man, seems to have been inordinately impressed by her.

He took over her entire view of babies and used it as a base for making assertions about how mothers feel. In one paper he wrote about the feelings of mothers almost as a side issue, explaining why psychoanalysts may hate their patients. But what he wrote has become widely known. His tone is light and teasing, which was a characteristic of his: "[The baby] is ruthless, treats her [the mother] as scum, an unpaid servant, a slave."[20] This reverses the traditional way of seeing mothers and babies. In a traditional home mothers had power, and children were sometimes treated like unpaid servants.

Other psychoanalysts grew interested in this unusual way of seeing babies. One was Rozsika Parker, a feminist who had published a most original study of embroidery before adopting the tenets of psychoanalysis. She comments: "Paradoxically, the dependent child seems to them [mothers] a powerful tyrant."[21] It is interesting that she mentions mothers in the plural—but just a single tyrant. It conveys the impression that one child is more than a match for a plurality of mothers.

The idea of a dominant baby seemed attractive to feminists. Jane Lazarre, in *The Mother Knot,* asked herself: "Who was this immensely powerful person, screaming unintelligibly, sucking my breast until I was in a state of fatigue the likes of which I had never known?"[22] Kate Figes complained: "[The baby] still needs to be dressed and fed, only now you need the physical strength of a professional wrestler, the spiritual knowhow of Mother Teresa and negotiating skills far superior to those of the UN in order to get anywhere near your goal."[23] Susan Maushart uses an ugly image in *The Mask of Motherhood:* "Yet we find, most of us, that our most heroic efforts to remain in charge and on top of things are as nothing compared to the juggernaut of a young child's needs."[24] Rachel Cusk gives another vivid visual picture: "Our daughter now sits on the bed between our broken bodies like some triumphal mini-Napoleon, waving her rattle in victory."[25] This is a complete reversal of the traditional view. Today, babies are presented giving their orders and cracking the whip.

The corollary of this is that these mothers don't see themselves as having adult power. They feel under the control of their babies. In this literature, mothers portray themselves in the victim role. Yet they call themselves liberated feminists. They are educated and articulate. Adrienne Rich argues, in *Of Woman Born,* that mothers were enslaved within a patriarchal system. It sounds, then, as if they think they have exchanged one form of slavery for another.

Rozsika Parker tries to explain the paradox in *Torn in Two*: "Mothers are bigger, stronger, adult, and yet socially and politically still the subjugated sex—and emotionally very vulnerable to their children."[26] Indeed, the very title of this book, *Torn in Two,* is interesting. It is a passive phrase with no subject. Who is tearing whom? The phrase, as the book makes clear, comes from a statement made by a particular mother about her feelings.[27] But who or what is tearing her feelings in two? Surely if these are her feelings, they express a conflict that is hers. However, the unspoken suggestion of the mother's words is that the subject of the violent tearing must be her (powerful) child.

Once the baby is seen as insatiable and powerful, the relationship becomes fraught. Adrienne Rich confessed: "My children cause me the most exquisite suffering of which I have any experience."[28] The point to note is that she sees her children as the active cause and herself as a passive sufferer. Kate Figes echoes this: "My children produce unrecognisable, terrifying depths of anger in me, not just the crossness they see."[29] Like Adrienne Rich, she sees the children as the subject, producing the anger, and herself in the victim role, experiencing it. Susan Maushart considered that: "Not surprisingly, the baby develops a whim of iron—necessitating ever-escalating cycles of maternal preoccupation. Somehow or other our guilt gets the better of us."[30] Susan Johnson puts it more strongly: "A new baby craves nothing less than the whole of its mother, a mother's arms, a mother's body, a mother's milk, a mother's sleep. A new baby takes the sleep from your eyes, the breath from your lungs, a new baby requires that you lay your body down as the bridge on which he will stand."[31] Understandably, a mother who feels dominated by her baby is not going to feel wholeheartedly loving toward him.

Hate comes up repeatedly in these mothers' accounts. It is not defined and may have different nuances for different writers. However, it sounds much stronger than the passing anger of a mother who screams in frustration that she hates her child, and immediately repents of using such harsh language. These writers voice a stronger and longer-lasting kind of hatred, founded on the frustration of feeling inadequate and powerless.

The gates seem to have been pushed open with the publication of the psychoanalytic paper mentioned earlier, by D. W. Winnicott. He wrote: "I suggest that the mother hates the baby before the baby hates the mother, and before the baby can know his mother hates him. The mother, however, hates her infant from the word go." "Let me give some of the reasons," he continued, "why a mother hates her baby."[32] A list follows of eighteen half-humorous reasons. The first is that "The baby is not her own (mental) conception," while the last is that "she mustn't eat him or trade sex with him." It's a provocative list, and it acts as a shrewd diversion. If we put the list aside, Winnicott is saying that ordinary mothers both love and hate their babies. On the next page, he adds that a mother can become masochistic or sentimental if she is too fearful of her hate. Yet where is his evidence for all this? Perhaps that is where the light teasing tone is so effective. Evidence sounds too heavy and cumbersome a request. Winnicott doesn't give any evidence. His paper is simply giving "some of the reasons." Many people have found it entirely convincing, and the paper is often quoted. Despite its total lack of evidence, admirers use it as if it were the definitive backup for saying that maternal hatred is the norm, and is beneficial for both mothers and babies.

When mothers themselves confess to feeling hate as well as love toward their children, their tone is not light or teasing. They sound distressed. Adrienne Rich writes in her journal that she felt: "caught up in waves of love and hate, jealousy even of the child's childhood."[33] She also claims: "every mother has known overwhelming, unacceptable anger at her children."[34] How she knows what "every mother has known" is not explained. Jane Lazarre also uses the word "hate": "Sometimes I hated him for rejecting me so completely" when her baby kept crying.[35]

Both Adrienne Rich and Jane Lazarre mention that they expressed violent anger to their children. Susan Johnson describes similar feelings. "He was a champion whinger, able to whinge nonstop for hours, ceaseless and monsoonal rain. At such moments I wanted to shake him until his teeth rattled, to shut him up, to stop him from ruining my life."[36] The novelist Joanna Briscoe describes her feelings for her baby: "In the predawn light, I feel like vomiting with hatred, just as hours earlier, I feared my love was so strong I might have to express it through cannibalism."[37]

These mothers don't sound easy with their moments of hate. All of them were intellectual women, with careers ahead of them. Winnicott sums up their dilemma in a sentence: "The baby is an interference with her [a mother's] private life, a challenge to preoccupation."[38] The women quoted here are all published writers, and all of them describe daily conflicts between wanting more time to concentrate on their work and feeling they ought to be caring for their children. It is important to realize that this needn't in itself set up a conflict. Another writer, Julia Darling, comments: "My writing at this time was furnaced by the great love I felt for my [small] daughters."[39] She found it difficult to be a mother, but she doesn't mention hatred or the feeling that her babies were making limitless demands on her. Susan Maushart, on the other hand, is more chilling: "We harbour no doubts that mothering our children is infinitely worth doing. It's only that we'd really rather be doing something else."[40]

Ambivalent love has been known for some time, but it has always been described as acutely uncomfortable. No one upgraded it into a desirable state, worth aiming for. Catullus, a classical Roman poet, pours the whole experience into two short lines:

I hate and I love. Maybe you ask how that can be.
I don't know, but I feel it happen and am in torment.[41]

"Torment" is a natural reaction to experiencing hate for a person one loves. Yet psychoanalytic writers have urged people to hold on to their feelings of both love and hate in order to love more truly. It must have seemed logical to extend this, as Winnicott did, to motherly love too.

For the first time, mothers are being encouraged to regard their ambivalent feelings as inevitable. Many mothers, say the authors of this literature, are afraid of their negative feelings and feel guilty when they acknowledge them. They need permission to experience their hate. Winnicott: "A mother has to be able to tolerate hating her baby without doing anything about it."[42] Jane Lazarre: "The only thing which seems to me to be eternal and natural in motherhood is ambivalence."[43] Winnicott, as we saw, gave eighteen reasons why a mother hates her baby. Rozsika Parker challenged Winnicott's need to provide reasons: "Once again, we end up dividing mothers into the good and containing, about whom nothing more need be said or done, and the mothers who require explaining. It is hard, but crucial, to hold on to the idea of mothers as necessarily ambivalent."[44]

Rozsika Parker and Susan Maushart argue almost like two missionaries that mothers need to acknowledge their feelings of ambivalence. Parker's book *Torn in Two* is devoted to this theme: "Recognition of maternal ambivalence, facilitated by reverie, is the basis for self-knowledge."[45] Further on she explains what this means: "My argument is that hate and rage mobilise fantasies of abandonment and separation that can have creative outcomes. The guilt induced by fantasies of repudiation and rejection can lead to productive concern—if these fantasies can be thought about."[46]

Susan Maushart is more concerned with social acknowledgment: "Experiencing ambivalence about motherhood is one thing. Expressing it—and, by extension, legitimising it—is quite another. The mask of motherhood ensures that the face of ambivalence, however widely or keenly felt, remains a guilty secret. . . . The evidence suggests that the willingness to acknowledge ambivalence and uncertainty—the courage to let the mask drop—is not . . . a sign of weakness, but an indicator of an unusual maturity and resilience."[47]

This literature is an advance on hiding or denying these feelings. Any of these books could encourage an ambivalent mother to be honest with herself about how she felt. But ambivalence is acutely uncomfortable. Rozsika Parker and Susan Maushart say they know the reason why. It's because these feelings are socially unacceptable and therefore frightening, they claim.

But this claim does not ring true. Mothers brave all kinds of fears and defy strong social norms if they believe their children will benefit. What evidence is there for assuming that ambivalence is too frightening for them? Mothers who describe their ambivalence sound not so much frightened as at odds with themselves. We have all been babies. On some level, hating a crying baby doesn't make sense. Certainly the honest acknowledgment of a mother's feelings is important. But it doesn't go far enough. It doesn't lead to a way of understanding and resolving the mother's dilemma.

But what exactly *is* the dilemma these mothers are describing? They sound as though they hate their babies at moments when their babies are an inconvenience to them. A typical moment of hate arises when the baby won't fall asleep just when his mother is desperate to get on with her book, poem, or article. Are we talking about a group of women who have picked up a sophisticated psychoanalytic concept—ambivalence—to dress up the fact that they are all so self-centered? Are they too selfish to be loving mothers?

At first sight, that is how they seem. They cover pages, complaining how miserable their babies make them. But a completely selfish woman would hire a babysitter and get to her desk without a qualm. These writers seem tormented. They are not cold women. They have intense feelings about their babies. But is their intense love mixed with hatred trailblazing a way for all of us? Or could they have taken a "wrong turn" along the way?

They describe a very specific kind of torment. Despite being such different women, the landscape they describe as mothers is very similar. For example, in order to comfort a crying baby, a mother, as we saw in chapter 5, usually assesses how serious the crying seems to be. To do this, she needs to be a little bit calm and detached. But these writers find that kind of detachment impossible. They don't seem able to assess their babies' crying. Their babies' crying *always* seems serious to them. It's as if they hear the crying on exactly the same level that their babies do.

These writers all describe feeling an intense closeness to their babies. Adrienne Rich writes that she felt: "but always, everywhere, in body and soul, with that child—because that child is a piece of oneself."[48] Jane Lazarre: "Yet I held him very close, stroked his skin, and imagined that we were still one person."[49] In her preface, she wrote: "For the separation is never total."[50] Kate Figes puts it: "My sensitivities merge with those of my children, their flesh feels like an extension of my own."[51] Susan Johnson's account is stronger: "Those two bodies who lived within me now live without, but they will always be part of me as long as I am alive and sentient, like some lost part of my own self."[52] Rachel Cusk recalls: "My daughter's small body, bundled in blankets, is handed to me, and as I take her I experience a moment of utter, almost visionary, clarity. In this moment I realise that a person now exists who is me, but is not confined to my body."[53]

These writers are describing, independently of one another, a similar way of relating to their babies. It's not the same as the overwhelming heart-opening feelings described by mothers on pages 178–80. Those mothers were opening up an emotional space for their babies. The mothers here seem to experience their babies as being so close to them that there is no separate baby-sized space for the babies to live in. One can't help wondering if their babies keep crying because they sense this. A baby is a separate person with a separate agenda, which is primarily about survival. If he doesn't get what he needs or if he gets too little of it, he becomes insistent. But it sounds as though the baby's insistence is the *result* of his mother's way of relating to him, not the cause of it.

All these mothers found this degree of closeness unbearable. However, they didn't question the way they saw their babies. Instead, after several months all of them strove to extricate themselves. Jane Lazarre resumed her university studies, which meant leaving her baby with a sitter at home in New Haven, so that "for two days every week I [could] be in New York attending classes."[54] Kate Figes returned to work "to feel attached to the real world again."[55] Her daughter then became very demanding at night. In the end, Kate Figes consulted the Hackney Sleep Clinic and trained herself to ignore her daughter's cries.[56] Susan Johnson took her four-month-old baby, Caspar, to a distressed-mothers' home. "Caspar was put in a cot in a tiny room across the hallway from me and I was told not to bother getting up if he cried."[57] Rachel Cusk got her husband to bottle-feed their three-month-old daughter but still felt her daughter "was everywhere, like something sweet but sticky on my life, like molasses, like glue. . . . What I wanted was to train her on something else."[58] In the end, her husband left his job to "look after the children while Rachel writes her book about looking after the children."[59]

Today, many health professionals state as a fact that mothers need time away from their babies. The idea that mothers should actively separate themselves is endorsed by psychoanalytic literature. Winnicott, for example, wrote that mothers needed to wean at around nine months, because their babies would show signs of being ready. At the same time, he wrote that mothers needed to be brave enough to withstand their babies' anger at being weaned.[60] One wonders why the babies would be angry if they were genuinely ready. An American psychoanalyst, Louise J. Kaplan, carefully delineates what she sees as the various stages of a baby's separation from his mother.[61]

But these discussions about how to separate mother from baby start from a false position. The two of them are separate anyway. A mother may *feel* merged with her baby. But this is an illusion. She isn't. Each one of us is unique. Mothers and babies learn to live alongside each other and get to know each other. Yet they keep being constant surprises to each other. A baby is separate and remains so. Mothers who enjoy physical closeness to their babies are usually in no doubt about this. For example, when they carry their babies close to their bodies in baby carriers, shawls, or slings, this closeness enables them to be sensitive to the messages from their babies. These mothers are not in a state of blissful oneness with their babies, as some writers suppose. They remain distinct people, continuously listening to each other and learning about each other.

The mothers writing about ambivalent motherly love frequently misunderstand this. They feel frantic. They look around to see if other mothers also experience motherhood as a battle, and are relieved to find some fellow travelers. But they are also puzzled to notice mothers who seem more wholehearted. They describe feeling envious and scornful of what looks to them like smug complacency. They are accomplished writers and use their verbal ability to draw caricatures of these other mothers. Often they seem to experience themselves as if spotlighted on the stage of a theater, watched by an audience of condemnatory mothers. These supposedly condemning mothers rouse them to fury.

Jane Lazarre talked to a local mother who "always . . . appeared to be even, serene, impenetrable. Once I listened at her baby's window for screams in the night. I heard none. I began to hate her and her baby."[62] Rozsika Parker quotes a mother who said: "'I'm thinking of one woman I know. . . . She always seems very calm and collected. She makes biscuits [cookies] with them [her children] every weekend. And she never seems to be hassled by them . . . and I just think YUK!'"[63] Allison Pearson, who based her fictional character Kate Reddy on the experiences of herself, her friends, and her colleagues, has Kate contrast a mocking description of "Mothers Superior" with "Mothers Inferior like me."[64] Part of the story is Kate's guilt-ridden struggle to pretend to "the local Muffia" of mothers that she is a competent mother.[65]

Guilt at being condemned by someone else for being an inadequate mother is a major preoccupation in this literature. But guilt is always described as the mother's feeling, which focuses her attention on herself. This is different from genuine guilt, which is not just an inward feeling. Genuine guilt is a painful recognition of having done a particular wrong. So it is bound to focus attention on the person one has wronged. This involves identifying the wrong, taking responsibility for one's share in it, repenting, and perhaps making amends. It is not a matter of feeling criticized by an audience of judgmental people. If a person experiences true guilt, she herself recognizes it. Acknowledgment of guilt leads to action. Whereas *feeling* guilty does not resolve anything.

Adrienne Rich seemed to backtrack on her ambivalence. "I could not begin to think of writing a book on motherhood until I began to feel strong enough, and unambivalent enough in my love for my children," she writes in her preface.[66] She concluded that "patriarchy" was the source of her difficulties, not her children. She states how much she regrets her outbursts of anger toward her children. She describes how she later left her husband, he then committed suicide, and she finally realized that her children were separate and interesting people. Her writing is explorative and personal. However, the text of *Of Woman Born* includes powerfully written accounts of maternal ambivalence. Despite her preface, this book must be acting as a catalyst to many.

Susan Maushart thought that an openly ambivalent mother would indicate her "unusual maturity and resilience."[67] But it sounds as though the opposite would be nearer the truth. Mothers in this position seem quite immature and rigid. It requires a certain maturity and elasticity for a mother to open herself and to welcome her baby. Ambivalent mothers may not be as self-centered as they sound. Their anxiety suggests that they don't have too much a sense of self but too little.

Rozsika Parker thought that if mothers would think about their ambivalence, this would be "the basis of self-knowledge."[68] Yet some of these writers think endlessly about themselves and their feelings, and they still sound trapped. Thinking doesn't seem to have made them wiser. Surely self-knowledge is difficult to attain through "reverie."[69] We benefit from the stimulation of talking to other people. But these mothers satirize precisely those more wholehearted mothers from whom they might learn.

It seems, then, that mothers differ. Some are tormented by ambivalent feelings, while others are not. Can their differences be explained by genetics, social situations, or other variants? One can't tell without having much more information. However, one of the mothers who describes her ambivalence has provided enough personal detail to allow us to piece together part of her story. It might seem intrusive if one was going to seek out data like this. But Jane Lazarre has volunteered some intimate information. *The Mother Knot* can show us a way to make sense of Jane Lazarre's ambivalent feelings when her baby son cried.

She tells us that when she was giving birth to her baby, Benjamin, she kept screaming. "I hadn't heard that kind of screaming since I had gone crazy as a child and heard my mother, dead from cancer, screaming in my head, breaking my eardrums from the inside."[70] The actual birth of her child seemed to bring back very painful memories of when she herself was a child. Later, when he cried, which he did frequently, she became distressed. She used to scream at him to be quiet. She noticed that she used to scream out not his name but her sister's.[71]

However, it is only right at the end of her book that she hints at how these memories might connect up. She recalls her sister, when they were both children, "crying because she could no longer remember what her mother looked like. She asked me if I could be her mommy. I laughed bitterly, even at nine, to think that at such an age all this should be expected of me. But I said yes."[72] This helps us to make sense of her distress. She sounds as though she was the older sister of the two. If her mother had died when she was seven, and her sister frequently cried when Jane was nine, the two girls must have spent two years bearing their grief (and Jane's going "crazy") without getting sufficient comfort from an understanding adult. Her sister turned to Jane for comfort, and Jane, at the young age of nine, seems to have struggled to give a comfort she was so clearly missing for herself.

This sense of desperate grief, which no one had comforted,

seemed to have been re-evoked when Benjamin cried. No wonder she automatically called out her sister's name. But Benjamin obviously couldn't be crying because his mother had died. A newborn usually cries for simple reasons that a mother can discover and put right. Jane Lazarre seemed unable to do this, perhaps because she associated urgent crying with the motherless years of her childhood. This suggests a possible explanation for how she felt as a mother herself. Perhaps she wasn't "necessarily ambivalent" toward her son. Perhaps she felt distressed for good reason. She believed that many mothers felt ambivalent toward their babies. Yet most other mothers have not been bereaved, gone uncomforted, or had to comfort their little sisters at so young an age.

It is not clear whether Jane Lazarre herself made this connection. However, her story certainly seems to fit together in this way. True, it is only one woman's story. Yet if it is relatively simple to make sense of one woman's distress, might not the distress of other mothers make sense if we really knew their circumstances? In that case, if ambivalent feelings arose in specific circumstances, then they would not appear to be universal. It would not be "honest" of every mother to say she experienced ambivalence. A mother in Jane Lazarre's position could then feel justified in saying she has a problem. She could consider seeking help and perhaps talk over her difficulties with a sympathetic friend or a counselor.

So how valid is the concept of motherly ambivalence? The ideas are spreading and obviously reflect the experience of some women. But ambivalence, as one can see from autobiographical literature, appears to arise when a mother feels that her baby is an extension of herself. There are many mothers worldwide who do *not* relate to their babies in this way. Ambivalence certainly doesn't seem a valid concept for them. It doesn't liberate them, because they never felt so merged with their babies in the first place. The concept of ambivalence has been helpful in enabling some mothers to identify how they feel. But this does not justify attributing it to every mother.

Meanwhile countless babies have started life with ambivalent mothers. How might it feel for a baby to have received ambivalent love? Ambivalence is different from a mother's burst of temper, followed by her apology. That tells her child that she sees her anger as a *lapse* of love. By contrast, the baby reared with ambivalent love would learn complex messages. His mother sometimes loves him and at other times hates him for demanding too much of her. A small baby is sensitive, yet too young to analyze his impressions in words. We can only guess his response. There are times when his mother seems to love him. At other times she switches mood and is either openly furious with him or withdraws from him. Yet she indicates that she sees this switch not as a lapse but as part and parcel of her love.

This is surely confusing if not downright frightening for a sensitive baby. From his mother, he is receiving his first experience of an intimate human relationship and learning what he can expect from another person. Through this relationship, he may well absorb the message that love includes adjusting to the beloved's inexplicable switches of mood. Instead of feeling accepted as the baby he is and therefore feeling safe and protected, he has found himself in a constant struggle with his own mother. The more this new view spreads, the more it is likely to produce adults who will both desire love and feel confused and frightened by it.

Wholehearted love is more straightforward. Babies seem to need enormous amounts of it, early on. They might seem greedy or insatiable to anyone schooled to expect less. However, if a mother can manage to love her baby (almost) as much as he wants, she suddenly realizes that he is returning the compliment. Then something momentous seems to flower between them. It lasts a lifetime. It must be the reason why the oldest people can still mention their mothers with tears in their eyes. These last observations by mothers were all spoken with great feeling:

> B lies on the bed and *bathes* us in his beautiful smiles. [B, 2 months]
>
> When I kiss B, he loves it so much he just closes his eyes for pleasure. [B, 6 months]
>
> B can walk quite well now, and he took my hand and we walked together and looked over a bridge. I thought: "This is heaven. Nothing is better than this. This is one of those perfect moments." [B, 15 months]

Generally, wholehearted love shows. A child loved wholeheartedly tends to enjoy relating to other people. Experience has taught him to expect a friendly response. So, even as a baby, he is often outgoing. Sure enough, passersby respond to the wide-eyed gaze of an interested baby. His mother suddenly hears the animated voice of a total stranger talking not to herself but to her child. Admittedly, having written this sentence, I can think of children who go through shy phases when they bury their faces in their mothers' arms and won't look at a new face. It's not easy to generalize. All the same, a child who has received plenty of wholehearted love has a sturdy and dignified bearing. Small though he is, he looks important, and people tend to talk to him with respect. If we notice a child like this, surely we should assume (unless we know otherwise) that his mother has given him great quantities of love. Many mothers struggle with all kinds of difficulties in order to do this.

Some mothers who have found the early months frustrating discover that they can relate to their child much better once he has learned to use words. Their separate identities then become more obvious. At this stage the whole relationship shifts into another gear. It usually becomes less physical, which suits some mothers more than others. To an outsider it can look casual. But the intimate base of their relationship is still there. A typical mother wants to know about her child's day at school. She is still keeping track of how he is but in a less detailed way. Many years later, when her child has left home, his mother may be able to hold out without news of him for a time. After that, the familiar interest builds up. There is obviously a fine line between wanting to know what her adult child is doing now—and being intrusive. Even so, at its best, her interest is one of the ways in which an older mother shows her love.

At this stage, the relationship can look effortless. But a mother's love did not drop into her lap ready-made from heaven. The beginning can seem almost painful, like a one-way conversation, because her baby simply is not ready to reply. Yet the mother's own love is undeniable. She continues to love him through her unspeakable tiredness, perhaps through times when one of them is ill and through all kinds of external pressures. It is almost as though her love is going through a test, pulling and tugging it this way and that, to make sure it will survive and prove strong enough to be trusted with the passionate love of her baby. Perhaps those first testing months are the secret of her love's lifelong strength.

ten

"I was surprised that I still had the same name"

If an expectant mother walked into a library and asked: "How will my baby develop?" the librarian could show her some books on infant development. If, however, she asked: "What about me? How will *I* develop as a mother?" the librarian would probably look surprised. The idea that *mothers* develop isn't a common subject for a book.[1] Almost the opposite. Many people seem to think that mothers risk stagnating. Especially if a mother isn't out at work, people assume she must be "stuck" at home doing boring and repetitive chores with little to stimulate her.

Certainly some mothers have described it this way. But do they all? Or do some mothers give us fragments of a different story that hasn't properly got into print?

> I had to sign a check the other day, and I was surprised that I still had the same name. I thought: "Have I really got the same name when I've been through all this?"

Well, I'm not sure if I thought those actual words, but that's how I felt. [B, 4 weeks]

People say: "Are you back to normal?" No, I'm not back to normal. I don't expect to be. Everything has changed since B was born. *Normal* has changed. [B, 6 weeks]

It develops me, having a baby. It pushes you forward into new areas. [G, 7 months]

I feel as if I'm in a different orbit. I used to be in another orbit, and then I only noticed things in *that* orbit. Now I'm in *this* orbit, and I go 'round in a totally different system. [B, 9 months]

It's like throwing a stone into a pond, and it creates ripples, layers and layers of them. The baby is like the stone and, once it's born, there's all these changes. It's *huge*. [B, 12 months]

These mothers don't sound as if they are stagnating. Rather, they appear to be describing a degree of change that seems almost too much for them. What kind of change is it and why does it make so much difference?

Mothers find it hard to explain. They sense the change, rather than recognize it consciously. We are short of words, as is so often the case. Perhaps we can adapt some ordinary words, such as "open" and "make space." Then we can sum up the process as being the way a new mother opens herself to provide enough space to accommodate her growing baby.

We can see how this process starts during pregnancy. The mother has to provide a physical space in her womb. This development is involuntary and does not owe much to what she does. Her uterus keeps growing to create the right amount of space for her developing baby. Giving birth requires a tremendous physical opening of the cervix. At this point, her voluntary cooperation can be helpful. This is especially important during the moments of birth, when her active and precise movements can enable her child to emerge safely. Afterward, the new mother's cervix closes again, and her uterus contracts down. But now the mother's conscious cooperation is essential. She has to open herself in a different way. Her awareness seems to open wide to encompass her baby, in a figurative sense, just as her womb did in a physical sense.

In time, the baby grows, so the intensity of the mother's attention gradually relaxes. People have described a mother's journey as a "letting go" process. But in a sense, she never completely lets go, and can never quite return to the woman she was. Once she opens herself to her child, something within her stays open. She has changed profoundly, and for her whole life.

Mothers tend to describe their sense of change in a particular way.

> I keep thinking ordinary things like: "I've got to brush my hair now and put on my jeans," and it's *weird*. It doesn't feel like me. I think that's the frightening thing. It's not the isolation. It's that I'm turning into a new person and that person is unknown. [B, 8 weeks]

> I keep turning over new pages of a new me. I don't really know what I am like anymore. [B, 4 months]

> I feel I have a new self, which is my mothering self. But what about my old working self and all my other selves?

> How will I get them back? *Will* I ever get them back? [G, 7 months]

> One night, I wept for the person I once was. She's gone. I felt I needed to mark her passing. I'm redefining myself as a mother. Who am I? I don't really know. And where is that person I used to be? [B, 16 months]

It's not only first-time mothers who experience this change:

> It feels relentless. I love it. But it feels, yes, relentless. And I wonder: where is the me? I know she must be there somewhere, but I can't find her. I said to F the other day: "Do you remember *M*, you know, that woman you once fell in love with and married?" [G, 3 years; B, 6 months]

The phrase mothers use to describe this change is significant. It is common to say that an event has changed one's *life.* But mothers spontaneously tell each other that having their babies has changed their actual *selves.* What can they possibly mean?

At the very least, a mother must be saying that becoming a mother doesn't mean living along a continuum, with a baby added onto her life. Rather, right from his birth, his presence changes her.[2] In order to make enough space in her life for her baby, she seems to make a momentous inner shift. No longer can she afford to keep only her own interests at the forefront of her consciousness. She has to share that special space with her baby. Sharing is not easy, especially at the beginning, when she finds she has to keep prioritizing the interests of the newborn.

Some women deeply resent the idea of this shift. Some refuse to make it and find ways around it. Yet many mothers do manage to put their newborns into the "attention space" that had been, till then, reserved for themselves. Good news about their babies is felt with intense joy and pride. Anything worrying sets off the loudest alarm bells. Even when her newborn is asleep or in someone else's care, his mother is intensely aware of him. If a mother has multiples or has older children or stepchildren, it takes time to work out how to prioritize.

At first, for safety's sake, she treats everything to do with her newborn as of life-and-death importance. The relationship often looks uncomfortably overbalanced in the baby's favor. Friends often beg the mother to remember her own needs. However, the balance changes gradually as mother and baby attune to each other. Eventually the mother is able to resume some of her personal life. Nevertheless, in an emergency, she can return to this shift of putting her child's interests first. If her older child, her adolescent, or even her fully adult offspring urgently wants her attention, a mother seems to be able to clear that same huge attention space. The familiar sound of her child's voice, and especially her child's tears, can reactivate all the mother's old, powerful protective feelings.

Surely this makes sense of why a mother says that her whole self is changing. Making this shift to create such an intimate space is a complicated process. But the most confusing part for a mother may well be the lack of a positive word to honor it. She may completely overlook moments when she is achieving it. She may chide herself for not "doing more," when she is quietly succeeding at one of the most difficult challenges of being a mother.

> I'm a very visual person and my job is all to do with how good I am at seeing. But now my vision has completely shrunk. I just see G's face, nine inches away from mine, and she's *all* I care about. A friend said to me that we

> were in a beautiful place—and I hadn't even *noticed.* [G, 2 months]

This change has been perceived but nearly always in a negative light. Many feminists deplore it as an example of maternal self-sacrifice.[3] Some psychoanalysts have described it as the "masochism" of mothers.[4] On the one hand, the image of an unhappy mother sacrificing her whole self to her child doesn't do justice to the intricate *balancing* of interests that the mother is doing when the relationship works well. On the other hand, feminists and psychoanalysts may have identified a way in which some women approach mothering.

It is possible to learn, from a strict upbringing, to give very little attention to oneself. This can make the shift to place the baby first almost too easy. It's like getting a room ready for the baby that is empty already. On one level, a mother in this position can seem extremely generous to her newborn. However, she may be using her child to fill up her own "empty space." This may be giving her baby too much "room" in her life. He then may sense that she wants him to compensate for her lack of self-fulfillment. It doesn't seem a good way to relate to a child. However, having a baby can give her a reason for thinking about this and perhaps asking herself whether she could relate to him differently.

But suppose a mother's "room" is not at all empty? Does she find any positive benefit from giving her baby so much attention space? Won't she deplete herself dreadfully if she does?

> I belong to the selfish generation. I was brought up to think that "I want it" equals "I should have it." But having B makes me think differently. It's given me a chance to review all those beliefs. [B, 8 months]

This doesn't sound like a sacrifice of the mother's self but a step that might lead to a new maturity. No longer is she thinking of herself as a self-contained "I." She is forming a relationship with her baby that calls into question many aspects of herself. Being a mother is not a matter of running through a succession of chores. The relationship is primary. It is not easy to adjust to sharing most of one's life, and the change can feel exhausting.

> You feel as if you can't go on anymore. It's too hard. And then, somehow, you find that you do it. [B, 7 months]

This mother has used the simplest language to express an age-old discovery. Many mothers say that just when they believe they are giving up in defeat over something, they stop struggling. It is then that they seem able to surrender to something more effortless and move forward.

What kind of surrender is it? Relating to a baby usually means that the pace of life slows down. Like having to make enough room, this slowing-down process often starts during pregnancy. It's hard to pack your day with action if you have a kicking baby and a heavy sac of amniotic water inside your abdomen. After the birth, a mother may be tempted to try to resume a quicker pace of life. She soon realizes that her baby does not enjoy being rushed around. He likes time to study and learn about the world. He becomes more content if she decelerates. Yet the pace of modern life is extremely fast. Being quick and active can keep a mother in step with the mainstream and encourage her to feel cheerful. By contrast, reducing her pace can leave a mother feeling sidelined and perhaps depressed and demoralized. Slowing down for a baby can never have been harder.

This process may sound very odd to an employed mother.

Slowing down may sound like an unattainable luxury, but someone has to look after her baby. Employers do not usually allow mothers to have their babies with them at work, so an employed mother has to leave her baby in someone else's care. There is then a vital third person, or several people, included in the relationship of mother and baby. It may be this third person who has had to slow down. Employed mothers sometimes say that they find themselves mothering their carers as well as their babies "like an older daughter," as one mother put it, even if the carers are much older than they are. So it may be useful to appreciate that their carers may not be outrageously lazy but simply trying to slow down. Not that "employed mothers" are a rigid, unchanging category. Mothers often decide to renegotiate. They give notice, or resume work, or arrange to work part-time. However, if a mother is employed full-time, she has limited time to come to meetings and talk. Most of the mothers quoted in this chapter were on maternity leave or were self-employed, part-time employed, or unemployed altogether. Some of their experiences may be recognizable to most mothers. All the same, a fully employed mother may well find that some statements here jar with her own experience.

> As soon as I got used to breastfeeding, I used to dash around, visiting all my friends. Then the clinic told me that G wasn't gaining enough weight. I was horrified. So I slowed down, and now I'm much better at going with the flow. That's what I've learned as a mother—flowing together. [G, 2 months]

> I've got my "power walk" like *this,* got to *get* somewhere. But with G, I can't do that anymore. I've completely slowed down. It's nice. My body feels more dense. [G, 5 months]

> Sometimes I've lots of things to do, but I just hold B and sort of mellow out. It's amazing. [B, 5 months]

> F and I have been in Babyland for seven months. But this friend came to see us. I used to study with her, and she was talking in this rush all about her latest exams. And I was thinking: "Has she changed? Or did *I* used to be like *her*?" [G, 7 months]

> I've changed a lot. I've always been very impatient and hated to wait for anybody. B's taught me patience. It was hard for me to learn it—but what else could I do? [B, 11 months]

Being a mother teaches the value of patience like nothing else. A mother soon learns that being patient turns out to be a shorter route than a flash of impatience, leading to a distressed baby who takes a long time to calm down again. So most mothers learn patience. The patience of mothers, if we could collect it and turn it into a visible substance, would surely fill *oceans*. It's priceless. It occurs when a stronger person doesn't try to impose her way by brute force but respects the wishes of a dependent person. This not only produces a better moment (and usually mothers find they still get what they want, only a bit later) but provides a role model for her child. Surely patience is one of the cornerstones of civilized behavior. Surely most of us first learn it from our mothers. Even a mother who rates herself as "very impatient" is probably overlooking all those tiny everyday occasions when she bit back an impulsive reaction and reminded herself how young and inexperienced her child still was.

Patience is part of the great process of slowing down. Slowing down makes a difference. It helps a mother to relax. It means that she can live at a tempo similar to her baby. It makes it possible for her to have time to notice details. Often the details she observes give her vital clues for understanding her baby. Many mothers report that they had never felt calm before. This might seem odd when we have seen how responsible they now are. But by living at a slower pace, a mother can recognize when to feel concerned. She is more on her baby's wavelength. Slowness brings a whole new awareness into her life.

Elderly people and those with long illnesses also slow down and reappreciate the simple elements of life. But they haven't necessarily got a baby to help them do it. It can seem a miracle to a mother when she sees the passionate excitement of her baby about something so everyday that she might hardly have noticed it.

For a newborn, perhaps lying flat on his back, the ceiling may seem important. An older baby, curious about what his mother is doing, may respond to the sound of dry rice pouring from a package into a metal saucepan, or of water rushing from a tap, or the flutter of a pigeon's wings, or the curve of a cat's tail. For a crawling or toddling child, the ground and everything close to it takes on new interest. A mother trying to understand her child may suddenly notice the astonishing beauty of an ordinary gravel path. From this perspective, it can seem amazing to see everyone else in time-conscious haste. Whatever is all the hurry for?

> *Mother:* I took G for a walk yesterday. *Me: Yesterday?* Didn't you get soaking wet? *Mother:* Yes, but G loves the rain. She pushes back her little hood, lifts up her face, and goes "*Aaahhhhh!*" [G, 6 months]

> You learn to slow down and enjoy the small things. [B, 12 months]

Women sometimes fear that slowing down and sharing life with their babies will drive them crazy or turn them into cows or cabbages. Some mothers do find it frustrating. Others say that adjusting their pace teaches them something new about life itself.

> When I'm "spinning" [by which she meant asking herself about the meaning of her life, so that the questions seemed to spin endlessly, without answers], I just look at G and she seems so grounded in the present that it heals me. When she looks at a pencil, her whole being is just exploring that pencil and nothing else. [G, 5 months]

> Being a mother puts you up against your own resistance all the time. Like when B wants me again, and I think: "You don't want me *again,* do you?" But he does. The difficulties come if I'm resisting. [B, 8 months]

> At first I felt a failure as a mother. I felt I wasn't cut out for it. Everyone else was talking about feeding schedules and sleeping schedules. I just couldn't. There was no way I could leave B to cry. And I'm so glad I persevered. Now I can see that he changes naturally. I don't have to do anything that a person like me would think was cruel. I suppose I'm not a very trusting person—and what I learned was to trust him. [B, 15 months]

> I feel G is a little nut, all growing inside herself. [G, 21 months]

> I've spent so long doubting myself over these last two years. Now it feels like there is an enormous amount of trust between us. [B, 24 months]

At first mothers worry and can feel responsible for everything. The mothers in the examples here found that slowly, as they learned about their babies, they learned how sensible their babies were. They wanted what they needed. It really *was* possible to trust them. This often went against the current fashion in childcare. At the time of writing, it is fashionable to believe that parents have to teach their children to go to sleep. A generation earlier, the main concern was persuading children to eat solid foods by a specific age. A generation before that, there was a mania for potty training. No doubt there will always be someone claiming that babies have to be trained to do something that human beings are capable of learning naturally, in their own good time.

This becomes a self-fulfilling prophecy. If a child is continually urged to do something, his mother is assuming responsibility for whatever it is and he is likely to depend on her to be responsible for it. This then serves to "convince" her that he would never have learned whatever it was without her. Meanwhile mothers who learn when to trust their children discover a vital truth. Children are individual. They want to become independent and don't need urging—they reach particular goalposts at a variety of different times. They "can't run before they can walk," as the fine old English proverb warns us.

A mother who trusts her baby is trusting *herself* to trust him. Suddenly, from being a sophisticated woman who feels in control of a fast-paced city life, she is learning about a slower way that is older and closer to nature. It's a more harmonious way in which one person relates respectfully to another. Once a mother discovers that she can trust herself to trust her child, she learns a new kind of calm.

This is surely the beauty of maternal serenity that Renaissance artists tried to show in paintings and sculptures. But it's not something many of us are born with, and it doesn't seem to be a permanent attribute of any mother. It's a momentary achievement. Mothers seem to have unexpected periods of this harmonious serenity, lose sight of it again, and renew it.

A mother may feel hot, tired, and sweaty, light-years away from a Raphael Madonna. With a young baby, most mothers have much less time to think about how they look. They often comment that now they no longer "dress to impress." Some like to shower, wash their hair, and make up their faces every day, but this, they explain, is for their own sakes. Other mothers find that at last they don't need to conform to social expectations.

> I'm a girl who never used to leave the house without lipstick on. [B, 2 months]

> My values got rearranged very quickly. Before I had B, having a haircut was very important to me. But last week I went to my hairdresser's, with my sister to hold B, and they asked me if I wanted a fringe. That would have been a *major* decision before, but suddenly I didn't care! [B, 2 months]

> I look at people in the street, taking so much care about their appearance, and I want to shout to them: "Why do you *bother*?" I don't want to sound arrogant, but I feel I've got past that stage now. [B, 6 months]

Mothers are sometimes thought to lose pride in their appearance and to "let themselves go." Perhaps some mothers do. The unofficial dress code for mothers today seems to be plain T-shirts and jeans. The soft, flowing muslin dresses, such as those worn by mothers in Mary Cassatt's paintings, are rare today. This is, after all, a generation of women who have been brought up to compete with men in the workplace. It's not surprising that their clothes are unisex. However, their expressions are not. No longer, as mothers, can they assume that air of cool and detached elegance, which is so greatly prized today. Instead, they glow with warm and tender expressions. Mary Cassatt might have recognized them after all. It seems to me that today's mothers may look incredibly feminine *because* they dress so simply.

Being a mother is surely the height of our sexual development. This is what all those changes during adolescence, when we started to grow breasts and have periods, were leading to. As mothers, we have reached sexual fruitfulness. Some mothers seem to feel this, but the majority clearly do not. Most mothers apologize for their appearances, as if we should expect to see fully groomed women in immaculate, dust-free homes. Part of this subject belongs to the next chapter. It's striking how few mothers feel they are beautiful and sexually attractive when they look hot and disheveled. Occasionally a mother will take a few tentative steps into what she obviously sees as an unfamiliar direction in which to develop.

> I was a tomboy all my childhood. I'd play with boys, or when I played with girls, I'd be the boyish one. At school, I was encouraged to compete with boys and show that I could achieve in a man's world. When I was pregnant, I was afraid of having a girl because I thought I'd be no role model for her. But now, motherhood has allowed me to realize my suppressed and stifled femininity for the first time. I even put on a skirt recently and I almost never do that. I feel . . . it's such a *relief!* [B, 2 months]

A new mother may long to confide in another woman about such profound changes. Her old friends are important. They can steady her because they remember what she was like before she became a mother. They help her to remember her "old self." However, once a woman becomes a mother, it usually adds an unexpected dimension to the friendship.

> A friend asked: "How are *you?*" and I just burst into tears. I'm not used to not being the unflappable, invincible me. I always *was.* [G, 4 weeks]

> My friend can't have a baby. I was apprehensive about meeting her again, but I didn't want to lose such a good friendship. In the end I went to see her, and she and B got on really well. It was such a relief. [B, 5 months]

> I think people think I'm much stronger than I am, so they don't offer to help me. I mean, when a friend rings the bell, I pull myself together, and they don't realize that I was feeling pretty low just before they came. So now I've realized that it's up to me to ask them for help. [B, 5 months]

Not all friendships survive. Becoming a mother can bring out deep convictions about how to bring up a baby. Mothers sometimes contact friends to whom they had once felt close but find that now the two of them feel divided from each other. Both say there is an unbridgeable gap between their opposite beliefs.

> I had a meal out last night with a really old friend, but I think she isn't, anymore. She told me, all doe-eyed, how she'd left her baby to cry when he was four months old and stood at the bottom of the stairs resisting the urge to

> go up. "I *had* to do it. I need my life back," she said. "We can't all be like *you,* M." I stayed awake half the night thinking about her and things I could have said. I was so upset. [B, 14 months]

A woman usually has a range of more casual friends as well as close ones. But just when she needs them the most, she realizes how many of her circle are busy working all day. Some of them may have chosen not to become parents, or perhaps not yet. Others may have had babies but are back at work with little time to talk. The wonderful ubiquitous network of feminine support that used to be flexible yet so reliable and effective now seems to operate at workplaces.[5] I have heard new mothers talk, almost in tears, about the office Christmas parties to which they are no longer invited.[6] Local mothers may chat to a new mother in the street as if she has now joined their informal club. But it's not the same as belonging to a network of people at work who are certain to meet each other every day. To whom does she now "belong"?

> I find it very hard to balance loneliness with getting enough company. I need to spend enough time alone with B, getting to know him. But also, if it's just him and me for hours till his dad gets back, it's too much. [B, 3 months]

> It was a beautiful day so I took G for a walk in the park, and I kept seeing these little groups of mothers, and everyone looked so happy. Suddenly I didn't feel happy myself anymore. I saw myself from the outside as a mother *alone* in the park. [G, 3 months]

> What's really helped me through this year is being friends with other mothers. At first, I kept myself to myself and couldn't relate to anyone. But then I found everyone so open and giving. Now I can be more open and giving myself, and I've got so many friends I can talk to. [B, 12 months]

These cooperative links with other mothers are vital. They tend to focus on immediate practical questions about child care rather than on intimate questions of the mother's identity. But at least there a mother can get understanding, reassurance, and comfort. Codes of conduct emerge, such as whether it is all right to borrow and share, or how late a mother might telephone another when she feels anxious. It is understood that a mother can easily panic about her own child yet be levelheaded about someone else's. These flexible groups of mothers are as warm and supportive today as they have always been. Being a mother can teach a woman the value of the generous support that other women can give her as never before.

The most pressing questions that mothers share are about their babies' health. Many new mothers have given hardly a moment's thought to infant health before. Suddenly they are confronted by it, especially the complex medical issue of infant vaccination. Few mothers have been educated for this. There are more variables facing this generation than previous ones, and it is difficult for a layperson to know what to trust. Mothers read what they can, but information is often not yet available to enable them to make well-informed choices. They are frequently compelled to make difficult decisions in unavoidable ignorance—decisions which they will be responsible for and which may have unforeseeable consequences for the children they love so much. This is extremely difficult. Other health questions can arise daily. Some mothers find themselves taking their babies to their doctors several times a week. At least a doctor can advise a mother whether there is something to worry about.

> B had eczema. His face was covered in a red rash, he puffed up and he was screaming. It was dreadful. I think I'm too sensitive to be a mom. [B, 8 weeks]

> I've read the literature for and against vaccinating. I got in a panic about the arguments. There seem to be dangers on both sides. [G, 2 months]

> I've been a nurse, but last week when B was ill, I just couldn't take his temperature. I couldn't trust my own judgment. I took him to the hospital and said to the doctor: "*You* do it!" [B, 4 months]

> B has been quite ill for about a month. I find it so hard to care for B when he is ill. I have all these visions of him dying. Before I had B I was a little girl turning to others for help, even though I'm nearly forty. Having B makes me become more mature. [B, 15 months]

One disabled mother described how her shower seat had collapsed that morning, "almost on top of B." As an afterthought, she added that the shower seat had wedged her so that, disabled as she was, she simply couldn't move. She was still shocked and kept talking about all the things that might have happened to B. I asked her three times whether she herself was all right. She never replied to my question!

It is a great pity that this kind of thinking is denigrated as "worrying," because if the child is ill, all his mother's ideas about his safety and health may turn out to be essential. In previous centuries, members of a household would consult the mother as we consult our local doctor. "It was to the mistress of the house that everyone turned whenever an accident occurred at home or on the farm, when feverish symptoms appeared in nursery or kitchen, or someone was smitten with epilepsy or an ague," wrote Christina Hole in *The English Housewife in the Seventeenth Century.*[7]

When I first read this, I took it for remote history. But it isn't, as mothers discover. They often find themselves thrown back on their own resources in the traditional way. With small children, emergencies arise unexpectedly. A mother's busy doctor may not be instantly available; nor is there time to check symptoms on the Internet, even if she has her own computer. She has to react as well as she can with the little she knows, just as mothers have always done. Then all the earlier crises she has been through, when other people were criticizing her for "always fussing over the baby," turn into invaluable experience and become her stepping-stones to help her respond as well as she can to this new situation.

As the baby grows into a small child, his mother may have more confidence in his immediate survival. But she starts to consider his future.

> I've been ill and still feel a bit weak and low. I started crying, thinking of all the pain B will go through in his whole life. Everyone suffers pain. [B, 10 months]

> There was a man knocked down by a car right outside my door. I suddenly started to worry about what might

happen to B. It was overwhelming. I couldn't think that way for very long. [B, 12 months]

She doesn't just worry about her baby. Her baby depends on *her.* A whole set of new anxieties arises when this idea occurs to her. Inevitably, mothers start to wonder what would happen to their babies if their own health failed. From poems and journals of mothers during earlier centuries, we can see how a mother's health always was a major concern. Today, a woman's chances of surviving childbirth are high. Before becoming a mother, a woman may have given scarcely a thought to her immediate mortality. But having a baby can bring that idea to the fore.

After B was born, I was so frightened of my own death. I suddenly realized how terrible it would be for *him.* [B, 5 months]

All these worries are often dismissed as morbid, but surely mothers are facing up to life's realities. Typically, they imagine a range of frightening scenarios. Thinking about them seems to be a method of preparation should they one day need to cope.

Mothers spend a lot of time wondering about the future. Especially if a mother is breastfeeding, she may spend hours with her baby asleep in her arms. Her eyes travel countless times up and down his body. Who is this unique and sensitive small person? Her curiosity leads her to make detailed observations of him. These can be at least as phenomenological as the data of psychology researchers. Most mothers haven't got degrees in child psychology, and they may sound humble about what they have noticed. But when they start talking, it is amazing to hear their close observations and insights.

As a psychologist, I'm finding things about my baby that are the opposite of all my training. [G, 6 weeks]

Mother: B wakes up in the night, thinking about crawling. *Me:* How do you know? *Mother:* He sort of kneels up on the bed and rocks himself backward and forward. [B, 5 months]

Why do all babies seem to touch each other's heads? It seems universal. [B, 7 months]

I don't think a child can be naughty and look at you at the same time. When B isn't sure, he looks at my face. But when he *knows* he's doing something I don't let him do, he won't look. [B, 14 months]

In learning about her baby, a mother learns about herself too. She is a vital part of the interaction.

I remember looking at B and thinking to myself: "Are you all right?" Then I thought: "No, this is ridiculous. I'm thinking that if *he's* all right, then *I* can feel all right." So I reversed it. And it works. If *I'm* all right, then B is in tune with me and he is all right too. [B, 6 months]

I've noticed that if I'm crabby, B's miserable, F's miserable, the cat's miserable, my *plants* are miserable, whereas if I'm happy, we're all all right. [B, 14 months]

I've learned to listen to myself. Often my feelings are *adding* to the problem. When B was four months old, my father died. I was very upset and cried a lot. B refused to breastfeed for eight hours. I'd put him to my breast and he'd just turn away. I realize, looking back, that he was sensitive to how I was feeling. [B, 2 years; G, 4 months]

Babies can show startling sensitivity toward their mothers. This is not detached or neutral. They can be passionately warm. Many mothers are self-critical people who tend to downplay the good that they do. From her baby, a mother can discover how it feels to be completely accepted by another person. Her baby may help her to recognize and to value the genuine good in herself.

To an outsider, all this may seem introspective. Aren't mothers getting too intense and too concerned about their babies? Haven't they got things out of proportion? One can hear the impatience in Dr. John Cobb's voice when he ordered mothers: "Do some non-baby thing every day. . . . Even if it is just half an hour of another kind of life, tear yourself away from that baby and that routine just once, and you can enjoy another dimension to your life besides motherhood."[8]

One can understand Dr. Cobb's reaction, but his choice of words shows that he does not appreciate the enormous changes that mothers go through. She may do "some non-baby thing," but she may find it hard to concentrate. A mother will not be preoccupied with her baby forever, but at the moment she is learning how to relate to him. Her whole system of mothering is taking shape. However, Dr. Cobb was not the only person to think that such preoccupation was absurd. Chekhov wrote a parody of this kind of mother. She is Natasha in *Three Sisters*. Natasha keeps coming onstage in the midst of the family drama, but she is oblivious of everything except her baby, Bobik.[9]

Chekhov is a great writer, and generations of audiences have laughed at Natasha. But is this fair to mothers? Can mothers be too absorbed in their babies and too little concerned with everyone else? We have only to listen. Looking after her baby usually increases a mother's awareness of the vulnerability of other people. Far from excluding the outside world, mothers often become acutely socially sensitive.

> You look at the down-and-outs on the streets, and you think: "They were *babies* once." You wonder who their parents were. [B, 8 weeks]

> I took G to the Anne Frank exhibition, and there was a talk. It affected me deeply. G is half Jewish, but it affected me anyway, and it still does. It sounded different, holding G in my arms. [G, 11 weeks]

> I've changed so much, being a mother. It's given me determination and direction. I wake up in the mornings and think about making life a better place for B. I always used to have woolly ideas, but now they are strong. [B, 9 months]

These feelings need to be understood. A mother may not have them for large and abstract issues. Because she is relating to one individual baby, she can see the world in much more personal terms. Large generalizations can seem untrustworthy. Instead, mothers are much more likely to focus on particular acts of unfairness. Having a baby often enables them to see society from a different angle, with much greater awareness of individual vulnerability.

Mothers can be suspicious of high idealism. After all, a good deal about being a mother is a coming-down-to-earth process. Most expectant mothers have nine months to consider the sort of mothers they intend to be. Most of us make noble resolutions to be patient with our children, to give them things we didn't have, along with many other heroic ambitions. However, becoming a mother is a quick cure for all that. We learn all kinds of humbling lessons about what is possible in reality.

> Before B was born, I bought some beautiful fabrics to sew. I wanted to bake bread. I thought you just put your baby down. I thought I'd get so much done. But I hardly get myself dressed! [B, 5 weeks]

> I look at B and it's like having a new frock. You don't want to wear it in case you drop food down it. But unfortunately, I can't keep B safely packed away on a cupboard shelf forever. [B, 3 months]

> I've been through a mourning process for the natural birth I didn't have and the breastfeeding I couldn't do. First I had a Caesarean, then I became anemic and got a blood transfusion. I just couldn't make enough milk. But now I'm starting to enjoy being a mother. [B, 4 months]

> I spent nine months before G was born trying to get emotionally perfect for her. I guess she just has to live with me as I am. [G, 6 months]

A second baby can underline this kind of realization.

> With my first baby, I "knew" I was pregnant, and I really noticed all the changes. Now I'm juggling work and looking after B, and my father's been ill, and I haven't had

time to *think* about this baby. It's all just happening. [B, 15 months; expected baby, 17 weeks]

I realize now that there is no Right Way. With my first child, I was making major decisions all the time. Now I'm much more easy and allow myself to make mistakes. [G, 2 years; G, 3 months]

That didn't seem to mean that mothers felt they could accept themselves no matter what they did. Many mothers seem to spend a lot of time reviewing and assessing what they do, not just in practical terms but in moral ones. Most expectant mothers have secret fears of the horrible mothers they might turn into. Usually a mother's worst fears are unfounded. But what happens when she fails a deeply held ideal? She can't pretend it's not important.

There's appropriate and inappropriate guilt. You'd be quite complacent if you didn't feel it at all. [G, 7 months]

You can learn quite a lot from the things you do wrong. You need to be aware of it. [B, 13 months]

Most of us underestimate just how much energy a mother can spend in struggling with her own quick temper. The temptation to stop being patient and to vent her frustrations onto her child is always there. Or, to be more exact, with a newborn, it is easier to see anger as inappropriate. But the more he grows into a lively child the more he can seem like an equal. It can be tempting for a mother to overlook how young he is and how devastated he becomes when she displays her anger. Mothers don't receive the recognition that they deserve for their daily efforts at self-restraint.

> B head-butted me the other day and I nearly passed out. It really hurt. I'm a volatile person, and I surprised myself that I didn't let fly. I *know* B. It was an accident. It wasn't his fault. He didn't mean to hurt me. [B, 8 months]

> I was stuck in traffic [in her car] and G was screaming. I needed to wee and I thought: "I can't pull over or I'll wet myself." I couldn't stand G's screaming. I was getting so upset, I was terrified I would do something to hurt G. Finally I wound down my window and yelled out into the road: "Will you SHUT UP!" The man in the next car gave me a funny look. Still, I felt better, but G was upset by me shouting and whimpered all the way home. I suppose babies get pissed off and they can let all their emotions out, but we're not supposed to. [G, 9 months]

> I got angry with B and then broke down and cried. He managed to make my washing machine get stuck in drying mode for about two hours. The only jeans that really fit me were in it, and a sweater knitted by my mother. They've both shrunk. It's not B's fault. It's his natural curiosity. But I couldn't help feeling angry and upset. [B, 11 months]

Learning to control her temper may be difficult, but it means that the mother at home with her baby is not necessarily "stuck" and "stagnating." Relating to her baby motivates her to develop in many directions.

Nor is she isolated from the rest of society. People sometimes assume that if a mother isn't earning her living, she is somehow "outside" society, without a social role. Yet mothers have a very precise social role. Because there is no word for it, mothers may not recognize it. They may be unaware not only of how often they fulfill it but also of how often they worry about whether they are doing it well enough. They are intermediaries. They relate both to their children and to other people. They often have to explain subtle social situations in simple language to their children. But they also find themselves explaining and sometimes apologizing for their children to other people.

Mothers do it all the time. Here is a mother with her twin girls outside a café on Hampstead Heath. I overheard her first trying to explain the feelings of one of her twins to an adult called Maggie, and then trying to explain her conversation with Maggie to the twin:

> G wants to say hello to your dog. She's scared of dogs, but in her own way she's trying to overcome it. Come here, G, *lovely* dog, good boy, good boy! All right, Maggie, we'll meet up later at the playground. Bye, see you there! Oh dear, oh *dear,* what a pity, G! Yes, I know, the dog's gone. Dog's gone with Maggie. It's all right, we'll see the dog later at the playground. We'll say hello to the dog again. Yes, we will. Oh, *poor* G, what a pity the dog's gone! Let's get packed up quickly and then we can go to the playground. [Twin girls, about 2 years]

Mothers often find themselves in this kind of position. It involves observation, sensitivity, and tact. They need to be quick to perceive misunderstandings and clear-thinking enough to sort them out.

> You become *porous* as a mother. I'd no idea I could be so sensitive to the way people react to me and my child. [G, 7 months]

Sometimes the patience, the sensitivity, and the tact snap. A mother who surprises herself by how patient she can be with her child can feel equally surprised by how much anger she can muster against other people in defense of her child. Mothers often say they had no idea they could be roused so powerfully.

> It makes me more assertive as a person. The little unimportant things fall away. I've even told my dad what I thought of him. I mean, before having B, I was a daddy's girl! [B, 9 months]

> I was getting on the bus with B in the stroller when two elderly ladies appeared from nowhere and started pushing me out of their way. B was nearly pushed into the road. It was mad. I got really angry, and put my arms out to stop them. I'd never have dared a year ago. [B, 10 months]

People sometimes suggest that it would be good for mothers to go out without their babies to get a break from all the care and responsibility. This sounds like a kind idea, but during the baby's first year it may not work. We saw in chapter 9 how strongly a mother may want to stay close to her baby. If she goes out without her baby, she often remains intensely aware of being a mother.

> I went out with a girlfriend to a pub. It was the first time I'd left G like that. It was half an hour before I could really listen to what my friend was saying—you know how totally

involved you are with the baby. And there were guys looking at us. My friend pointed it out to me. I really didn't notice. I'm not in the market now. I'm a *mom!* [G, 7 weeks]

When G was younger, I was out with my friend and I said: "I'll have to get back now. G is crying." Then I really heard what I was saying. I was surprised at myself. How could I *possibly* know that G was crying? But we went back home, and she *was.* [G, 7 months]

I went to a hardware shop, and I felt funny without G. I ended up buying everything wrong: wrong paint, wrong stripper, and wrong brushes. [G, 7 months]

It is when a mother tries to bridge her two worlds that she realizes how much she has developed. She may have rethought many of her earlier assumptions. Her pace of life may be slower, and she may feel more practical, grounded, and better able to focus on issues that she perceives as important. Her employer may not realize or appreciate this. In *Toward a New Psychology of Women,* Jean Baker Miller argues that mothers develop new abilities that make them very capable employees.[10] But few employers seem to welcome them back as *mothers.* So many mothers feel there is an unbridgeable gap between mothering and, as one mother phrased it, "the jagged and sharp world of work."

I had to go to a meeting at my old job. I felt overwhelmed. It was like my two lives meeting. I couldn't connect them. It was an overwhelming experience. [B, 4 months]

I've completely lost my confidence. That's what being a mother has done to me. I think back to my old life—I did acting and stuff—and no way could I do that now! [G, 6 months] [But she was wrong. Soon after saying this, she was chosen to act the part of a mother in a play, and her acting career took off from there.]

I went back to work for a few weeks, for the first time, after four years of being a mother. I work with a lot of equipment, so I quickly set it all up. But everyone else was really leisurely and asked if I wanted a coffee. Then—I couldn't *believe* it—they decided they'd all go out for a drink. My boss has three children under five, and I bet his wife is at home thinking he's having a hard day at work. I used to think it was hard. But now, after being a mother, it seems incredibly slow and easy. [B, 4 years; G, 1 year]

An essential difference is that employment usually means working to agreed dates and times. Meanwhile the slow-paced life with a baby may feel rhythmical rather than organized by the clock.

I used to love my work. Now it's not the same. I see my clients for one hour, and it's a room that is only along a corridor. But by the end of the hour, I'm desperate to hold B. And something's changed. It takes me half an hour to calm down and be with him again. I keep feeling it's only an hour of work, and I shouldn't feel this. But I start to "tune out" the night before. I think: "I'd better get my clothes ready and get a good night's sleep. I'm *working* tomorrow." So I'm not being together with B. And this day will never repeat. I'm hoping to have another baby in a few years. But another baby will be a different baby, not

> B. Life with a baby goes in waves like the sea. [She gestured a slow, wavy motion with her hand.] And work is all . . . [She briskly gestured slicing bits of something.] [B, 6 months]

Again, this is not a permanent change. Becoming a mother does not turn a woman off her work for the rest of her life. Many mothers describe times when they "surface." They seem to emerge from a more gentle state with new energy and want to resume working. This seems to be when they feel their children have reached a particular level of independence. Mothers who don't want to return to work seem, when one listens to them, to feel needed by their children. We should not assume that they are neurotically clinging to motherhood. They belong to a generation of women who take their working lives for granted. When they feel ready, their desire to return to work sounds like a passionate one.

> I work for a few hours a week. It makes a huge difference. It's like coming out of a bubble. It's a complete shift of focus. [G, 7 months]

> I feel that B is a real person now. He's not the same as me. And now, for the first time, I'm not thinking about him all the time. I've started to think about me, and what to do with my life. [B, 9 months]

Mothers who are ready to resume work have come a long way from being shocked beginners with newborn babies.

> Every week I say to myself: "It's better now." Next week I'll probably say it again. [G, 4 months]

> It's like when you've been ill and you say: "I'm *much* better now." Then, a month later, you realize that you weren't really better, even then. Being a mother is like that. I feel it's much easier now. But I'll probably move on and have to say it again. [B, 11 months] [That's exactly what she did.]

Part of this change is accepting her new identity. On the surface, she has become a mother, and this should be an obvious truth. But it takes some getting used to.

> My mom came with me to the hospital for B's birth. Just before B was born, I heard a doctor say: "Let's lift Mom onto the delivery table." I know it sounds weird, but I was like: "Why are they lifting my *mom* onto the delivery table?" I wasn't thinking of myself as a mom. [B, 4 months]

> I don't feel like a mommy yet. Then I hear myself say: "Sorry, darling, Mommy's going to change your diaper. I know you hate it. Isn't Mommy silly, doing such a stupid thing!" And I have to do a double-take. On some level, I *am* G's mother. [G, 3 months]

> It's been dreamlike, becoming a mother. I can't really believe it's me. Now G says "Mommy!" and it's beginning to sink in that it's not *my* mother. G means *me!* [G, 16 months]

Then, as they look back, mothers find that their previous lives, before they had their babies, now seem remote and unreal.

> Now, when I look back, I can't think what I used to do on the weekends before I had B. [B, 4 months]

> I can't imagine how I used to be. What did I do in the evenings before I had G? I must have had so much time. [G, 12 months]

This is not a mechanical failure of memory. Mothers change profoundly. It then becomes hard to recall the women they used to be.

> It's like shedding an old skin. I'm amazed at who I am now. [B, 7 weeks]

> I love my profession and I used to think I wouldn't want a child. But the moment G was born, I thought: "This is the Real Me." [G, 5 months]

> It's made me a nicer person. I've become much more understanding of other people. [G, 10 months]

> I feel fulfilled. I was going to take two weeks settling G and then start my business, which I would love to do. But I haven't started yet. Being a mother is a whole different mind-set, and I've found that it helps to accept that this is a change in my whole life. [G, 13 months]

It seems a paradox that a mother can start by feeling that she is losing herself in her new life with her baby. Yet, a few months later, she may realize that she has discovered more of her self.

These last four months have been the best months of my life. I've learned a richer kind of happiness than I knew before. [B, 4 months]

People used to say I hadn't got a sense of humor. I don't know. There never seemed very much to laugh about when I was younger. But now I laugh every day. G makes me laugh. We have such *fun* together. [G, 9 months]

I wouldn't sing by myself. I wouldn't go dancing through the house by myself, singing: "Oh, you're such a *lovely* baby." [B, 11 months]

B is such a joy to be with. I haven't laughed so much since the day I was born. Every day he does something new, and I love him so much. [B, 11 months]

I've done all sorts of jobs, and I've enjoyed them. But motherhood is the first thing I've done to the best of my ability. I'm not perfect, but I feel I'm doing the best I can. I thank God for motherhood, for letting me have the chance to work like this. [B, 2 years; B, 6 weeks]

I want to sum up this change, but the right words are eluding me. Whenever I'm sitting with a group of mothers, everything seems so obvious that there doesn't seem anything to explain. Back home at my desk, it's so different that I feel I have lost it.

It is only by remembering some of the negative statements that have been published on the experience of being a mother that my anger is roused and, with it, some words. There is a book by Jane Price, a psychiatrist and psychotherapist, for example, titled *Motherhood: What It Does to Your Mind.* Chapter 9 is called

"The Devastating Effects of Motherhood."[11] There is no balancing chapter on the beneficial effects of motherhood for a woman's mind. It seems an outrageous omission.

Babies and children are highly intelligent. It is their job to take nothing, absolutely *nothing,* for granted. It is extremely beneficial for our minds to try to keep pace. "Nature speaks with a thousand voices, and we have only begun to listen," write Ilya Prigogine and Isabelle Stengers in *Order Out of Chaos.*[12] But mothers certainly haven't "only begun to listen." Mothers who study their babies have been making order out of chaos for millennia before present-day chaos theory scientists have attempted to do so. As their children grow, mothers find themselves faced with the most unexpected questions about technology, spirituality—especially life after death—semantics, moral philosophy . . . anything. Surely this means that we are not devastating our minds. We are really using them.

> *Child:* Mommy, how does this [concrete] step be so flat? Does a man roll it?
>
> *Mother:* Yes. No, I've got no idea. I don't know how to answer. How *do* steps get so flat? B's always asking me questions that I can't answer. [B, 3 years]

The wisdom we learn from our children is that we don't need to be encyclopedias of information. We don't need to be perfect. This mother took her child's question seriously and gave him an honest reply. Walking down the steps behind the two of them, I could see B looking completely relaxed and satisfied at her answer. I could sense his warm affection for her. From his point of view, she was perfect enough.

This is a brief look at an exciting field. There is so much more one could say. But surely we have to acknowledge that having a baby *can't* mean a woman must be "stagnating" or "stuck at home" in "mind-numbing" activities. Relating to her baby provides infinite opportunities to develop herself in many directions.

Moreover, as she changes, all her other relationships change with her. New mothers mention especially their relationships with the fathers of their babies and with their own mothers. We consider both in the next two chapters.

eleven

snapping at my partner

Many women say that with hindsight they can see how unprepared they were to become mothers. Is it the same for men? The sociologist Brian Jackson interviewed a sample of one hundred first-time fathers. He commented: "The unreality of their preparation for parenthood was breathtaking."[1] Whatever happens when such an unprepared couple has a first baby?

From talking to mothers and from reflecting on what they describe, I have been able to draw a few general conclusions. This chapter is a tentative step into a large subject. Conversations with mothers are inherently biased because the father is not there to offer his view. Mothers often use the safety of a discussion circle to voice strong and negative feelings. Sometimes they add: "But that's only part of the picture." This chapter is written with this assumption. I feel certain that many mothers take for granted their basic love for their partners. But their love does not seem problematic, so mothers leave it unsaid.

Mothers often describe how tender and close they felt to

their partners before the birth of their first-borns. The coming baby felt like a natural affirmation of their love. Also, long before the baby's birth, many first-time mothers felt awash with maternal feelings, which they then showered on their partners. They were shocked at the sensational headlines that journalists use, such as: HAVING A BABY CAN RUIN YOUR MARRIAGE. Surely their love, which generated their babies, would be enhanced when those babies were born.

After the baby's birth, couples quickly discover their minimal level of preparation. During a home visit that I carried out as a breastfeeding counselor, a father put the whole situation especially clearly:

> *Father:* We were very well prepared for the birth. We'd read everything, we'd been to a childbirth workshop, and we'd talked through our birth options with each other. But we hadn't turned the page and got onto the next chapter. Suddenly reality was upon us. [G, 1 week]

This father talked about "we" and "us." In the weeks that followed, he would be more likely to say "I" and "she." A couple can feel as though they are walking on separate roads. It may seem unbelievable that they feel more separate than close and tender to each other now that they have a joint child. Some people have compared the baby to a "wedge" driving the couple apart. But it's easy to blame the baby. True, the couple relationship feels different. However, there may be a different way to explain it. What few parents mention is the momentous change that comes about when a two-person relationship suddenly opens out into a three-person one. It can be a surprise to discover what a strong presence the newborn is. He is a definite person, not to be discounted, right from his birth.

A two-person relationship is radically different from one of three people. A two-person relationship has a kind of elegant symmetry, whereas this three-person one is complex. It is not symmetrical. The two parents have a biological relationship with their child but a consensual relationship with each other. In addition, the three-person relationship can operate as three separate individuals, or one set of three people, or three sets of pairs (mother/father, mother/child, and father/child). Additional children increase the complexity, but the change is not as great as the two-into-three change. This doesn't necessarily drive a "wedge" into the marriage. But it certainly changes it.

New parents don't often consider this change. Their attention is usually on practical matters, so they may continue to think in two-person terms for months. In this, the "other" person is especially important, whereas in a three-person relationship, *two* other people are especially important. Typically, a new father may try to hold on to the old couple relationship, as it was before their baby was born, whereas a new mother may form an exclusive dyad with her baby, which closes out her partner. This situation makes it easy for one partner to feel undervalued by the other.

It is confusing because a mother is usually trying to create enough "attention space" for their newborn (see pages 214–21). Before the birth, the father may have enjoyed some of the "attention space" himself. His expectant wife may have lavished her motherly feelings on him and kept his wishes at the front of her consciousness. So after the baby is born, the father can feel rudely and inexplicably ejected. Suddenly the baby can seem to be occupying "his" special place. Instead of both parents trying to identify the father's own new and unique place in the triangle, both may perceive the father as competing for affection with his baby.

F was coming toward me to give me a kiss, but what I saw was this pockmarked face with all these wrinkles. It shows what my frame of reference has become. I'm besotted with B. I feel as if I've swapped one man in my life for another. [B, 2 months]

We were so close before the birth. Now all my love is for G. F is losing out. [G, 6 months]

Sometimes F says: "Oh, that's what you *used* to cook." I used to make things for him. Now if I cook, it's for B. [B, 12 months]

A mother and her partner might be able to make intelligent adjustments to their relationship, if only they understood it. After all, couples make all kinds of similar physical adjustments. For example, a breastfeeding mother may decide she needs to have their baby in bed with her at night. This is a visible change. The father can see what the mother has decided. He can challenge it, adapt to it, or even enjoy the novelty. Some fathers cuddle up as a threesome, while others decide they must get undisturbed sleep on the sofa. However, one can't solve a problem if one hasn't identified what it is. Many mothers report that their partners experience the intimate mother/baby relationship as a personal affront. This misunderstanding may continue long after the early months.

I don't think F has made the shift. To me, G is the center of our lives. To F, she's still an add-on. [G, 7 months]

A while back, F and I went to a movie. On the drive back, F started telling a story, and we almost had a quarrel

> about it because I couldn't listen. I was like . . . [she gestured someone running.] . . . to get back to G. [G, 8 months]

> My husband keeps complaining that when he's in the middle of talking to me, if B makes a noise, I turn my head to see what he's doing. But I *need* to check if B is all right. [B, 14 months]

It can't be easy for the father. At first, he may imagine that his partner is close to their baby, whereas he is not. Yet his baby has been listening to his (the father's) voice, even in the womb. There are many reasons why a father could feel close to his newborn. But this is not generally recognized. "In our culture," wrote Ursula Owen, "mothering is a job and fathering is a hobby."[2] His own father may well have only seen his children in his leisure time. But fathers today often seek a much more active fatherly role than hobby making. Charlie Lewis, a psychologist who conducted a research study on fathers, wrote that "the experience of fatherhood is usually intense."[3] So there may be a time when a father is struggling to pioneer his new role.

A new father can feel short of love. He may be at work during the day and come home in the evenings, tired and no doubt associating home with a place of comfort. Unknown to him, his partner may have spent hours of love, patience, and self-restraint with their baby, with no adult to witness and confirm how well she has done. She can feel impatient with herself for having spent all day "doing nothing." She is glad to see her partner, but on another level, he can seem like a criticism of her. He returns from the "at work" world that they used to share. He has had an entire day of "doing something." Many women are astonished at how furious they can feel toward their partners. The partner searches his conscience and cannot imagine what he has done to deserve this reception.

> I'm just watching the clock for F to come home. Only when he gets in, I let fly at him: "Get me some food! *NOW!*" It's only just occurred to me, as I speak, that I'm doing to him what G's been doing to me all day. I'm passing it on. I want F to mother me. [G, 5 weeks]

> F belongs to the work community. He comes home and it's after five-thirty, so he likes to stretch out and relax. But for me, now I'm a mother, five-thirty *never* comes! [B, 4 months]

> *First mother*: I was furious with F. I went for him with a knife. He has a high-flying city job. He doesn't understand what I do. [B, 2 months]
>
> *Second mother*: Sex on the sofa, dinner on the table, and intelligent conversation? [B, 4 months]
>
> *First mother: Exactly!*

> I envy F. He gets up and he has his bath and puts his suit on. And off he goes. I can't do that. [B, 7 months]

We have already seen how much a mother has to learn about her baby. In moments of anxiety, she may no longer have the traditional female support network to comfort her. There are few words to tell her she is doing as well as anyone could expect at this stage, so she can suppose that she should be managing much better. She has heard of "terrible twos" and temperamental teens. Yet here she is, failing at the "easy" part, caring for a tiny baby. Many mothers admit that they displace their sense of inadequacy onto their partners.

> When B is crying, my confidence seems to go and I shout at F. [B, 3 months]

> We had a row this morning, because F complained that I spoke sharply to him. I said: "I *know* I talked to you sharply. I can't help it. I'm worried about G." [G, 4 months]

> G woke up a lot last night, and this morning when I woke up, I wanted to *kill* my partner. [G, 7 months]

> When G keeps crying and there's nothing I can do to calm her, I find I want to snap at my partner. [G, 14 months]

Mothers can be shocked by the strength of their feelings. Maybe the journalists were right after all. It can be especially difficult if a couple regard their mutual tiredness and irritability as final, rather than as a stage of adjustment. Mothers can feel reassured when they compare notes with each other. They can laugh at themselves and regain a sense of proportion.

> I am a new person, and F is a new person, and I'd really like some time for these two new people to learn to know each other. [B, 6 months]

> Men have difficulty coming to terms with having a baby—and no one talks about it, and there's nothing to help them. [9 months]

> But I know F's as tired as I am. I can see he works his socks off to bring in money to support us. I wish I could bite my tongue. [B, 11 months]

New parents often apologize for getting angry with each other. Frequently, the underlying difficulty is getting used to the three-way nature of their new relationship. It is easy to get stuck here because a tired and underconfident new parent may not feel like facing something new. So it's simpler to have another shout at the partner.

Many couples try to restrain their anger when their sensitive babies are present, but this means there isn't much opportunity to explore feelings. Also the ultimate option of walking out would now cause pain to this new and innocent little person.

> I had a flaming fight with F. After he'd left for work, I felt like walking out and leaving a note saying: GONE TO PARIS. Then I looked at G—and I suddenly realized that I *couldn't*. [G, 7 months]

Learning to be a parent is a challenge. Before their baby was born, the couple probably dealt with challenges by affirming each other. Now, as parents, both feel uncertain. Neither may feel strong enough to affirm the other. It is easy for a mother both to hurt and to be hurt by her partner.

> Some partners ignore their babies. Mine is just the opposite. He comes bounding in after work, gives me a peck on the cheek, and says: "Oh, *G,* I'm *back*!" G gets a real kiss and a cuddle, and I'm sitting there thinking: "Is that all *I* get?" [G, 7 months]

> When we thought G had whooping cough, I thought she was going to die. It was really awful. But when we got back from the hospital and the crisis was over, F and I were furious with each other. He shouted at me: "How can you be such a drama queen?" And I shouted back: "Why can't you be more sympathetic?" And the next day we talked about divorce. It was awful. [G, 8 months]

> F gets home truly exhausted, and he checks his post and e-mails first. I *do* understand that. And I bite back my impatience for him to be nice to me. It lasts about a *minute*. And then I've said something horrid about him putting B and me last. But F works so hard, it makes me cry to see him working so hard. We spend our precious time together, which is so short, just snapping each other's heads off. [B, 12 months]

But surely the liveliest baby has to get some sleep sometime. Then, can't the parents make up, jump into bed, and make love? New parents can be surprised to discover that sex, which enabled most of them to become parents, may have become another source of misunderstanding. It can be very hard for a woman to see her partner's perspective or to imagine how he could seem so obtuse about her own.

After the baby's birth, the father's life often has not radically altered. He usually retains the same job as before. His body, especially, remains unchanged. There is more continuity. It is understandable that a father might see sex as a reaffirmation of the couple's earlier relationship. He may feel tired and disoriented, and may long for the reassurance and pleasure of their sexual association.

The mother, however, has been pregnant for nine months and has recently given birth. This means a major physical change. Some women want sex soon after they have given birth and get irritable because having a baby offers much less opportunity for it. But most new mothers today need to recover after the birth, physically and emotionally. They often say that they feel as if they no longer desire their partners sexually. This absence of desire may be partly a form of natural self-protection, ensuring that women are not overwhelmed by sexual passion and don't try to make love before recovering. Some women are afraid to try sex again, especially if they have had stitches after the birth. The typical quarrel arises when the parents feel close and affectionate, so the father suggests or indicates that they make love. The mother replies or indicates that she still doesn't feel like it. He concludes that he no longer has the power to excite her, while she is sure he cares only about his pleasure and has no sympathy for her physical well-being.

> Where has the couple gone? F and I make a good team for looking after B. But that's *it*. There's no time for romance. [B, 5 months]

> When F and I are talking and I can feel a cuddle coming up, I feel so afraid it will lead to something else that I quickly jump up to fetch something. F is much more keen to make love than I am. And yet I keep thinking of all those mothers whose husbands walk out, after the baby. It has crossed my mind that it could happen to us. I don't want to be one of those. [B, 6 months]

> After breastfeeding B all night, I long for F to touch me, but not a sexy, fluttery touch. That sexy feeling is all gone.

I yell at him if he tries that; I can't help it. A firm touch is all right. [B, 9 months]

I've lost all libido. F is very understanding. He's got past the angry stage. He doesn't even ask for it anymore. But I feel terrible. I don't feel I want it. Every night, I think: "Tonight, I'll do it." But I never want to. [G, about 12 months]

F thinks we'll never have sex again. I keep explaining that we *will*, when I stop feeling so tired. [B, 12 months]

Mothers often complain that they are "too tired" for sex. Many feel exhausted from broken sleep. But, in addition, from the way they talk about sex, it is clear that they feel demoralized and confused. In more traditional cultures, motherhood is a desirable state, something to be proud of. A mother is regarded as the embodiment of female mystery and beauty. Childbirth is seen to enhance her, both spiritually and physically. Breastfeeding reveals her power to nourish their child. This means that while the relationship opens out to include the baby, there is also a new and exciting development between the couple.

This doesn't seem to happen to many mothers in the West today. As girls, they have been encouraged to develop more masculine abilities. So when they become mothers, instead of feeling beautiful, women often say they feel overweight, out of condition, tired, and unkempt. How can any woman whose body feels changed, yet who perceives herself in these negative terms, respect herself? How can she be in a good mood for sex? One mother approached this subject from a feminist angle when she said:

> I can tell from the way F looks at me that he's thinking: "My woman produced this baby." He's proud of something I couldn't help. And I can play into that. I say: "Oh, F, this fuse has blown." And he's flattered and fixes it. Of course, if I was on my own, *I'd* do it. [B, 8 months]

But surely her partner was right to feel proud of her. Childbirth both is and isn't "something I couldn't help." There are all kinds of reasons for feeling proud of giving birth. Even if it didn't go according to plan, I know from working as a counselor that one can usually find plenty to enable a woman to hold up her head again, and see that, given the challenges that the birth gave her, she responded well. Childbirth is both ordinary—and a miracle—every time. A couple could be amply justified for feeling proud of their initiation into parenthood.

Unfortunately, this is not how either may feel, especially a new mother. As a culture, we do not seem to value maturity. We admire endlessly the new and unused. This goes for sexuality too. A mother may look at a groomed woman who hasn't experienced childbirth yet and see this less mature woman as somehow more "sexual" than she is. The groomed woman is regarded as "beautiful" and therefore sexually desirable. New mothers often talk about all the cosmetic aids they think they ought to use to make themselves look "desirable again." As mothers, they seem to feel they have become *less* attractive.[4] It is heartbreaking to discover how few of them seem to feel that despite their tiredness and lack of cosmetics, they *are* beautiful. This does not seem to be any one mother's individual problem but an attitude that is inhibiting a whole generation. This demoralized sense of a mother's sexuality surely contributes to feeling "too tired for sex."

Unlike their mothers and grandmothers, women are generally relaxed and honest about discussing sexual practice. This encourages them to laugh at themselves, and some of them discover how much they do want to resume making love.

> I was missing sex. So we've got a "shag rota." You find a friend with a baby that you can be honest with, and they take your baby for an hour and a half one Sunday afternoon, and you have theirs on the alternate one. That really works for us. It used to be "our" time before B was born. I really felt the need to make sex a priority. [B, 3 months]

> I had a nice cuddle with F last night. We'd been bickering a lot. It was important for us to be more than just B's parents. [B, 7 months]

> I come really quickly now. I don't know how to put it into words. It's a wonderful thing. Sex seems really potent since having G. [G, 8 months]

However, for mothers today, sex is definitely not a cure-all. It can leave too many feelings unacknowledged. Yet when couples manage to talk about their feelings the tension can resolve, even after all the hasty insults exchanged. They feel close again. Talking seems to be the crux of it.

When a father expresses his understanding and appreciation of his wife in her new role as mother, it moves her profoundly. His kind words, as she quotes them, can bring tears to the eyes of a whole circle of mothers. Each wants that kind of affirmation. Fathers speak from a unique perspective, and their praise is dynamic.

> My partner went abroad for a week, and when he came back, he could see how content B was, and then it was

obvious that it was all because of me. He said some really nice things about me. I *treasure* them. It was fantastic. I felt such energy, being appreciated. Suddenly nothing was too much for me. [B, 2 months]

F looks after G for three hours, and he expects praise afterward. I look after G all *day.* So one day I asked F to praise me. So he said: "I think you're a wonderful mother." I said: "No, no, tell me *exactly* what you see me doing that you think is wonderful." So now he tells me without my asking, in the middle of the night, when I'm tearing my hair out. He'll say: "I don't know how you do it. You hold G so patiently—I just wish you'd been my mother and I could have been your baby." Then I feel I'm in the stars. [G, 6 months]

When B was seven months old, I thought that F might be having an affair. I've spoken to several of my friends since, and this seems quite a common reaction. He didn't treat me in the way he used to, and he always came back from work very late. I was *sure* there was someone else. So one evening, we had a long conversation. I told him how much I saw he had changed toward me. I said maybe it was time to separate and go different ways. Then he said he was very surprised, and he said to me: "How *could* you think that I don't . . .?" [She was clearly going to finish ". . . love you?" But there was a sudden flurry among the mothers listening to her story, as if each was trying to control a welling up of tears. Perceiving this, the mother stopped. It looked to me as if this group of listening mothers, most of whom had described bickering with their own partners, suddenly recognized that the underlying love that the mother was describing was probably true of their own partners too.] [B, 4 years]

The reverse can be equally and horribly true:

My husband told me off the other day. It was only a tiny thing. The baby was wet and I hadn't noticed. But you feel so vulnerable as a mother. I went to pieces when he told me that, I really did. [G, 8 weeks]

Well, if it's that simple, why aren't men falling over themselves to tell their partners what good mothers they are? Surely there is a lot of good in every mother. The difficulty is the one of language, described in chapter 1. Most fathers are at work all day. Many find that the birth of each baby increases their sense of responsibility, which leads them to work harder, for longer hours than before. Then, if a father is absorbed by his work, it becomes difficult for him to know what there is to praise. His wife finds it hard to explain. Her achievements are subtle and often have no word to alert him to all she has learned. Her daily life with their baby can seem remote from his daily life. He can feel a stranger when he comes home to her.

Me: Do you think your boyfriend feels unsafe, being left in charge of G?

Mother: Oh, it's a *shame* because he used to be the same as me. When G was born, he took three weeks off. We did everything together. Then he went back to work, and he works a really long day. He only gets back at eleven at night. He's a step behind me now, and I think he's lost all his confidence. He does things we *used* to do, and I have to stop myself saying: "Well, actually, we don't *do* that anymore." [G, 7 weeks]

My partner had one week off for paternity leave, and it was great. He loved it, and he loved being with B and me. When he had to go back to work, I think he felt *bereaved.* [B, 3 months]

Mothers often find it hard to tell their partners what they have learned about caring for their babies. Fathers can quickly feel discouraged about their own competence. If a new father only has short periods (awake) at home, his partner can seem so much more capable than himself.

My husband always brings G to me when she cries. [G, 5 months]

My partner says: "I can't get G's cardigan on. Oh, I give up!" I say: "You *can't* give up. G's got one arm in a sleeve. You've got to finish it." [G, 9 months]

I went to an evening class on Wednesday, and I think F got into a panic. G has learned to scream, and she screamed for an hour. She was asleep when I got home, and F was in a state. He forgot to offer her food. He forgot that I was only ten minutes' walk away. G's crying really *got* to him, and he couldn't think what to do. [G, 9 months]

F has two children from an earlier marriage. Before B was born, he was always telling me he was an experienced father. But after we had B, I noticed there was none of this "experienced father" bit. When B cried, he was as confused as I was, and he'd pass B to me and say: "*You* deal with it!" [B, 11 months]

It is tempting for a mother to criticize her partner for knowing even less about child care than she does. Some mothers recognize the need to resist this temptation.

It's so hard not to keep checking: "Have you done what I asked? Have you done it *properly?*" [B, 3 months]

You have to bite your tongue, sometimes, when F dresses B and you see he's put unmatching socks on. It's not the important thing. [B, 6 months]

Mothers often describe how reluctant they feel to trouble their partners with requests for help with child care. They can remember the stresses of going to work themselves. Most feel that they ought to protect their partners. At the same time, this self-imposed protectiveness doesn't seem fair to themselves.

I begged my partner to use our car to get to the station. Then I walked to the station to pick up the car afterward. I kept thinking: "Hey, I shouldn't be doing this. I've just given birth to a premature baby. Why can't *he* walk to the station?" But I feel I have to look after him. [B, 4 weeks]

When G cries and F can't comfort her, I say: "Oh, give her to me!" because I know F has to go to work the next day. And I feel quite benevolent at the moment I say it. But when F actually hands G to me and walks out of

> the room, I feel this *unbelievable* resentment. And our relationship's been going down and down. It's not just my baby. It's *his* baby too. [G, 8 weeks]

Yet when fathers do share the care of their babies, they get better at it, and their confidence increases. This is not to promote any idea of the "new man" or to tell any man how to be a good father. Not all men feel easy about sharing child care, and very few men seem to have had fathers who modeled this way of being a father. There must be a spectrum of ways for fathers to show their love. However, when you listen to what mothers say, it is clear that they feel they shared a lifestyle when both were earning money. They were part of the traditional "man's world." So now it seems logical to expect their partners to take a share in the traditional "woman's world."

> When F comes home in the evening, my attitude is that I've been doing a full-time job all day, looking after B. And he's doing a full-time job, earning money. So the evenings are shared, fifty-fifty, looking after B. [B, 4 months]

When men share in child care, they can start to appreciate its nameless difficulties. This helps them to appreciate their partners much better.

> The good part about our holiday is that my partner really understands now how hard it is looking after a baby. He used to *say* he understood, but he obviously hadn't *really* understood. He said to me: "I thought you could just leave her to play for two hours while you did everything." He found he couldn't go down to the beach when he wanted to or read a book. Or he wanted to go out, and she

started crying. So we couldn't go till we'd sorted her out. He understood, then. [G, 4 months]

Again, it might seem that the solution to the quarrels is for men to take part in child care. But sometimes this leads to another misunderstanding. Mothers often assume that the "right" way to look after the baby is *their* way, whereas many men develop styles of their own. Obviously we aren't all alike. But, for example, women frequently complain that men seem to focus on one task at a time, whereas they do many tasks simultaneously.

My husband's a computer engineer. He's not used to babies. I think he thinks that if you just tinker around with the baby for a bit, you can find out what's wrong and put it right. But B keeps crying. I think F has had enough after half an hour. He'd like to pack B away in a box and send him back. [B, 3 weeks]

F can cut off. I can't watch the news the way he can. Half of me is thinking of G and if she's all right. [G, 5 months]

Men are so different. I come home when F has been looking after B, and the dirty dishes are still there, and how come B's socks are both lost? [B, 10 months]

I think F has a kind of chip missing. He loves B, but he never remembers to do things. I have to leave him a list when I go out, like to make sure to get some food into B. [B, 14 months]

But often this seems to be based on a misunderstanding. A baby doesn't need two mothers. The father's alternative style may be exciting. Often a baby seems to associate eating with his mother. He enjoys being entertained by his father and seems willing to hold out for the next eating session until his mother comes back. So the baby may well not be giving his father "I'm hungry" signals. The father starts to develop some happy, carefree ways of being with his child—and is suddenly reprimanded by his anxious partner. It takes time to realize that the baby is relating differently to each of them.

Some men respond sensitively to the needs of their babies. Occasionally this can knock the precarious confidence of a mother, as in the next example. But usually it enables her to value him as a father, whom she can trust.

> I feel terrible because I can't stop B crying. My husband can calm him much better than I can. Already I hear this voice in me [she pointed her finger dramatically at her own head] calling: "Failure, *failure!*" [B, 4 weeks]

> G had reflux. It was terrible. She cried nonstop. I couldn't have coped without F. I never thought it would be like that. I saw F as the weaker party. I thought I was the strong one. But after a day with G, I wanted to hurl myself out of a window, while F was calm. [G, 4 months]

> G nearly asphyxiated herself in a restaurant. It was the worst moment of my life. I can't talk about it too much because it still upsets me so much. I really thought I'd lost her. F was in America, and he's usually very laid back. But that night he was trying desperately to telephone us [after she and her mother had taken the baby to a local hospital]. He'd had a dream that G was dead. That's what he dreamed. [She felt immeasurably close to him for

what seemed to her more than mere coincidence.] [G, 6 months]

F and I both love kissing B. And I said I'd be so sad when B got too big and didn't want to be kissed. F said he felt exactly the same. I was really moved that we both felt the same. [B, 6 months]

F has ideas I'd never have thought of. He puts B in the sling, gets on his bike, and goes cycling off with him. I haven't got the confidence to get on a bike. But B really loves it. [B, 8 months]

F can get B to sleep without me. B has an energy surge just before nighttime. F does some serious play with him, and it wears him out. Then B's ready for bed. [B, 14 months]

As well as the baby, the mother may need more looking after. Especially if a mother is breastfeeding, it may be difficult for her to get up, fetch herself some food, and complete the housework as perhaps she used to. Most babies like to be held and carried. This means that a mother is probably holding her baby with one hand for much of the day and trying to do everything else with the other. Two-handed tasks become problematic. Women often describe feeling guilty in the evening if they make demands on their husbands for themselves.

When F gets home and sits down, I can see he looks so tired. And I'm parched, as if I'll die of thirst if I have to wait another minute [a very common sensation after breastfeeding]. So I ask for a drink of water. Then, when he's given it to me, he sits down again, and I can't *bear* to

> ask him to get up again. But there's so many things I want him to do. [B, 3 weeks]

> When F's away [working], it's awful because he's my source of food. [G, 2 months]

> I wish my partner understood what I needed without my having to ask for everything individually. I can hear myself rattling on: "Could you do *this?* Could you do *this?*" And I sound terrible. It's not that he minds. It's just that he doesn't understand. [G, 9 months]

Another change to the relationship is over money. Most women today earn independent incomes. If they decide to care for their own babies, many find themselves financially dependent on their partners. Their morale is low because they feel exhausted and feel that they "look a mess," while "getting nothing done." So the loss of financial independence can be strongly felt.

> I used to earn more than F does. Now I feel I have to go to him, cap in hand, and ask permission to spend *his* money. [G, 6 weeks]

> I like to have all the bills paid. I'd rather *starve* than owe debts. But F owes lots of money. He says: "Leave it to me. Just trust me." But I feel my trust was misplaced. [B, 6 months]

> I thought whatever F earned was *our* money, but now B is here I don't feel that anymore. I think: "I mustn't buy that. *I* didn't earn the money for it." I feel really guilty, though I know F doesn't want me to. So I'd like to get

back to work, to feel my professional self again, and to bring back some money. [B, 9 months]

This dilemma is new. In the past, women had less opportunity to earn, and it was generally accepted by everyone that husbands had to provide for their families. The guilt that so many mothers describe today is unprecedented. It seems to me that mothers might feel more deserving if mothering was appropriately valued. Caring for others combines "a dazzling array of skills in an endless variety of circumstances," as one writer put it.[5]

Some of the most painful disputes between couples arise over how to bring up their child. Their joint ignorance means that these issues were unlikely to have been talked over beforehand.

I feel I've crossed a bridge, and now I'm confident about what I'm doing. But looking back, I realize that the problem was that F and I never sat down and discussed the future. We talked about the birth. But not about having B in our bed, or demand feeding, or whether either of us agreed with sleep training. [B, 6 months]

I realized over Christmas that F and I had never stopped to consider our long-term plans for G. But when we really talked issues through, we both agreed. F was saying he wanted G out of our bed and in a crib, but he doesn't like leaving her to cry or sleep training. So now we are both happy about our style of parenting. It makes everything so much easier. And people keep telling me how happy G looks. [G, 8 months]

I thought F and I knew each other well and talked about everything. But having a baby revealed things we didn't

> know about ourselves or each other, and it would have been so easy just to carry on without talking about them. [G, 9 months]

Most of the arguments seemed to get resolved, provided the couple could make time to talk them over. Listening to each other seemed to restore their trust in each other.

> I was getting very irritable with my partner. We should have talked, but we didn't. Often, I was just so busy looking after B. I was always short of sleep and hungry. Also, I was like: "B's the new person in my life. I don't care about *you* anymore." Then, one day, we had this furious row. We were shouting and crying. It was horrible. But the upshot was that we *did* want to live with each other, and we *did* want our baby. So now things are good between us. [B, 3 months]

> We kept having these competitive arguments of "*I'm* more tired than *you*." "No, *I'm* more tired than *you*!" We both wanted appreciation before we could give it to each other. Deep down, I knew how hard he was working, and he says he knew how hard I was working too. It was really difficult to make the leap from this argument to compassion. I don't know how we did it, or what changed. But it's fabulous now. I'd thought of leaving, but I'd never do that now. [G, 9 months]

Slowly, a new development occurs. The baby starts to express a much more adventurous interest in his father. Once this happens, the father is usually delighted, and the baby seems thrilled to discover a new friend. This makes the threesome more obvious.

In the evenings, my boyfriend and I always chat. Now G joins in! [G, 2 months] F comes home from work, and I can see from his face that's it's been very stressful. Then I give him G, and he goes up and gives her her bath. And when he brings her back down, I can see that he's all . . . [She gestured smoothing her forehead and cheeks.] [G, 7 months]

My daughter cries when her father goes out to work. She crawls in and out of all our rooms, looking for him. [G, 8 months]

B really wants F's admiration, and he always tries to copy what F does. With me, he won't *look* at a glass of water. But when F comes home and he drinks water, B demands a glass—no baby cup for him—and as he drinks he keeps looking at his father as if to say: "Watch me do this!" F's got a court case on, and it's very difficult, but B cheers us both up. [B, 8 months]

We all three sleep in the same bed. B has taken to lying across F's chest and falling asleep. F *loves* it. He's so proud. He says: "B fell asleep on my chest." [B, 9 months]

In countless magazines and manuals for parents, women are advised to nurture the couple relationship. They are told to organize times to be alone with their partners, when they can feel romantic and forget about being parents. But is it so easy to forget such a huge change to their lives?

We celebrated our first wedding anniversary. My mom looked after B, and he was fine. We just went out for dinner for two hours. And—it was probably a bit weak of us—we missed B, and all we could do was to talk about him, and we absolutely *rushed* back afterward. [B, 3 months]

If you can't share your baby with your partner, you can't share all that joy. [B, 4 months]

People say we should get a babysitter and go out and give ourselves a break for a change. But I always think I didn't have a baby to get rid of her in the evenings. We like to have her with us. [G, 6 months]

When F and I went out for our anniversary, all we could talk about was B. [B, 9 months]

This kind of conversation sounds not so much a weakness as a vital event. In it the parents go over and begin to assimilate the reality of their baby. By the simple method of exchanging anecdotes, they can put together some of the daily details into a joint story that makes sense of what they are doing and how they feel as parents. They marvel at their baby, and this helps them to feel more confident about themselves and each other.

Not all parents snap at each other. Some couples regard angry words as purely negative and destructive. They can certainly cause pain. But snapping words can also act like small keys to open the door to greater honesty. When a couple calm down enough to listen to each other and allow each other to qualify or even retract some of their complaints, they find it easier to understand their individual journeys into parenthood. Usually their relationship becomes stronger. The angry words, which might have seemed eternally unforgivable at the time, lose their sting when seen as part of the efforts each is making to turn into a good parent.

twelve

closer to my mother

When a person dies, she or he leaves an empty space among the living. When a baby is born, the opposite happens. A dense family network of people jostle each other to create enough space for the newcomer.

There ought to be a word to describe a family's reshuffle every time a new member is born. One little baby can turn a couple into a family or a "small family" into a larger one. Individuals receive new identities. The baby can make someone his sister, another person his uncle, a third his step-grandparent. In addition, all these people are brought into familial relationships with one another. They get to know each other better, and new friendships may form. But at the same time differences that could be ignored before may now become problematical, precisely because the relationship has become closer.

I've never got on with F's sister, but it didn't matter before. Now I've just realized that she's B's aunt. And their

> mother, whom I don't much like either, is B's other granny. [B, 3 weeks]

As the family starts to redefine their alignments, new dilemmas can arise.

> I know it's crazy, but I'm worrying already [in July] about Christmas dinner. My parents assume that of course we'll have it with them. Whereas my husband says: "*We're* the parents now. Let's have it with us. It's our first Christmas as a new family." Only my mom's already said: "I can't wait for this Christmas," meaning that she expects that *we'll* be there. [B, about 3 months]

As her husband realizes, their baby has turned them into a new family unit, and this means that they add the identities of "father" and "mother" to their existing identities as "son" and "daughter." Both may consider their own parents from this new perspective. A woman's relationship with her mother is usually the oldest relationship that she has known. Up till now, "mother" meant her own mother. Suddenly, this evocative name also refers to herself.

> About ten days before B was born, I was staring at my face in the mirror and I thought: "Soon someone will be looking at this face and this face will mean 'Mommy!' to them. That's unbelievable." [B, 1 week]

> Could my baby ever feel for me what I feel for my mom? [G, 2 months]

A woman's relationship with her mother has a long history and is often complex. Some mothers establish warm friendships with their daughters when they are little. Some are more self-absorbed, and the daughter learns to be concerned for her mother and not to ask much for herself. Sometimes it's the other way around, and the mother effaces herself while all her attention flows to her daughter. A mother may keep comparing herself with her daughter and resent her daughter for being different.

On her side, the daughter probably starts by accepting her mother as the norm. Then she starts to notice the mothers of her friends and begins to see her own mother as one variant among many. She may wish she could patchwork together the best of several mothers to create a perfect one. But there's no such thing as a mother made to order. Instead, her mother, faults and all, may become the most permanent person in the daughter's life. A few mothers walk out on their children. Some adult daughters break off contact with their mothers. But the biological and historical connection remains.

Perhaps the daughter falls in love, as an adult. This shifts her resilient relationship with her mother again. Now the daughter may refer back to what she has learned from her first relationship. Adrienne Rich reflects: "Perhaps all sexual or intimate physical contact brings us back to that first [i.e., maternal] body."[1] The daughter may reassess her childhood as either a good or an inadequate preparation for a mature relationship. In time, it turns out that not all relationships are permanent, and some of these partners may turn into exes. But "mother" does not describe a consensual relationship, so a mother cannot become an ex-mother. Single mothers especially often say that their own mothers provide the most stable relationships of all.

Perhaps the couple conceives a baby just when mother and daughter feel distanced from each other. But once a woman learns that she is pregnant, she can be surprised at how urgently she wants to contact her mother. It doesn't always happen, but it is common.

This may sound strange. Most expectant mothers today are working women. They have learned to become independent and resourceful. Some have more than a decade of career experience to their credit. Yet many were brought up by full-time mothers who, unlike their daughters, had never been financially self-supporting. Many of these daughters have traveled far more than their parents. They have observed different cultures and had their assumptions challenged. They feel they have "outgrown" the world they grew up in. All the more surprising, then, that so many women, when they learn they are pregnant, describe an urgent need to contact their own mothers. If they have grown beyond their parents' world, why are they so determined to reconnect with it? What do they want?

Partly, by definition, an expectant mother's mother is experienced. She has had at least one baby. A first-time mother is a beginner. But if that was all, a woman could turn to any experienced mother. This is more personal. The incredible longing that so many women describe, even those who previously felt estranged from their mothers, seems to happen for several reasons.

First, when a woman bears a baby, she is creating his earliest home, as her mother once created a home for her. Phyllis Chesler describes a mother as "the woman who will always mean 'home' to us."[2] As the expectant mother tries to eat a healthy diet and get enough exercise and sleep to make a good home for her child, and as she tries to help her baby to feel at home after the birth, she may long for the relaxation of being "at home" with her own mother, and for her mother to take care of her. By touching "home base," a woman can draw unexpected strength.

> I was ill and my mom came. I really wanted my mom. I thought: "My mom can handle us." And that made me feel: "*I* can handle us." And she was brilliant. It was great to have her. [B, 12 months]

Perhaps there can also be a deeper sense of coming home. A woman can feel she has enjoyed more opportunities in life than her own mother. For years, she may have seen motherhood as a second-class option. How can motherhood compare with the excitement of holding down a difficult job and affording exotic holidays? But when a woman becomes a mother herself, she can feel herself returning to, and revaluing, the previously despised values of mothering. Suddenly, these values become significant and interesting. Instead of feeling light-years ahead of her mother, she may find her mother a useful guide to help her find her way in a strange new world.

> I've moved a long way away from the way I was brought up. But my mother helps me to see G in a positive way. Sometimes G thrashes about at my breast and hits me with her hand. My mom said: "She's full of energy, she's got character, she's feisty." I find that helps a lot. [G, 4 months]

Part of mothering is slow and wordless. While her baby is in her arms sinking into sleep, a mother often finds she needs to relax and be still, or she will disturb him. Some grandmothers remember doing this themselves. Others discover only as grandmothers how to relax into this stillness, whereas some women always experience it as alien to them. It can be wonderful for a mother if her own mother is one of those who can sit quietly with her at such a moment.

Another reason a woman may long for her mother concerns

all the physical changes that come with pregnancy and childbirth. With her own mother, a woman is often returning to a familiar relationship. Her mother may have taken care of her health all through her childhood and nursed her through a variety of illnesses. This is a tested relationship. Now it will have an added dimension. The daughter needs to find out how much she can ask of her mother on behalf of her child. Some grandmothers are generous, while others can be more demanding.

> When G was born, she had to be held upright all through every night for the first two weeks. My mom took shifts with us [her boyfriend and herself]. She didn't complain. She was brilliant. [G, 2 months]

> My mom is not available for babysitting. I have to laugh at the *idea*. That's just not my mom. When she visits, we have to do what she wants, which means a lot of sitting in restaurants for B. [B, 9 months]

All this can lead to changes in their relationship. The mother's mother belongs to the older generation, though she may not necessarily settle down in that position. Some get into fierce competition with their sons-in-law to prove that they are more successful at looking after the new mother. Others seem to feel equally driven to compete with their daughters to demonstrate that they are "better" mothers. For a new mother who wants nothing but love, comfort, and support, these complications can be exhausting and disappointing.

Most expectant mothers feel anxious about giving birth. They are amazed at how much they can recall details, both good and frightening, which they once heard their mothers describe. In some families, there is a silence over the subject, which usually leaves the impression that it must be too frightening to be talked about. The positive experiences of the mother's mother can definitely help. Sheila Kitzinger remembered how she took confidence from the example of her own mother. She wrote: 'My mother was very small, but gave birth to babies of more than nine pounds. I knew that if she could do it I could do it.'[3]

After the baby is born, the mother may find she spends days and nights simply feeding him. Breastfeeding, which looks so simple, can take time, especially in the early months. Perhaps that is why breastfeeding mothers appreciate the chance to meet in cafés. At last someone else is making tea and sandwiches for them. This used to be the traditional province of the mother's mother. New grandmothers who could offer some care of their daughters were much appreciated.

> *Mother:* When B was born, my mother phoned and said: "I'm coming to see my baby. And I don't mean B."
>
> *Me:* Was that nice or not nice?
>
> *Mother:* Oh, *nice.* You can get so absorbed in your baby, you forget that you exist too. [B, 5 months]

> My mother visited for a week, and she was amazing. I didn't have to wash a single dish. She cleaned and cooked, so I could be with G. [G, 8 months]

Sometimes the mother's mother assumes she knows what kind of help her daughter wants. She doesn't check that her daughter really wants it, and her daughter feels awkward about explaining to her mother that it wasn't what she most needed.

> My mother was staying with us for a week. She did housework. She ironed things. She ironed everything.

> As a result, my partner and I both have drawers of ironed pants and socks. I mean, *I* never iron those anyway. After she'd left, I realized that I'd much rather she'd made lots of meals that I could put in the freezer. Maybe, if she came again, I could mention it to her. [G, 4 weeks]

There is also a fine line between caring for the new mother and infantilizing her.

> My mother thought I should have a rest. I didn't want to, but she insisted and put me down for an hour and a half. Then she woke me up, and I was really bad-tempered, partly because of being woken up and partly because of not wanting to be put down in the first place. [G, 4 months]

A new mother may feel and appear very unsure of herself. Her own mother may feel unnerved by her daughter's uncertainty. She can find it difficult to stand back and recognize that she is now a grandmother, not the mother of the new baby. Some new grandmothers seem to find this impossible. They rush in to give practical help and don't seem to notice how much it expresses their lack of confidence in their daughters.

> My mother really took over my baby. One night she decided it was time he went to bed, and she scooped him up and I was left sitting there. [B, 2 months]

> My mom put G down, and little *rat* here [shaking her baby] fell asleep right away! [G, 4 months] [This mother seemed to have displaced onto her baby her annoyance with her own mother for seeming so much more competent than herself.]

Theories about child care keep changing. This can become a sensitive area. The mother's mother is experienced and knows what worked for her. The new mother is not experienced and is trying out her ideas. The grandmother may feel criticized because her daughter is not doing things the way she did, whereas the new mother may be hurt that her mother keeps "knowing better." The two can get locked into arguments about the best ways of feeding, whether babies need routines, whether a working mother is being selfish at her child's expense, and plenty more. The underlying argument is about whether the mother's mother can support her daughter as she turns into a mother, without feeling that her own way of being a mother was the *only* way.

> Everything is perfectly all right if it's just B and me. But my mother is relentless. She keeps making little comments implying that I'm doing it all wrong. So then I feel as though I am. [B, 2 months]

> My mother's a midwife. That has its good side and its downside. Last week she rang me and asked if B was on solid food yet. I said he didn't seem ready, but her suggestion of baby rice somehow *iggled* its way into my head, and I found it hard to feel confident about my own way of mothering after that. [B, 4 months]

> My mother told me I was "drifting" because I'm at home with B all day. She thinks I should go back to work. I'm not going to phone her again. I can't deal with her. [B, 4 months]

> My mother asked where I was and someone told her I was breastfeeding B. They were all in the next room, and

I could hear my mother say: "*Again?*" B must have got a shock, because my milk supply went bang. [B, 6 months]

I get into a state every time after my mother's visited us. I didn't connect it at the time. I ought to know by now. It leaves me feeling exhausted and that there's nothing good to life. [G, 7 months]

Occasionally a mother breaks off all contact with her mother, soon after the birth of the baby. Usually in such cases the relationship was strained already, before the baby's birth. This is a drastic step, and mothers feel shaken by it. Almost invariably, whatever the long-standing reasons, mothers complain how much their own mothers criticize them as mothers. This seems the final straw. Even then, most daughters describe plans to rebuild part of the relationship later on, if only for their babies' sakes.

The mother's mother often seems unaware that she is now an important person in her daughter's life. Her negative verbal remarks, even light or jocular ones, can feel extremely painful. This is a pity. An experienced mother is a unique resource for her daughter. Even if she is not physically present, memories of her example can provide important contrasts to current ways of mothering. Today, for example, there is strong pressure on women, especially from employers, to return to work soon after childbirth.

My mother always seemed calm and peaceful. She was never in a chaotic rush like me. Our home was tidy, and she was always there. [B, 3 months]

My mother used to keep everything tidy and ordered. I knew where everything was. And she always seemed to

> have time for us. Whereas I always seem stressed. I feel I was brought up with a real sense of home and I wish I could pass that on. [B, 15 months]

Neither grandmother had criticized her daughter. If they had, their daughters might have felt devastated. Both worked, and neither could see any way of re-creating her mother's home. Even so, these memories inspired them. Mothers are good at adapting, and I feel sure that both will have looked for other ways to re-create that vital sense of home that they both remembered.

A mother-in-law's comments can be important too. Before having a baby, the daughter-in-law may not have had much contact with her. Once she has a baby, she is producing a grandchild for both sides of the family. So she becomes more sensitive to what her mother-in-law thinks. A mother-in-law does not have the same biological connection and lifelong relationship with her as with her own mother. Mothers-in-law are usually expected to keep more of a distance. Some new mothers find that their mothers-in-law offer invaluable practical help and bring in welcome fresh ideas on mothering to the family. When the new mother finds their relationship problematic, it is usually because she finds her mother-in-law's behavior intrusive, especially if there seems too little respect for her as the baby's mother.

> My mother-in-law visited last night, and she said: "G will get really spoiled, being picked up whenever she cries." I didn't say anything at the time, but I was awake till two o'clock this morning thinking about it. She upset me. [G, 6 weeks]

> My mother-in-law comes, and B is her first grandson. She's very intense and in his face, talking and singing all

the time. F and I don't exist for her. It's as if we're not there. [B, 2 months]

I call my mother-in-law my *monster*-in-law. She's taken to insulting me. She wants to see G every weekend, and she can't understand why I don't want her to. [G, 3 months]

When my mother-in-law makes pointed remarks like: "B really knows his own mind" or "He can twist you round his little finger," I laugh it off at the time. Then I come home and keep repeating her words and absolutely *seethe*. [B, 5 months]

All these responses show how much a new mother cares about how her mother and mother-in-law perceive her as a mother. Her husband may protest: "I'm the father. Isn't my approval good enough for you?" But her position is many-sided. As well as being related to him, she also belongs to the current generation of mothers. Every generation makes its distinctive contribution to ideas about bringing up children. Yet even when a mother sounds proud and confident about what she and her whole generation are doing, she probably doesn't feel as certain as all that. Until her child is older, she can't tell whether she is doing a good job or not. In her uncertainty, it is understandable that she would value the steadying reassurance of her experienced mother and mother-in-law.

Some women cannot contact their mothers. Especially when their mothers have died, they are very aware of how much they are missing. Often a motherless new mother will explain how fervently she seeks out experienced maternal women to comfort and reassure her.

> [Tears, before this mother could speak] I miss my *mom*. She died ages ago, and probably if she *was* here, it wouldn't be so good as I think. But B's still skinny compared to other babies, and I just want my mom to sit with me and tell me I'm doing all right. [B, 3 months]

Isn't this what every mother wants? Women surely aren't expecting their mothers to walk in with all the answers, as if they were still children. A new mother is living through an unavoidable period of responsibility and uncertainty. Her mother and mother-in-law can give invaluable help if they can find ways to be calm and to learn to have faith in her.

The mother's mother can also provide vital details of the daughter's earliest years. The daughter is now going to extend the family story. From her mother she can learn insights into the story to date. Women whose mothers have died often feel very aware of a hiatus of information which no other person can give them.

> She told me what I had been like when I was little. It was amazing! [B, 2 months]

> B was crying, and my mom was saying it was my fault for taking him into bed with me and being too soft on him. I said: "Look, you're really hurting my feelings. I've been a mother for six months, and you're saying that in six months I'm doing it all wrong." Then she could see how upset I was, and to comfort me, she said that when I was little, she used to have me in bed with her and she'd wrap a bottle of warm milk in a jumper for me, and everything. She was just the same sort of mother underneath! [B, 6 months]

At the same time, a new mother is often fascinated to notice all kinds of details in the way her mother or her mother-in-law is helping her with her baby. Now she starts to imagine how they might have been as mothers.

> My mother keeps trying to keep B happy. He adores her, so it does no harm. But I reckon that's how she was with us. We weren't allowed to be anything that wasn't happy. [B, 11 months]

Mothers also looked back at the mothering they had received. Many had either had counseling and psychotherapy or had learned about it from books or friends. This enabled them to re-evaluate their childhoods, and sometimes to resolve to parent their own children differently.

> I was called a difficult baby. My mother said I cried for a whole year. I feel, if I was insensitive to B, he could easily become what I was. [B, 4 months]

> My mother never cuddled me much. It was never a physical relationship. So I'm trying to put that right for G. I really have to *think* about it. I ask myself: "Would this be a good moment to hold you, G?" It's not spontaneous. [G, 6 months]

> I've been thinking about my parents, especially my mom. I come from a very conventional background, and I am quite a disappointment to my parents. But I went to the same training institute as my mom, and I qualified in the same profession at the same age as her. I married at

> the same age as she did. I've been thinking of her childhood too. She was very unhappy. Maybe what I have done is to repeat the life that she had but to find a different way. Thinking about all this has made me feel much closer to my mom. [G, 10 months]

> My mother was like *her* mother. But I'm trying to break the cycle. I'm different from her. I see it as important to fulfill B's needs. But it's hard to come to terms with the mothering I had. It leaves a void inside, in adulthood. [B, 12 months]

At the same time, this new understanding of themselves helped them to make more sense of their mothers and sometimes grandmothers. A whole history of mothering that stretched back several generations sometimes opened out. New mothers felt able to consider the lives of their own mothers with more compassion than before. They often said they felt they had advantages that their mothers didn't. They saw themselves as part of an unfolding and meaningful story.

> My mother was twenty-one when she had me. I've had B at thirty. When my sister was a baby, she was very ill. My mother went over to the clinic and said: "You've got to help me. I'm afraid of damaging my child." I can see, now, how terrible she must have felt. She meant well. She was just *so* young. [B, 2 months]

> My mother's given me the keys to their house. She seems to perceive me as grown-up now, and that she can trust me. And of course I can understand her so much better now, myself. [B, 3 months]

> It must be hard for them. When we become mothers, we turn them into grandmothers, and maybe many of them don't want to go. I know mine says: "Don't call me 'Granny' It sounds so *old*." [G, 8 months]

Just *because* many mothers had so much paid work and travel experience, they felt they could rediscover their own mothers and appreciate them with new eyes.

> My mother's helped me with B all week. She's absolutely sweet to him. At the end of the week I thanked her for it. And she replied: "That's all right. After all, *you* used to be *my* baby." Then I felt terrible. I'd been a rebellious teenager, and there were all those years when I was so horrible to her. When I was twenty, I screamed at her that I hated her. I thought I meant it then. But when she said that, I suddenly realized. She loves *me* the way I love *B*. [B, 4 months]

This last account brought a rush of tears to the eyes of the mothers listening to her. It crystallized what many of them felt. Several admitted how much they too regretted the way they had treated their mothers. They could understand and respect their mothers so much more now. They saw their mothers not as failed models of perfection but as figures in an episode of the family story, restricted by a particular era. The next installment was in their own hands. They were humbled by their awareness of how difficult mothering could be and were very ready to appreciate all that their mothers had managed to achieve.

epilogue

circles of mothers

Today, a mother can enjoy some freedom of choice over how she brings up her child. While she is finding her feet, at the beginning, this freedom might seem more of a burden than an advantage. However, it allows her to learn not just what "works" but also what her deepest values are and how she can express them in creating her family. This, then, is a precious freedom. It may feel heavy, but it's surely worth it.

Yet mothers themselves sometimes undermine each other's freedom. Over breastfeeding, for example, women can become evangelical. La Leche League has maintained a careful policy of respecting each mother's decision about how she feeds her baby.[1] However, at another, more general breastfeeding meeting that I once went to, the news that a group of expectant mothers had been collectively "converted" to breastfeeding raised a round of loud applause and cheering. This seems shortsighted. Mothers need information to help them make decisions. If the person giving the information also pressures the mothers to decide in a particular way, our precious freedom is undermined.

Two individuals who have chosen differently do not have to be a threat to each other. A mother's real enemy is not the mother who seems to have made all the "wrong" choices. If they can sit down together, relax and talk and laugh, that "wrong" mother can turn into an ally or even a friend. Their joint enemy is anyone who claims that there is only *one* right way to bring up a child. Plato's grand scheme has fortunately remained safe inside the covers of his book, and few people seem aware of it.[2] But Frederic Truby King was authorized[3] to launch a worldwide program for mothers. It's surely just a matter of time before someone else offers to homogenize mothers again.

Truby King was born in New Zealand in 1857. His book *Feeding and Care of Baby* first came out in Britain in 1913 and was reprinted there twenty-four times. Truby King visited Britain and created a training center for mothers in Highgate, North London. He set up other training centers in several English-speaking countries, and also in Russia, Poland, Palestine (as it then was), and China.

Truby King's book provided the basis for training. It amounts to a virtual encyclopedia on the minutiae of child care, and little is left to question. Even the relationship of mother to baby was regulated. Breastfeeding had to be every four hours by day and was forbidden for twelve hours at night. Also "the baby should be picked up at regular intervals and carried about . . . but much harm is done by excessive and meddlesome interference and undue stimulation."[4] I interviewed two women who had been students at the Truby King Centre for Training Mothers in Highgate, which survived until 1951. One of them remembered: "We always had to pick the babies up and turn them from one side to the other in their cribs, by the clock. I used to cuddle them if no one was looking. You got told off if you were seen doing that."

Truby King's influence went far beyond his training centers. Through staff at baby clinics it reached large numbers of new mothers. I recall a woman who bore four children between the 1940s and 1950s, telling me: "Your generation is so lucky. We weren't allowed to pick our babies up when they cried. I can remember standing in the next room, listening to my baby crying, with tears running down my cheeks, because there was half an hour to go before the next feeding." She was alone in her home. No one had the power to see her or prevent her from picking her baby up. But Truby King's regime demanded total obedience from mothers—and often got it.

For centuries there has been a heated debate over whether every mother should look after her children herself or whether all or some mothers should delegate child care to professionals. Jean-Jacques Rousseau, for example, was adamant that mothers should bring up their own babies.[5] Florence Nightingale, a century later, believed babies should be brought up in communal crèches.[6] Like so many adamant people, neither was a mother. Today, new research is reported, often on the front pages of national newspapers, several times a year, promoting one side or the other. Fortunately for all of us, this debate has never been settled. This ought to leave mothers free to make personal choices.

However, today this debate has a special slant. Surely there will always be some mothers who want children but whose commitment to their work is primary. They are aware of making difficult choices when they delegate child care to professionals. Surely there will also always be other mothers who prefer to care for their babies themselves. They try to fit their work around their babies or put their work on hold. But when the subject is debated today, there seems to be an unquestioned assumption that it should be the babies whose lives should be fitted around their mothers' careers. Today, the *majority* of mothers in Britain seem to have joined the first group.[7] They resume work within their child's first year. Is this because virtually all women now prefer work to child care?

A woman mothering her baby is doing something that no professional person can do as well as she can. Women who have worked in child care professions frequently say how different they feel once they become mothers themselves. As professionals, they often thought mothers were being "overanxious." Now, with their own vulnerable and beloved babies in their arms, those mothers make sense. The most hardworking professional is often the first to acknowledge that she is not the child's mother, meaning that she perceives a crucial difference. A mother's knowledge of her child is unique. In traditional societies this is a truth that is obvious to everyone, but in societies where women have achieved greater equality with men, this apparently so-obvious truth has been ignored.

Women have been educated to believe that after six months with a baby they will be in a state of cabin fever and desperate to resume work again. To what extent does this become a self-fulfilling prophecy? Kate Figes writes: "I needed to get back to work to feel attached to the real world again."[8] In her eyes, being a mother is not being attached to "the real world."

For decades there has been a consistent denigration of genuine mothering. Women can be dismissed as "earth mothers" if they express pleasure in caring for their babies. It sounds as though these mothers are thought to have some weird ability to achieve what "normal" women cannot. This seems unlikely. Most women seem able to turn themselves into mothers even if they are ill, or are refugees, or are in all kinds of difficult situations. Mothering is adaptable and definitely not the prerogative of only a few. But do women really know this?

Many books for mothers, for example, convey a false picture of what being a mother really involves. They play down the importance of relating to babies. Yet it is dishonest to reduce the intimacy of mothering to a series of practical techniques. Too much literature today implies that being a mother is about changing a baby's "inconvenient" behavior. Gina Ford, author of the bestselling *The Contented Little Baby Book,* offers to help parents do this. "What is so different about my book," she writes in her introduction, "is that it comes from years of hands-on experience. I have lived with and cared for hundreds of different babies. . . . My advice will teach you how to listen to what your baby is really saying."[9]

Mothers who follow Gina Ford's advice are said to have "Gina Ford babies." Since Gina Ford's book "will teach" mothers what their babies are "really" saying, mothers are encouraged to attend to the book before their babies. But babies are not like machines that can be repaired by following instructions in a manual. They are living beings in complex relationships with their parents.

There are small indications that genuine mothering is slowly beginning to inch its way back into fashion. By the time it does, today's mothers will probably be grandmothers. Perhaps they will tell their daughters or granddaughters: "Your generation is so lucky. We weren't allowed to look after our babies ourselves."

It is alarming to discover how few mothers have confidence in their own ability to learn how to mother. They often speak and write as if they *depend* on professional child care. They have surely received a biased picture of motherhood. In order to make a balanced decision about when to return to work, a mother needs to be able to hear arguments supporting *both* sides of this controversial question.

This kind of debate shows us that there is a political dimension to what mothers do. An early exploration of this subject was initiated by a brilliant man. The great Athenian playwright Aristophanes pioneered a whole way of thinking in *Lysistrata,* written in 412 B.C. In this comedy, women manage to bring the long-running Peloponnesian War to a sudden end. Lysistrata, an Athenian mother, wins the cooperation of her Spartan counterparts. Her plan is for women on both sides to withhold sex from their men until the men end the war. In one scene, an Athenian magistrate sneers at Lysistrata for supposing that, as a mere woman, she could understand matters of war. Lysistrata protests that mothers do understand. They mother the men who are killed as soldiers. "*Silence!*" snaps the magistrate. She has clearly touched a raw nerve. This is comedy, and the actors, representing both Athenian and Spartan men, soon stagger onto the stage with what appear to be gigantic erections under their tunics. Peace is declared within days.

This must have sounded farfetched in the large theater in fifth-century B.C. Athens, where both the actors and the audiences were made up of men. Women were socially subservient to men, with rare exceptions. Yet today this farfetched idea has been realized. There have been recent times when women really have grouped together for this kind of purpose. Mothers have begun to discover that they have political power. It is interesting that they use it mostly to protest against injustice. There are a growing number of international movements with names that begin "Mothers Against," such as Mothers Against War, Mothers Against Violence in America, Mothers Against Gangs, Mothers Against Drugs, Mothers Against Drunken Driving, Mothers Against Sexual Abuse, Mothers Against the Death Penalty, Mothers Against Genetic Engineering. A list like this may sound negative, but all these causes are rooted in thoroughly positive maternal values.

Any mother who supposes she is isolated at home without any political identity is overlooking her importance as a mother. She is extremely important. As she starts to create a family, it embodies her values. This is both her private affair and also her political base. She can create a good base, especially through the way that she uses her power to relate to her children. The political values around her do not have to be hers. Equally, her silence and subservience can act as passive endorsements of whatever is the status quo.

Anyone who doubts this could usefully look at the role mothers have played in many societies. If a government is tyrannical and corrupt, then mothers can unwittingly buttress it up. It is an uncomfortable discovery, but mothers' support seems to have been crucial for the enforcement of racist policies in the Third Reich, which culminated in the Final Solution. There has been much heart-searching to ascertain how humans could act with such lack of humanity. Nazi psychiatrists relied on a simple support system. They encouraged perpetrators to "rehumanize" themselves by spending plenty of leisure time with their wives and children.[10]

In democratic societies, this kind of exploitation may be less obvious. However, an experienced mother may find that adults as well as children like her to mother them, not only at home but also at her place of work. It can take some vigilance on her part to recognize whom she is mothering and what values she is supporting by doing so. Without realizing it, she may be "rehumanizing" people whose values she does not share.

It seems to me that the best antidote to all these large and small pressures on mothers are circles of mothers, either at regular meetings or in spontaneous gatherings in shops or on the street.[11] Here a mother can exchange views and have her assumptions challenged. People often ridicule mothers for talking. They may attend regular work meetings themselves but dismiss mothers as "just chatting."

Women have always been good at conversation, and mothers develop a particular style. They are often short of sleep and distracted periodically by their babies. So topics tend to be dealt with in (what an outsider might criticize for being) a somewhat disorganized and rambling way, in which questions can be addressed on many levels.[12] I notice this especially at La Leche League meetings because each meeting always has a specific title. The title is addressed, though not methodically. Yet afterward, mothers say as they leave how much they have learned from the meeting. They have clearly used the meeting as a way of reviewing their work as mothers.

Mothers usually find or create local groups where they can meet. At Mothers Talking, the weekly discussion group that I began more than twelve years ago, there are no set topics. Over the years, mothers often tell me what they value about talking to other mothers. It seems to "work" on many levels.

> I feel better sitting here, listening to you all. I feel so much better. I wish I could take you all home with me. Because that's where it's difficult, being alone with B at home. [B, 3 weeks]

> *Mother of a baby with Down's syndrome:* I was afraid I'd turn out to be the neediest person in the group. But listening to you all talking, I can see that other people have difficulties that I haven't had. [B, 2 months]

> Everything that all the mothers have said before me affects me. I recognize every single problem. I never knew that other people worried about their babies like I

> do. I've got so much to say, but I can't stop crying because now I know I'm *normal*. I thought I was mad. But it's normal to feel all these things. [B, 2 months]

> Talking here is very nourishing. I leave feeling energized. The most important thing, as a mother, is to be listened to. [B, 6 months]

> This is a very honest group. It's nice to be able to say how you really feel. When I get ready to come here, I start to get ready all my really honest feelings. [G, 8 months]

Although new mothers can be so appreciative, they are not always easy to facilitate. They are at a sensitive stage in their lives. They often feel very short of confidence. They are easily hurt, and a thoughtless joke or remark can cause pain that the same women, at previous stages of their lives, say they would hardly have noticed. Yet for exactly this reason, their sensitivity to each other and their capacity for understanding can be heightened.

There doesn't seem to be any word to refer to this wonderful ability to reach across the differences to understanding. Yet if mothers feel safe together, that's what they do. It's very moving. The earliest example I have found (which I noticed because of the coincidence of my own name) is that of Naomi in the Book of Ruth in the Bible. This tells the story of a famine in Bethlehem, which led Naomi and her family to emigrate to Moab. Here, after several years, Naomi's husband and two sons died, and she returned to Bethlehem, accompanied only by Ruth, widow of one of her sons.

The Hebrew language, in which the original story was written, is like French in one respect. Its verbs take the masculine ending, not only when the subjects are all men but even when many women and just *one* man are the subjects of the verb. At this point in the story, the verbs (very unusual for the Bible) all have feminine endings. So, from the original Hebrew, we can tell that not a single man was present. We are in a gathering entirely of women. "Is this Naomi?" they (the women of Bethlehem) ask, and Naomi replies: "Call me not 'Naomi.' Call me 'Marah,' for the Almighty has dealt very bitterly with me. I went out full and the Lord has brought me back empty. Why do you call me 'Naomi,' seeing the Lord has testified against me, and the Almighty has afflicted me?" The next sentence begins: "So Naomi returned . . ."[13]

What happened? We are not told how the women of Bethlehem responded. Did they put their arms around Naomi and weep with her or cold-shoulder her (because she and her family had abandoned Bethlehem during the famine), or what? I suspect they were silent because I have seen situations like this at Mothers Talking. A mother will start to speak with exactly that bitterness to which Naomi gave voice. The listening mothers form themselves into a kind of containing basket—I'm not sure how to explain this process. There is a moment of tension when we cannot be sure that the basket will hold and be strong enough. The mother starts crying and perhaps another mother passes her a tissue. The others murmur, "That must be so hard," or other sympathetic comments. But the overall response is a profound silence in the face of another mother's suffering.

It took me many failures to realize that this silence is healing. It acts as a kind of shock-absorber. No more needs to be said. The crying mother feels less alone, and the listening mothers feel they have taken on a tiny fraction of her lot. All feel lighter and stronger, despite the pain they have shared. After some time, the bitter mother will dry her eyes, thank everyone, and the meeting moves on to something else.

Silence often works better than words. Mothers sometimes

use meetings to seek or share advice, but this can easily go wrong. Each mother's situation is specific to herself. Often when one mother learns something from another, it's a tiny bit of information that she finds useful, not the informant's entire system. But when a mother has survived the early months of uncertainty, she can be tempted to believe that she can rescue newer mothers from this difficult time.

> I was standing at the checkout of our supermarket, and I could see the woman after me was expecting. I thought to myself: "Oh, *wow,* I've got all this wealth of motherly experience!" And then I said to myself: "M, she hasn't asked your advice. Just keep quiet!" It wasn't easy, but I bit back the words. [G, 6 months]

> There was a mother, this morning, whose baby was ten months old, and she was having similar problems to mine. I said: "Would you like me to explain what I've done, which has really worked for us?" So I started telling her, and she kept saying: "Oh, I've tried that." "No, I don't want to do that." So after about five minutes, I just stopped telling her, because she didn't want to hear. But I feel really *terrible* when I think of her. [Meaning that she so much wanted to help the other mother.] [G, 10 months]

Most of the time, what mothers seem to want from each other is compassion—without any advice. That's why their stories can sound harrowing. The harrowing quality is to elicit pity. A mother may often give a more one-sided picture than is truly the case. This is because the mother longs to be bathed in her listener's compassion. She has probably spent all morning being patient and compassionate toward her child and craves some attention for herself. However, her harrowing story may make her listener feel so sorry for her (as in the example above) that the listener feels pressured into helping her by giving her practical advice. This makes the first mother try harder to reassert her need for compassion by sounding even more harrowing, but that in turn pressures the listener harder to come up with some acceptable advice. Neither mother can understand why her efforts aren't working. These conversations are very common. I can still fall into the just-one-word-of-advice role, in spite of myself, even after so many years.

Mothers are never short of troubling subjects to discuss with each other. Perhaps it has never been easy to be a mother. But today the whole meaning of motherhood seems to have been twisted inside out. Just as youth is said to be "much too good to be wasted on the young," so mothering seems to be considered much too good to be wasted on babies. Adults value mothering—but often for themselves. When mothering concerns babies, it is frequently belittled. Babies are often caricatured as nothing but sources of dirty diapers and sour regurgitated milk. In Britain, mothers are expected to keep their children from making too much noise, from getting "under the feet" of other adults, from being a nuisance or causing "trouble." "Is he a good baby?" usually refers (if you ask what this question means) to a baby who appears to be no trouble. By these standards, genuine mothering, which means taking enormous trouble to ease the child's journey into the complexities of life outside the womb, can be seen as a failure. If a mother is doing all this, she is clearly *allowing* her baby to cause her trouble.

The title of this book, *What Mothers Do Especially When It Looks Like Nothing,* is a reflection of this negative outlook toward mothers. If we see "nothing" when we look at a mother who is quietly being a mother, it is easy for *her* to feel as if she is doing nothing too. If she thinks she is doing nothing, and *we* think she is doing nothing, there is only the speechless baby to experience how much good she is doing.

What *do* mothers do?

In a bathroom, a tube of toothpaste lies open on the floor. Its top has rolled goodness knows where. A toothbrush with some paste on it lies unused on the rim of the sink. Someone must have been disturbed who was about to brush their teeth. That person is in the next room. She's a woman, a mother with her baby. What is she doing? Well, how you answer depends on you yourself and what you see when you look at her.

Putting two and two together, you may see an unfortunate woman with a very demanding baby who couldn't even wait *two minutes* while his mother brushed her teeth but cried and cried until she had to go and pick him up. You may offer to hold the baby, but the baby is so unreasonable that he clings to his mother and won't trust you or anyone else. You may ask yourself why babies were ever invented. This probably isn't you. You will have your own unique way of seeing. I'm going to end this book by telling you what I see.

I see a totally exhausted-looking mother, pale with dark shadows under her eyes, who miraculously has the energy to sing and rock her baby in a way that he is starting to recognize. I see him relax, and his tense body seems to melt into her arms. He isn't crying now. His whole being is attentive to the music and wonderful rhythm of the mother who is comforting him so well. It takes a long time until he finally reaches sleep. When he does, the entire room seems at peace. Something momentous seems to have changed. It has been a journey, a transition from distress into harmony. The mother looks up with a warm smile. The miracle was hers, but perhaps you and I helped her by being there and seeing what she did as "something."

notes

one. who understands?

1 Griffin, Susan (1982), *Made from This Earth: Selections from Her Writing 1967–82*, London: Women's Press, pages 70–71.

2 Cusk, Rachel (2001), "The Language of Love" in *Guardian, G2*, September 12, 2001, page 8.

3 Gansberg, Judith M., and Mostel, Dr. Arthur P. (1984), *The Second Nine Months: The Sexual and Emotional Concerns of the New Mother*, Wellingborough, England: Thorsons, page 86.

4 Klaus, Marshall H., and Kennell, John H. (1983), *Bonding: The Beginnings of Parent-Infant Attachment*, St. Louis: C. V. Mosby, page 2.

5 Bowlby, John (1988), *A Secure Base*, London: Routledge, page 29.

6 Klaus and Kennell, *Bonding*, page 64.

7 Ibid., page 56.

8 See, for example, Daniel Stern's much-quoted *The Interpersonal World of the Infant: A View from Psychoanalysis and Developmental Psychology* (1985), New York: Basic Books, pages 207–19.

9 Personal verbal communication from Kittie Franz, Director, Breastfeeding Infant Clinic, Los Angeles County, to Naomi Stadlen. The other health professional is Chloe Fisher, now retired from the Breastfeeding Clinic at the John Radcliffe Hospital, Oxford. Kittie Franz said the word arose out of a discussion they were having on a beach in 1970, and she could not remember which of them used it first.

10 Priya, Jacqueline Vincent (1992), *Birth Traditions and Modern Pregnancy Care,* Shaftesbury, England: Element Books, page 116.

11 See especially Spender, Dale (1980), *Man Made Language,* London: Pandora, pages 54–58.

two. "nothing prepares you"

1 See, for example, Kitzinger, Sheila (1992), *Ourselves as Mothers,* London: Bantam, pages 197ff.

2 Cobb, John (1980), *Babyshock,* London: Hutchinson, page 13.

3 Reprinted from *Weavers of the Songs: The Oral Poetry of Arab Women in Israel and the West Bank,* compiled, edited, and translated by Mshael Maswari Caspi and Julia Ann Blessing. Copyright © 1991 by the authors. Reprinted with permission of Lynne Rienner Publishers, Inc. See page 94.

4 White, Amanda, Freeth, Stephanie, and O'Brien, Maureen (1990, 1993), *Infant Feeding,* London: HMSO, pages 27 and 69.

5 Johnson, Rachel, "Real Women Don't Need Degrees," *Daily Telegraph,* February 21, 1998.

6 Elkind, David (1981, 1988), *The Hurried Child: Growing Up Too Fast Too Soon,* Reading, MA: Perseus.

7 Breen, Dana (1981, 1989), *Talking with Mothers,* London: Free Association, page 116.

8 Nigella Lawson's column in the *Observer,* March 28, 1999.

three. "all the responsibility"

1 Tolstoy, Leo, *The Kreutzer Sonata and Other Stories,* translated by David McDuff (Penguin, 1985), translation copyright © 1985 David McDuff. London: Penguin, pages 70–71. Reproduced by permission of Penguin Books Ltd.

2 Stern, Daniel N., and Bruschweiler-Stern, Nadia (1998), *The Birth of a Mother: How Motherhood Changes You Forever,* London: Bloomsbury, pages 96–97 (published in New York by Basic Books).

four. "being instantly interruptible"

1 Olsen, Tillie (1980), *Silences,* London: Virago, pages 18–19.

2 Karmiloff-Smith, Annette (1994), *Baby It's You,* London: Ebury, describes how babies as young as six to eight weeks of age sometimes go quiet after a bout of crying and seem to listen for their parents' footsteps. If they can't

hear these sounds, they will resume crying (page 168). In other words, in order for a baby to succeed, he has first to realize that his parents come when he cries.

five. the power of comfort

1 Dunn, Judy (1977), *Distress and Comfort,* London: Fontana/Open Books, page 32.

2 Isaiah 66:13. A literal translation from the Hebrew Bible is: "As a mother comforts a man . . ." This reveals the long-lasting value of maternal comfort. Isaiah was comparing the comfort of mothers to divine comfort.

3 Glynn, Laura M.; Christenfeld, Nicholas; and Gerin, William (March 1999), "Gender, Social Support, and Cardiovascular Responses to Stress," *Psychosomatic Medicine* (Baltimore), pages 234–42.

4 See Davies, Susan Shannon, "Nursing Twins," in *New Beginnings,* Schaumburg, IL: La Leche League International, May–June 1997, page 73.

5 See Lester, Barry M. (1985), "There's More to Crying than Meets the Ear," in *Infant Crying: Theoretical and Research Perspectives,* ed. Lester, Barry M., and Boukydis, C. F. Zachariah, New York: Plenum Press, page 7; and Gunner, Megan R., and Donzella, Bonny (1999), "Looking for the Rosetta Stone: An Essay on Crying, Soothing and Stress" in *Soothing and Stress,* ed. Lewis, Michael, and Ramsay, Douglas, Mahwah, NJ: Lawrence Erlbaum Associates, page 39.

6 Plato (1984), *Laws* (1926, 1984), tr. R. G. Bury, Cambridge, MA: Harvard University Press, and London: Heinemann, Book VII, 790D, page 11.

7 Dunn, *Distress and Comfort,* page 28.

8 La Leche League International (1958, 2004), *The Womanly Art of Breastfeeding,* Schaumburg, IL: La Leche League International, page 94.

9 See, for example, Parker, Rozsika (1995), *Torn in Two,* London: Virago, page 1.

10 Maushart, Susan (1999), *The Mask of Motherhood,* London: Pandora, page 125.

11 Donovan, Wilberta L., and Levitt, Lewis A. (1985), "Physiology and Behaviour: Parents' Response to the Infant's Cry," in *Infant Crying: Theoretical and Research Perspectives,* ed. Lester, Barry M., and Boukydis, C. F. Zachariah, New York: Plenum Press, page 253.

12 Lester, "There's More to Crying Than Meets the Ear," pages 23, 25.

13 Simpson, John, with Speake, Jennifer, eds. (1982), *The Oxford Concise Dictionary of Proverbs,* Oxford: Oxford University Press, page 43.

six. "I get nothing done all day"

1 Parkinson, Christine E., and Talbert, D. G. (1987), "Ways of Evaluating the Mother-Infant Relationship," in Harvey, David, ed., *Parent-Infant Relationships,* Chichester, England: John Wiley & Sons, page 17.

2 Olsen, Tillie (1980), *Silences,* London: Virago, page 19.

3 Stern, Daniel N. (1985), *The Interpersonal World of the Infant,* New York: Basic Books, chapter 9.

4 Klaus, Marshall H., and Kennell, John H. (1983), *Bonding: The Beginnings of Parent-Infant Attachment,* St. Louis: C. V. Mosby, page 41.

5 See, for example, Parkinson and Talbert, "Ways of Evaluating the Mother-Infant Relationship," pages 18–19; and Klaus and Kennell, *Bonding,* page 60.

6 Prigogine, Ilya, and Stengers, Isabelle (1985), *Order Out of Chaos,* London: Fontana; and Abraham, Frederick David, and Gilgen, Albert R., eds. (1995), *Chaos Theory in Psychology,* Westport, CT: Greenwood.

7 Winnicott, D. W. (1964), *The Child, the Family and the Outside World,* London: Penguin, page 15.

8 Plato, *Laws,* in *The Collected Dialogues,* ed. Edith Hamilton and Huntingdon Cairns (1961); New York: Bollingen Foundation/Pantheon, page 1362.

9 Bernard, Jessie (1975), *The Future of Parenthood,* London: Caldar and Boyars, page 277.

seven. so tired I could die

1 Hartmann, Ernest L. (1973), *The Functions of Sleep,* Oxford: Oxford University Press, page 3.

2 Coren, Stanley (1996), *Sleep Thieves,* New York: Free Press, page 114. See also Pinilla, Teresa, and Birch, Leann, "Help Me Make It Through the Night," *Pediatrics* 91(2), February 1993, pages 436–44.

3 Kleitman, Nathaniel (1939, 1963), *Sleep and Wakefulness,* Chicago: University of Chicago Press, page 112.

4 Ibid., pages 219ff.

5 Jensen, Susan, and Given, Barbara A., "Fatigue Affecting Family Caregivers of Cancer Patients," *Cancer Nursing* 14(4), 1991, page 182.

6 Milligan, Renee A., and Pugh, Linda C., "Fatigue During the Childbearing Period," *Annual Review of Nursing Research,* 12, 1994, pages 34 and 43. See also Lee, Kathryn A., and De Joseph, Jeanne F., "Sleep Disturbances, Vitality, and Fatigue Among a Select Group of Employed Childbearing

Women," *Birth* 19(4), December 1992, page 208: "Little research has been done to examine the phenomena of fatigue and sleep disturbances during pregnancy and the postpartum."

7 Benn, Melissa (1998), *Madonna and Child,* London: Jonathan Cape, page 241.

8 Hobson, J. Allan (1989), *Sleep,* New York: Scientific American Library, page 4.

9 McKenna, James J., "Rethinking 'Healthy' Infant Sleep," *Breastfeeding Abstracts,* Schaumburg, IL: La Leche League International, 12(3), February 1993, page 27. Two other pioneering books on this solution are Thevenin, Tine (1987), *The Family Bed,* Wayne, NJ: Avery, and Jackson, Deborah (1989), *Three in a Bed,* London: Bloomsbury.

10 Daugherty, Steven R., and Dewitt, C. Baldwin, "Sleep Deprivation in Senior Medical Students and First-Year Residents," *Academic Medicine,* 71(1), January 1996 (supp.), page S93.

11 Ibid., page S95.

eight. what do babies seem to want?

1 Kagan, Jerome (1984), *The Nature of the Child,* New York: Basic Books, page 24.

2 The La Leche League guideline is clear about this: "Breastfeeding is not a guarantee of good mothering, and bottle feeding does not rule it out. The most important thing is the love you give your baby and the fact that you are doing your best to be a good mother." La Leche League International (1958, 2004), *The Womanly Art of Breastfeeding,* Schaumburg, IL: La Leche League International, page 16.

3 Karmiloff-Smith, Annette (1994), *Baby It's You,* London: Ebury, pages 168–69.

4 Freud, Sigmund, *Introductory Lectures on Psychoanalysis* (1916), in *The Standard Edition of the Complete Psychological Works of Sigmund Freud* (1953–74), London: Hogarth Press and Institute of Psycho-Analysis, vol. 16, page 314.

5 Aristotle, *On Poetry and Style,* tr. G. M. A. Grube (1958, 1997), Indianapolis: Hackett, chapter 4, pages 7–8.

6 Freud, *Standard Edition, Jokes and Their Relation to the Unconscious,* vol. 8, page 223.

7 See, for example, Nightingale, Florence (1859, 1952) *Notes on Nursing,* London: Duckworth, page 127, paragraph 1.

8 Elkind, David (1988), *The Hurried Child: Growing Up Too Fast Too Soon,* Reading, MA: Perseus.

9 See Stadlen, Naomi, "Temper Tantrums," *Nursery World,* January 24, 1984.

10 Aristotle, *The Nichomachean Ethics,* Book VIII.1, ed. Ross, W. David (1971), Oxford: Oxford University Press, page 192. Reprinted by permission of Oxford University Press.

11 Wollstonecraft, Mary, *A Vindication of the Rights of Women,* ed. Miriam Brody, London: Penguin (1992), pages 273–74.

nine. what is motherly love?

1 Erman, Adolf (German original, 1923), *Ancient Egyptian Poetry and Prose,* tr. Aylward M. Blackman (1927, 1995), New York: Dover, page 239.

2 Freud, Sigmund, "On Narcissism: An Introduction" (1914), in *The Standard Edition of the Complete Psychological Works of Sigmund Freud* (1953–74), London: Hogarth Press and Institute of Psycho-Analysis, vol. 14.

3 See, for example, Lidz, Theodore (1968), *The Person,* New York: Basic Books, page 131.

4 See, for instance, Odent, Michel, (1999), *The Scientification of Love,* London: Free Association; and Hrdy, Sarah Blaffer (1999), *Mother Nature,* London: Chatto & Windus.

5 Text from Schlein, Miriam, *The Way Mothers Are* © 1963, 1991 by Miriam Schlein. Reprinted by permission of Albert Whitman & Company, Morton Grove, IL.

6 For a good description, see Stern, Daniel N., (1985), *The Interpersonal World of the Infant,* New York: Basic Books, page 43.

7 Brazelton, T. Berry, and Cramer, Bertrand G. (1990), *The Earliest Relationship,* London: Karnac, page 160.

8 For example, "'I don't think of Sam as being disabled, he's just Sam to me with his character and personality' (Sam's mother)," quoted in Bridge, Gillian (1999), *Parents as Care Managers: The Experience of Those Caring for Young Children with Cerebral Palsy,* Aldershot, England: Ashgate, page 51.

9 I Kings, 3:16–27. Hebrew editions of the Bible have singing marks that emphasize the phrase about the mother's womb warming up.

10 *Daily Telegraph,* September 6, 1997, page 15.

11 *Daily Telegraph,* August 12, 1997, page 33.

12 Cassandra Eason (1998) gives examples in "Maternal Sacrifice," in her book *Mother Love,* London: Robinson.

13 Cobb, John (1980), *Babyshock,* London: Hutchinson, page 175.
14 Johnson, Susan (2000), *A Better Woman,* London: Aurum, page 80.
15 Ibid., page 220.
16 Rich, Adrienne (1977), *Of Woman Born,* London: Virago, page 23.
17 Figes, Kate (1998), *Life After Birth: What Even Your Friends Won't Tell You About Motherhood,* London: Viking, page 102. Reproduced by permission of Penguin Books Ltd.
18 Ibid., page 98.
19 Cusk, Rachel (2001), *A Life's Work: On Becoming a Mother,* London: Fourth Estate/HarperCollins, page 103.
20 Winnicott, D. W. (1958), "Hate in the Countertransference" (1947), in *Through Paediatrics to Psychoanalysis: Collected Papers,* London: Tavistock, page 201.
21 Parker, Rozsika (1995), *Torn in Two,* London: Virago, page 213.
22 Lazarre, Jane (1977), *The Mother Knot,* London: Virago, page 34.
23 Figes, *Life After Birth,* page 125. Reproduced by permission of Penguin Books Ltd.
24 Maushart, Susan (1999), *The Mask of Motherhood,* London: Pandora, page 123.
25 Cusk, *A Life's Work,* page 186.
26 Parker, *Torn in Two,* page 200.
27 Ibid., page 4.
28 Rich, *Of Woman Born,* page 21.
29 Figes, *Life After Birth,* page 99. Reproduced by permission of Penguin Books Ltd.
30 Maushart, *The Mask of Motherhood,* page 145.
31 Johnson, *A Better Woman,* page 43.
32 Winnicott, "Hate in the Countertransference," pages 200–201.
33 Rich, *Of Woman Born,* page 22.
34 Ibid., page 224.
35 Lazarre, *The Mother Knot,* page 36.
36 Johnson, *A Better Woman,* page 141.
37 Briscoe, Joanna, "I Have to Keep Telling Myself It'll Get Better," *Guardian, G2,* February 5, 2003, page 17.
38 Winnicott, "Hate in the Countertransference," page 201.
39 Darling, Julia, "Small Beauties," in ed. Sumner, Penny, *The Fruits of Labour, Creativity, Self-Expression and Motherhood* (2001), London: Women's Press, page 3.
40 Maushart, *The Mask of Motherhood,* page 128.

41 Catullus, Quintus Valerius, *Odes,* ode 85. "*Odi et amo. Quare id faciam, fortasse, requiris? Nescio, sed fieri sentio et excrucior.*"

42 Winnicott, "Hate in the Countertransference," page 202.

43 Lazarre, *The Mother Knot,* page ix.

44 Parker, *Torn in Two,* page 99.

45 Ibid., page 98.

46 Ibid., page 120.

47 Maushart, *The Mask of Motherhood,* pages 111–12.

48 Rich, *Of Woman Born,* page 22.

49 Lazarre, *The Mother Knot,* page 35.

50 Ibid., page viii.

51 Figes, *Life After Birth,* page 102. Reproduced by permission of Penguin Books Ltd.

52 Johnson, *A Better Woman,* page 146.

53 Cusk, *A Life's Work,* page 95.

54 Lazarre, *The Mother Knot,* page 62.

55 Figes, *Life After Birth,* page 71. Reproduced by permission of Penguin Books Ltd.

56 Ibid., page 120. Reproduced by permission of Penguin Books Ltd.

57 Johnson, *A Better Woman,* page 91.

58 Cusk, *A Life's Work,* page 143.

59 Ibid., page 7.

60 Winnicott, D. W. (1964), *The Child, the Family and the Outside World,* London: Penguin, chapter 12.

61 Kaplan, Louise J. (1978), *Oneness and Separateness,* London: Jonathan Cape, 1979.

62 Lazarre, *The Mother Knot,* page 72.

63 Parker, *Torn in Two,* pages 3–4.

64 Pearson, Allison, "Good Mum Bad Mum," *Daily Telegraph,* magazine, June 15, 2002.

65 Pearson, Allison (2002), *I Don't Know How She Does It,* London: Chatto & Windus, page 91.

66 Rich, *Of Woman Born,* page 15.

67 Maushart, *The Mask of Motherhood,* pages 111–12.

68 Parker, *Torn in Two,* page 98.

69 Ibid.

70 Lazarre, *The Mother Knot,* pages 6–7.

71 Ibid., page 74.

72 Ibid., page 185.

ten. "I was surprised that I still had the same name"

1 T. Berry Brazelton wrote a book with the promising title *Infants and Mothers: Differences in Development* (New York: Dell, 1969, 1983). I remember rushing out to read it in a library only to discover that it was a book on how three *infants* developed. Dr. Brazelton does write that mothers develop but doesn't explain how. There is also Daniel N. Stern's (1995) *The Motherhood Constellation* and his more recent work with his wife, Nadia Bruschweiler-Stern (1998), *The Birth of a Mother: How Motherhood Changes You Forever,* New York: Basic Books. This is a unique book on maternal development, though its tone tends to be didactic rather than exploratory.

2 Rachel Cusk has described this state, for example, when she writes: "After my first child was born, I used to wonder when I would be once more the person I had been and feel things that were familiar to me. I felt a sort of homesickness for myself, and a terrible sense of the unreality of everything." "The Language of Love," *Guardian G2,* September 12, 2001, page 9.

3 A few obvious examples: Dally, Ann (1976), in *Mothers, Their Power and Influence,* London: Weidenfeld, chapter 12, "Circles"; Rich, Adrienne (1977), *Of Woman Born,* London: Virago, chapter 2, "The "Sacred Calling"; Badinter, Elisabeth (1981), *The Myth of Motherhood,* London: Souvenir, page 300; Figes, Kate (1998), *Life After Birth,* London: Viking, chapter 4, "Working and the 'Good' Mother"; Maushart, Susan (1999), *The Mask of Motherhood,* London: Pandora, pages 144ff.

4 A few examples are Deutsch, Helene (1947), *Psychology of Women,* London: Research Books, vol. 1, chapter 7, "Feminine Masochism"; Price, Jane (1988), *Motherhood: What It Does to Your Mind,* London: Pandora, chapter 9, "The Devastating Effects of Motherhood"; Parker, Rozsika (1995), *Torn in Two,* London: Virago, chapter 6, "Unravelling Femininity and Maternity."

5 A good example comes from chapter 2 of D. H. Lawrence's semiautobiographical novel *Sons and Lovers.* This describes how, during Paul Morel's birth, his mother depended on an efficient system of neighborly support. Today, these neighbors and perhaps even Mrs. Morel would be more likely to be at work than at home during the day.

6 Gansberg, Judith M., and Mostel, Dr. Arthur P. (1984), *The Second Nine Months: The Sexual and Emotional Concerns of the New Mother,* Wellingborough, England: Thorsons, page 82.

7 Hole, Christina (1953), *The English Housewife in the Seventeenth Century,* London: Chatto & Windus, page 79.

8 Cobb, John (1980), *Babyshock,* London: Hutchinson, page 146.

9 Chekhov, Anton, *Three Sisters,* Act 2.

10 Miller, Jean Baker (1978), *Toward a New Psychology of Women,* London: Penguin, pages 58–59.

11 Price, *Motherhood.*

12 Prigogine, Ilya, and Stengers, Isabelle (1984, 1985), *Order Out of Chaos,* London: Fontana, page 77.

eleven. snapping at my partner

1 Jackson, Brian (1983), *Fatherhood,* London: Allen and Unwin, page 96.

2 Owen, Ursula (1983), "Introduction" to *Fathers, Reflections by Daughters,* ed. Ursula Owen, London: Virago, page 13. Chapter 1 of Jackson, *Fatherhood,* has the revealing title "The Invisible Man." Claudia Nelson gave a similar title to her research study: *Invisible Men: Fatherhood in Victorian Periodicals 1850–1910,* Athens: University of Georgia Press, 1995.

3 Lewis, Charlie (1986), *Becoming a Father,* Milton Keynes, England: Open Universities Press, page 41.

4 Sheila Kitzinger (1992) sums this up: "In contrast to traditional cultures, when a woman turns into a mother she is treated suddenly as less, not more." *Ourselves as Mothers,* London: Bantam, page 7.

5 A spirited account of mothers' work is given in "Appendix V: Women Count—Count Women's Work" in *The Milk of Human Kindness* by Solveig Francis, Selma James, Phoebe Jones Schellenberg, and Nina Lopez-Jones, London: Crossroads Women's Centre, 2002, pages 188–90.

twelve. closer to my mother

1 Rich, Adrienne (1977), *Of Woman Born,* London: Virago, page 243.

2 Arcana, Judith (1981), "Introduction," *Our Mothers' Daughters,* London: Women's Press, page xv.

3 Kitzinger, Sheila (1997), *Becoming a Grandmother,* London: Simon & Schuster, page 107.

epilogue: circles of mothers

1 For example, see La Leche League International (4th rev. ed., 2003), *Leader's Handbook,* pages 16–17.

2 Plato, *Laws,* in *The Collected Dialogues,* ed. Edith Hamilton and

Huntingdon Cairns (1961), New York: Bollingen, Foundation/Pantheon, page 1362.

3 Truby King was authorized by the government of New Zealand.

4 Truby King, Frederic (undated), *Feeding and Care of Baby,* Oxford: Oxford University Press, page 42.

5 Rousseau, Jean-Jacques (1762), *Emile, or On Education,* Book 1.

6 See Chapple, J. A. V. (1980), *Elizabeth Gaskell: A Portrait in Letters,* Manchester; England: Manchester University Press, page xii.

7 Some useful statistics at the time of going to press can be found in "Key Indicators of Women's Position in Britain," by Angelika Hibbert and Nigel Meager, in *Labour Market Trends,* Norwich, England: The Stationery Office, 3 (10), October 2003, page 507. Also see Hamlyn, Becky; Brooker, Sue, Olejnikova, Karin, and Wands, Sarah (2002), "The Employment Status of Mothers," *Infant Feeding Report 2000,* Norwich, England: The Stationery Office, page 138.

8 Figes, Kate (1998), *Life After Birth: What Even Your Friends Won't Tell You About Motherhood,* London: Viking, page 71. Reproduced by permission of Penguin Books Ltd.

9 Ford, Gina (1999), *The Contented Little Baby Book,* London: Vermilion, page 10. Used by permission of Random House Group Ltd.

10 For details, see "Consequences" in Claudia Koonz's pioneering *Mothers in the Fatherland,* London: Methuen, 1988.

11 Claudia Koonz describes how, on Hitler's rise to power, women formed sewing circles to read and discuss *Mein Kampf* (ibid., page 70). This sounds like a tantalizing opportunity, because how free would these discussions have been? Rozsika Parker's *The Subversive Stitch* (London: Women's Press, 1984) gives examples of how challenging women's discussions can be in the apparently gentle setting of a sewing circle, when there are no external constraints on their speech.

12 Jennifer Coates, in *Women Talk,* Oxford: Blackwell, 1996, gives an original analysis of how women's conversation "works." It would be wonderful if she had time to write specifically on the conversation of mothers.

13 This translation of the Book of Ruth, chapter 1, verses 19–22, is based on that by Rabbi A. J. Rosenberg, in *The Five Megilloth* (1946, 1984), ed. Rev. Dr. A. Cohen, New York: Soncino, pages 120–21.

bibliography

Aristotle. *The Nichomachean Ethics,* ed. W. David Ross, Oxford: Oxford University Press, 1971.

———. *On Poetry and Style,* trans. G. M. A. Grube. Indianapolis: Hackett, 1989.

Balaskas, Janet. *Natural Baby,* London: Gaia, 2001.

———. *Preparing for Birth with Yoga.* Shaftesbury, England: Element Books, 1994.

Benn, Melissa. *Madonna and Child.* London: Jonathan Cape, 1998.

Bernard, Jessie. *The Future of Parenthood.* London: Caldar and Boyars, 1975.

Bowlby, John. *A Secure Base.* London: Routledge, 1988.

Brazelton, T. Berry, and Bertrand G. Cramer. *The Earliest Relationship.* London: Karnac, 1990.

Breen, Dana. *Talking with Mothers.* London: Free Association, 1981, 1989.

Caspi, Mshael Maswari, and Julia Ann Blessing. *Weavers of the Songs: the Oral Poetry of Arab Women in Israel and the West Bank.* Boulder, CO.: Lynne Rienner, 1991.

Chapple, J. A. V. *Elizabeth Gaskell: A Portrait in Letters.* Manchester, England: Manchester University Press, 1980.

Chekhov, Anton. *Three Sisters.* (Many translations.)

Coates, Jennifer. *Women Talk,* Oxford: Blackwell, 1996.

Cobb, John. *Babyshock.* London: Hutchinson, 1980.

Coren, Stanley. *Sleep Thieves.* New York: Free Press, 1996.

Cusk, Rachel. *A Life's Work: On Becoming a Mother.* London: Fourth Estate/HarperCollins, 2001.

Dunn, Judy. *Distress and Comfort.* London: Fontana/Open Books, 1977.

Eason, Cassandra. *Mother Love.* London: Robinson, 1998.

Elkind, David. *The Hurried Child: Growing Up Too Fast Too Soon.* Reading, MA: Perseus, 1988.

Erman, Adolf. *Ancient Egyptian Poetry and Prose,* trans. Aylward M. Blackman. New York: Dover, 1927, 1995. (German original, 1923.)

Figes, Kate. *Life After Birth.* London: Viking, 1998.

Ford, Gina. *The Contented Little Baby Book.* London: Vermilion, 1999.

Francis, Solveig, James Selma, Phoebe Jones Schellenberg, and Nina Lopez-Jones. *The Milk of Human Kindness.* London: Crossroads Women's Centre, 2002.

Freud, Sigmund. *Jokes and Their Relation to the Unconscious* (1905) in *The Standard Edition of the Complete Psychological Works of Sigmund Freud,* vol. 8. London: Hogarth Press and Institute of Psycho-Analysis, 1953–74.

———. "Lecture 20: The Sexual Life of Human Beings" (1916) in *The Standard Edition of the Complete Psychological Works of Sigmund Freud,* vol. 16. London: Hogarth Press and Institute of Psycho-Analysis, 1953–74.

———. "On Narcissism: An Introduction" (1914) in *The Standard Edition of the Complete Psychological Works of Sigmund Freud,* vol. 14. London: Hogarth Press and Institute of Psycho-Analysis, 1953–74.

Gansberg, Judith M., and Dr. Arthur P: Mostel. *The Second Nine Months: the Sexual and Emotional Concerns of the New Mother.* Wellingborough, England: Thorsons, 1984.

Gaskin, Ina May. *Spiritual Midwifery.* Summertown, TN: The Book Publishing Company, 1978.

Gopnik, Alison, Andrew Meltzoff, and Patricia Kuhl. *How Babies Think.* London: Weidenfeld & Nicolson, 1999.

Griffin, Susan. *Made from This Earth: Selections from Her Writing 1967–82.* London: Women's Press, 1982.

Hartmann, Ernest L. *The Functions of Sleep.* Oxford: Oxford University Press, 1973.

Harvey, David. *Parent-Infant Relationships.* Chichester, England: John Wiley & Sons, 1987.

Hobson, J. Allan. *Sleep.* New York: Scientific American Library, 1989.

Hole, Christina. *The English Housewife in the Seventeenth Century.* London: Chatto & Windus, 1953.

Hollway, Wendy, and Brid Featherstone, eds. *Mothering and Ambivalence.* London: Routledge, 1997.

Hrdy, Sarah Blaffer. *Mother Nature.* London: Chatto & Windus, 1999.

Jackson, Brian. *Fatherhood.* London: Allen and Unwin, 1983.

Jackson, Deborah. *Three in a Bed.* London: Bloomsbury, 1989.

Johnson, Susan. *A Better Woman.* London: Aurum Press, 2000.

Kagan, Jerome. *The Nature of the Child.* New York: Basic Books, 1984.

Kaplan, Louise J. *Oneness and Separateness.* London: Jonathan Cape, 1978.

Karmiloff-Smith, Annette. *Baby It's You.* London: Ebury, 1994.

Kitzinger, Sheila. *Becoming a Grandmother.* London: Simon & Schuster, 1997.

———. *The Experience of Childbirth.* London: Penguin, 1962.

———. *Ourselves as Mothers.* London: Bantam, 1992.

Klaus, Marshall H., and John H. Kennell. *Bonding: The Beginnings of Parent-Infant Attachment.* St. Louis: C. V. Mosby, 1983.

Kleitman, Nathaniel. *Sleep and Wakefulness.* Chicago: University of Chicago Press, 1939, 1963.

Koonz, Claudia. *Mothers in the Fatherland.* London: Methuen, 1987, 1988.

La Leche League International. *The Womanly Art of Breastfeeding.* Schaumburg, IL: La Leche League International, 1958, 2004.

Lazarre, Jane. *The Mother Knot.* London: Virago, 1977.

Lester, Barry M., and C. F. Zachariah Boukydis. *Infant Crying: Theoretical and Research Perspectives.* New York: Plenum Press, 1985.

Lewis, Charlie. *Becoming a Father.* Milton Keynes, England: Open Universities Press, 1986.

Lidz, Theodore. *The Person.* New York: Basic Books, 1968.

Maushart, Susan. *The Mask of Motherhood.* London: Pandora, 1999.

Miller, Jean Baker. *Toward a New Psychology of Women.* London: Penguin, 1978.

Nightingale, Florence. *Notes on Nursing.* London: Duckworth, 1859, 1952.

Odent, Michel. *The Scientification of Love.* London: Free Association, 1999.

Olsen, Tillie. *Silences.* London: Virago, 1980.

Owen, Ursula. *Fathers, Reflections by Daughters.* London: Virago, 1983.

Parker, Rozsika. *The Subversive Stitch,* London: Women's Press, 1984.

———. *Torn in Two.* London: Virago, 1995.

Pearson, Allison. *I Don't Know How She Does It.* London: Chatto & Windus, 2002.

Plato, *Laws,* trans. R. G. Bury. Cambridge, MA: Harvard University Press, and London: Heinemann, 1926, 1984.

Price, Jane. *Motherhood: What It Does to Your Mind.* London: Pandora, 1988.

Prigogine, Ilya, and Isabelle Stengers. *Order Out of Chaos.* London: Fontana, 1984, 1985.

Priya, Jacqueline Vincent. *Birth Traditions and Modern Pregnancy Care.* Shaftesbury, England: Element Books, 1992.

Rich, Adrienne. *Of Woman Born.* London: Virago, 1977.

Rousseau, Jean-Jacques. *Emile, or On Education,* 1762. (Many translations.)

Schlein, Miriam. *The Way Mothers Are.* Morton Grove, IL: Albert Whitman & Company, 1963, 1991.

Salter, Joan. *Mothering with Soul.* Stroud: Hawthorn, 1998.

Spender, Dale. *Man Made Language.* London: Pandora, 1980.

Stern, Daniel N. *The Interpersonal World of the Infant: A View from Psychoanalysis and Developmental Psychology.* New York: Basic Books, 1985.

———. *The Motherhood Constellation.* New York: Basic Books, 1995.

Stern, Daniel N., and Nadią Bruschweiler-Stern. *The Birth of a Mother: How Motherhood Changes You Forever.* London: Bloomsbury, 1998, 1999. (Published in New York by Basic Books.)

Sumner, Penny, ed. *The Fruits of Labour, Creativity, Self-Expression and Motherhood.* London, Women's Press, 2001.

Tolstoy, Leo. *The Kreutzer Sonata and Other Stories,* tr. with introduction by David McDuff. London: Penguin, 1985.

Truby King, Frederic. *Feeding and Care of Baby.* Oxford: Oxford University Press, n.d.

Winnicott, D. W. *The Child, the Family and the Outside World.* London: Penguin, 1964.

———. *From Paediatrics to Psychotherapy: Collected Papers.* London: Tavistock, 1958.

Wollstonecraft, Mary. *A Vindication of the Rights of Women,* ed. Miriam Brody. London: Penguin, 1992. (Original edition, 1792.)

index

about the author

Naomi Stadlen has had the unique experience of listening to hundreds of mothers talk about their experiences, both in her weekly discussion group Mothers Talking, which she founded more than fifteen years ago at the Active Birth Centre in London, and in her private practice as a psychotherapist specializing in parenting issues. A former breastfeeding counselor for the National Childbirth Trust and now for La Leche League, Stadlen is the mother of three adult children and has a grandson.